ABOUT THIS PUBLICATION

FOR SERVICE ASSISTANCE

Customer Service
1.704.898.0770

www.visionbooks.org

TID: 5106026
ISBN (10) digit: 1503230740
ISBN (13) digit: 978-1503230743

123-4-56789-01239-Paperback
123-4-56789-01239-Hardback

First Edition

090520140547

Printed in the United States of America

1

2015 EDITION

North Carolina Criminal Law

And Procedure-Pamphlet # 73

Printed In conjunction with the Administration of the Courts

North Carolina Criminal Law and Procedure
Pamphlet Reference Guide

8

11

13

§ 131E-99. Confidentiality of health care contracts.

Except for the information a hospital or an ambulatory surgical facility is required to report under G.S. 131E-214.12, the financial terms and other competitive health care information directly related to the financial terms in a health care services contract between a hospital or a medical school and a managed care organization, insurance company, employer, or other payer is confidential and not a public record under Chapter 132 of the General Statutes. Nothing in this section shall prevent an elected public body which has responsibility for the hospital or medical school from having access to this confidential information in a closed session. The disclosure to a public body does not affect the confidentiality of the information. Members of the public body shall have a duty not to further disclose the confidential information. (1995 (Reg. Sess., 1996), c. 713, s. 2; 1997-123, ss. 1, 2; 2013-382, s. 10.5.)

Article 6.

Health Care Facility Licensure Act.

Part 1. Nursing Home Licensure Act.

§ 131E-100. Title; purpose.

(a)   This Part shall be known as the "Nursing Home Licensure Act."

(b)   The purpose of the Nursing Home Licensure Act is to establish authority and duty for the Department to inspect and license private nursing homes. (1983, c. 775, s. 1.)

§ 131E-101. Definitions.

As used in this Part, unless otherwise specified:

(1)   "Adult care home", as distinguished from a nursing home, means a facility operated as a part of a nursing home and which provides residential care for aged or disabled persons whose principal need is a home with the shelter or personal care their age or disability requires. Medical care in an adult care home is usually occasional or incidental, such as may be required in the home of any individual or family, but the administration of medication is supervised.

Continuing planned medical and nursing care to meet the resident's needs may be provided under the direct supervision of a physician, nurse, or home health agency. Adult care homes are to be distinguished from nursing homes subject to licensure under this Part.

(1a)   "Combination home" means a nursing home offering one or more levels of care, including any combination of skilled nursing, intermediate care, and adult care home.

(2)   "Commission" means the North Carolina Medical Care Commission.

(3)   "Community advisory committee" means a nursing home advisory committee established for the statutory purpose of working to carry out the intent of the Nursing Home Patients' Bill of Rights (Chapter 131E, Article 6, Part 2) in accordance with G.S. 143B-181.1.

(4)   Repealed by Session Laws 1995, c. 535, s. 21.

(5)   "Medical review committee" means a committee of a State or local professional society, of a medical staff of a licensed hospital, of physicians having privileges within the nursing home or of a peer review corporation or organization which is formed for the purpose of evaluating the quality, cost of or necessity for health care services under applicable federal statutes.

(6)   "Nursing home" means a facility, however named, which is advertised, announced, or maintained for the express or implied purpose of providing nursing or convalescent care for three or more persons unrelated to the licensee. A "nursing home" is a home for chronic or convalescent patients, who, on admission, are not as a rule, acutely ill and who do not usually require special facilities such as an operating room, X-ray facilities, laboratory facilities, and obstetrical facilities. A "nursing home" provides care for persons who have remedial ailments or other ailments, for which medical and nursing care are indicated; who, however, are not sick enough to require general hospital care. Nursing care is their primary need, but they will require continuing medical supervision.

(7)   "Peer review committee" means any committee appointed in accordance with G.S. 131E-108, "Peer review."

(8)   "Quality assurance committee" means a committee, agency, or department of a state or local professional organization, of a medical staff of a

16

licensed hospital, nursing home, of nurses or aides on the staff of a nursing home, or adult care home, of physicians having privileges within the nursing home, or adult care home, or of a peer review corporation or organization that is formed for the purpose of evaluating the quality, cost of, or necessity for health care services under applicable federal and State statutes, regulations, and rules. (1961, c. 51, s. 3; 1981, c. 833; 1983, c. 775, s. 1; 1995, c. 535, s. 21; 2004-149, s. 2.1.)

§ 131E-102. Licensure requirements.

(a)   No person shall operate a nursing home without a license obtained from the Department. Any person may operate a nursing home or a combination home, as defined in this Part, in the same building or in two or more buildings adjoining or next to each other on the same site. Both a nursing home and a combination home must be licensed by the Department under this Part.

(b)   Applications shall be available from the Department, and each application filed with the Department shall contain all necessary and reasonable information that the Department may by rule require. A license shall be granted to the applicant upon a determination by the Department that the applicant has complied with the provisions of this Part and the rules promulgated under this Part. The Department shall charge the applicant a nonrefundable annual license fee in the amount of four hundred twenty dollars ($420.00) plus a nonrefundable annual per-bed fee of seventeen dollars and fifty cents ($17.50).

(c)   A license to operate a nursing home shall be annually renewed upon the filing and the Department's approval of the renewal application. A license shall not be renewed if outstanding fees and penalties imposed by the State against the home have not been paid. Fines and penalties for which an appeal is pending are exempt from consideration. The renewal application shall be available from the Department and shall contain all necessary and reasonable information that the Department may by rule require.

(d)   Each license shall be issued only for the premises and persons named in the application and shall not be transferable or assignable except with the written approval of the Department.

(e)   In order for a nursing home to maintain its license it shall not intentionally impede the proper performance of the duties of a lawfully appointed

17

community advisory committee as set forth in G.S. 131E-128(h). (1961, c. 51, s. 3; 1963, c. 859; 1983, c. 775, s. 1; 1993, c. 530, s. 1; 2003-284, s. 34.3(a); 2005-276, s. 41.2(c); 2009-451, s. 10.76(g).)

§ 131E-103. Adverse action on a license.

(a)   Subject to subsection (b), the Department shall have the authority to deny a new or renewal application for a license, and to amend, recall, suspend or revoke an existing license upon a determination that there has been a substantial failure to comply with the provisions of this Part or the rules promulgated under this Part.

(b)   The provisions of Chapter 150B of the General Statutes, the Administrative Procedure Act, shall govern all administrative action and judicial review in cases where the Department has taken the action described in subsection (a). A petition for a contested case shall be filed within 20 days after the Department mails the licensee a notice of its decision to deny a renewal application, or to recall, suspend, or revoke an existing license. (1961, c. 51, s. 3; 1983, c. 775, s. 1; 1987, c. 827, s. 1; 1991, c. 143, s. 2, c. 761, s. 24.)

§ 131E-104. Rules and enforcement.

(a)   The Commission is authorized to adopt, amend, and repeal all rules necessary for the implementation of this Part.

(b)   The Commission shall adopt rules for the operation of the adult care portion of a combination home. The rules shall provide that for each requirement applicable to freestanding adult care homes or freestanding nursing homes, the combination home may choose to operate the adult care portion of the home in compliance with either the requirement applicable to freestanding adult care homes or the higher standard applicable to freestanding nursing homes.

(c)   The Department shall enforce the rules adopted or amended by the Commission with respect to nursing homes. (1961, c. 51, s. 3; 1973, c. 476, s. 128; 1981, c. 614, s. 1; 1983, c. 775, s. 1; 1995, c. 535, s. 22; 2000-154, s. 6.1.)

§ 131E-105. Inspections.

(a)   The Department shall inspect any nursing home and any adult care home operated as a part of a nursing home in accordance with rules adopted by the Commission.

(b)   Notwithstanding the provisions of G.S. 8-53, "Communications between physician and patient," or any other provision of law relating to the confidentiality of communications between physician and patient, the representatives of the Department, when necessary for investigating compliance with this Part or rules promulgated by the Commission, may review any writing or other record in any recording medium which pertains to the admission, discharge, medication, treatment, medical condition, or history of persons who are or have been patients of the facility being inspected unless that patient objects in writing to review of that patient's records. Physicians, psychologists, psychiatrists, nurses, and anyone else interviewed by representatives of the Department may disclose to these representatives information related to any inquiry, notwithstanding the existence of the physician-patient privilege in G.S. 8-53, "Communications between physician and patient," or any other rules of law, if the patient has not made written objection to this disclosure. The facility, its employees, and any person interviewed during these inspections shall be immune from liability for damages resulting from the disclosure of any information which is provided without malice or fraud to the Department. Any confidential or privileged information received from review of records or interviews shall be kept confidential by the Department and not disclosed without written authorization of the patient or legal representative or unless disclosure is ordered by a court of competent jurisdiction. The Department shall institute appropriate policies and procedures to ensure that this information shall not be disclosed without authorization or court order. The Department shall not disclose the name of anyone who has furnished information concerning a facility without consent of that person. Neither the names of persons furnishing information nor any confidential or privileged information obtained from records or interviews shall be considered "public records" within the meaning of G.S. 132-1, "`Public records' defined." Prior to releasing any information or allowing any inspections referred to in this subsection, the patient must upon admission be advised in writing by the facility that the patient has the right to object in writing to the release of information or review of the records and that by an objection in writing the patient may prohibit the inspection or release of the records.

(c)   Authorized representatives of the Department with identification to this effect shall have at all times the right of proper entry upon any and all parts of the premises of any place in which entry is necessary to carry out the provisions of this Part or the rules adopted by the Commission. It shall be unlawful for any person to resist a proper entry by an authorized representative upon any premises other than a private dwelling. (1981, c. 586, s. 1; c. 614, s. 1; 1983, c. 775, s. 1; 1995, c. 535, s. 23.)

§ 131E-106. Evaluation of residents in adult care homes.

The Department shall prescribe the method of evaluation of residents in the adult care portion of a combination home in order to determine when any of these residents is in need of professional medical and nursing care as provided in licensed nursing homes. (1963, c. 859; 1981, c. 833; 1983, c. 775, s. 1; 1995, c. 535, s. 24.)

§ 131E-107. Quality assurance, medical, or peer review committees.

(a)   A member of a duly appointed quality assurance, medical or peer review committee shall not be subject to liability for damages in any civil action on account of any act, statement or proceeding undertaken, made, or performed within the scope of the functions of the committee, if the committee member acts without malice or fraud, and if such peer review committee is approved and operates in accordance with G.S. 131E-108.

(b)   The proceedings of a quality assurance, medical, or peer review committee, the records and materials it produces and the materials it considers shall be confidential and not considered public records within the meaning of G.S. 132-1, " 'Public records' defined", and shall not be subject to discovery or introduction into evidence in any civil action against a nursing home or a provider of professional health services that results from matters that are the subject of evaluation and review by the committee. No person who was in attendance at a meeting of the committee shall be required to testify in any civil action as to any evidence or other matters produced or presented during the proceedings of the committee or as to any findings, recommendations, evaluations, opinions, or other actions of the committee or its members. However, information, documents, or records otherwise available are not immune from discovery or use in a civil action merely because they were presented during proceedings of the committee. Documents otherwise available as public records within the meaning of G.S. 132-1 do not lose their status as public records merely because they were presented or considered during proceedings of the committee. A member of the committee or a person who testifies before the committee may testify in a civil action but cannot be asked about the person's testimony before the committee or any opinions formed as a result of the committee hearings. (1983, c. 775, s. 1; 2004-149, s. 2.2.)

§ 131E-108. Peer review.

It is not a violation of G.S. 131E-117(5) for medical records to be disclosed to a private peer review committee if:

(1)   The peer review committee has been approved by the Department;

(2)   The purposes of the peer review committee are to:

a.   Survey facilities to verify a high level of quality care through evaluation and peer assistance;

b.   Resolve written complaints in a responsible and professional manner; and

c.   Develop a basic core of knowledge and standards useful in establishing a means of measuring quality of care; and

(3)   The peer review committee keeps such records confidential. (1979, c. 707; 1983, c. 775, s. 1; 1997-456, s. 27.)

§ 131E-109. Penalties.

(a)   Any person establishing, conducting, managing or operating any nursing home without a license shall be guilty of a Class 3 misdemeanor, and upon conviction shall only be liable for a fine of not more than five hundred dollars ($500.00) for the first offense and not more than five hundred dollars ($500.00) for each subsequent offense. Each day of a continuing violation after conviction shall be considered a separate offense.

(b)   Any person acting under the authority of the Department who gives advance notice to an operator of a nursing home of the date or time that the nursing home is to be inspected shall be guilty of a Class 3 misdemeanor. The inspection of a nursing home for initial licensure shall be exempt from the prohibition of prior notice. All subsequent inspections must comply with the provisions of this subsection.

(c)   The Secretary or a designee may suspend the admission of any new patients or residents at any nursing home or domiciliary home where the conditions of the nursing home or domiciliary home are detrimental to the health or safety of the patient or resident. This suspension shall remain in effect until the Secretary is satisfied that conditions or circumstances merit the removal of the suspension. This subsection shall be in addition to authority to suspend or revoke the license of the home. Any facility wishing to contest a suspension of admissions shall be entitled to an administrative hearing as provided in the Administrative Procedure Act, Chapter 150B of the General Statutes. The petition for a contested case shall be filed in the Office of Administrative Hearings within 20 days after the Department mails a written notice of suspension of admissions to the facility.

(d)   Except as otherwise provided in this Part, any person who violates any provision of this Part or who willfully fails to perform any act required, or who willfully performs any act prohibited by this Part, shall be guilty of a Class 1 misdemeanor: Provided, however, that any person who willfully violates any rule adopted by the Commission under this Part or who willfully fails to perform any act required by, or who willfully performs any act prohibited by, these rules shall be guilty of a Class 3 misdemeanor.

(e)   The clear proceeds of civil penalties provided for in this section shall be remitted to the Civil Penalty and Forfeiture Fund in accordance with G.S. 115C-457.2. (1977, c. 656, ss. 1, 2; 1981, c. 667, ss. 1, 2; 1983, c. 775, s. 1; 1991, c. 143, s. 3; c. 761, s. 25; 1993, c. 539, s. 960; 1994, Ex. Sess., c. 24, s. 14(c); 1998-215, s. 78(c).)

§131E-110. Injunction.

(a)   Notwithstanding the existence or pursuit of any other remedy, the Department may, in the manner provided by law, maintain an action in the name of the State for injunction or other process against any person to restrain or prevent the establishment, conduct, management or operation of a nursing home without a license.

(b)   If any person shall hinder the proper performance of duty of the Secretary or a representative in carrying out the provisions of this Part, the Secretary may institute an action in the superior court of the county in which the hindrance occurred for injunctive relief against the continued hindrance, irrespective of all other remedies at law.

(c)   Actions under this section shall be in accordance with Article 37 of Chapter 1 of the General Statutes and Rule 65 of the Rules of Civil Procedure. (1983, c. 775, s. 1.)

§ 131E-111: Recodified as § 131E-255 by Session Laws 1995 (Reg. Sess., 1996), c. 713, s. 3(a), as amended by Session Laws 1995 (Reg. Sess., 1996), c. 713, s. 3(b).

§ 131E-112. Waiver of rules for health care facilities that provide temporary shelter or temporary services during a disaster or emergency.

(a)   The Division of Health Service Regulation may temporarily waive, during disasters or emergencies declared in accordance with Article 1A of Chapter 166A of the General Statutes, any rules of the Commission pertaining to facilities or home care agencies to the extent necessary to allow the facility or home care agency to provide temporary shelter and temporary services requested by the emergency management agency. The Division may identify, in advance of a declared disaster or emergency, rules that may be waived, and the extent the rules may be waived, upon a disaster or emergency being declared in accordance with Article 1A of Chapter 166A of the General Statutes. The Division may also waive rules under this subsection during a declared disaster or emergency upon the request of an emergency management agency and may rescind the waiver if, after investigation, the Division determines the waiver poses an unreasonable risk to the health, safety, or welfare of any of the persons occupying the facility. The emergency management agency requesting temporary shelter or temporary services shall notify the Division within 72 hours of the time the preapproved waivers are deemed by the emergency management agency to apply.

23

(b)　　As used in this section, "emergency management agency" is as defined in G.S. 166A-19.3. (1999-307, s. 1; 2007-182, s. 1; 2012-12, s. 2(u).)

§ 131E-113. Immunization of employees and residents.

(a)　　Except as provided in subsection (e) of this section, a nursing home licensed under this Part shall require residents and employees to be immunized against influenza virus and shall require residents to also be immunized against pneumococcal disease.

(b)　　Upon admission, a nursing home shall notify the resident of the immunization requirements of this section and shall request that the resident agree to be immunized against influenza virus and pneumococcal disease.

(b1)　　A nursing home shall notify every employee of the immunization requirements of this section and shall request that the employee agree to be immunized against influenza virus.

(c)　　A nursing home shall document the annual immunization against influenza virus and the immunization against pneumococcal disease for each resident and each employee, as required under this section. Upon finding that a resident is lacking one or both of these immunizations or that an employee has not been immunized against influenza virus, or if the nursing home is unable to verify that the individual has received the required immunization, the nursing home shall provide or arrange for immunization. The immunization and documentation required shall occur not later than November 30 of each year.

(d)　　For an individual who becomes a resident of or who is newly employed by the nursing home after November 30 but before March 30 of the following year, the nursing home shall determine the individual's status for the immunizations required under this section, and if found to be deficient, the nursing home shall provide the immunization.

(e)　　No individual shall be required to receive vaccine under this section if the vaccine is medically contraindicated, or if the vaccine is against the individual's religious beliefs, or if the individual refuses the vaccine after being fully informed of the health risks of not being immunized.

(f)   Notwithstanding any other provision of law to the contrary, the Commission for Public Health shall have the authority to adopt rules to implement the immunization requirements of this section.

(g)   As used in this section, "employee" means an individual who is a part-time or full-time employee of the nursing home. (2000-112, ss. 3, 4; 2007-182, s. 1.3.)

§ 131E-114. Special care units; disclosure of information required.

(a)   A nursing home or combination home licensed under this Part that provides special care for persons with Alzheimer's disease or other dementias in a special care unit shall make the following disclosures pertaining to the special care provided that distinguishes the special care unit as being especially designed for residents with Alzheimer's disease or other dementias. The disclosure shall be made annually, in writing, to all of the following:

(1)   The Department, as part of its licensing procedures.

(2)   Each person seeking placement within a special care unit, or the person's authorized representative, prior to entering into an agreement with the person to provide special care.

(b)   Information that must be disclosed in writing shall include, but is not limited to, all of the following:

(1)   A statement of the overall philosophy and mission of the licensed facility and how it reflects the special needs of residents with dementia.

(2)   The process and criteria for placement, transfer, or discharge to or from the special care unit.

(3)   The process used for assessment and establishment of the plan of care and its implementation, as required under State and federal law.

(4)   Typical staffing patterns and how the patterns reflect the resident's need for increased care and supervision.

(5)   Dementia-specific staff training.

(6)   Physical environment features designed specifically for the special care unit.

(7)   Alzheimer's disease and other dementia-specific programming.

(8)   Opportunities for family involvement.

(9)   Additional costs or fees to the resident for special care.

(c)   As part of its license renewal procedures and inspections, the Department shall examine for accuracy the written disclosures made by each licensed facility subject to this section.

(d)   Nothing in this section shall be construed as prohibiting a nursing home or combination home that does not offer a special care unit from admitting a person with Alzheimer's disease or other dementias. The disclosures required by this section apply only to a nursing home or combination home that advertises, markets, or otherwise promotes itself as providing a special care unit for persons with Alzheimer's disease or other dementias.

(e)   As used in this section, the term "special care unit" means a wing or hallway within a nursing home, or a program provided by a nursing home, that is designated especially for residents with Alzheimer's disease or other dementias, or other special needs disease or condition, as determined by the Medical Care Commission, which may include mental disabilities. (2000-154, s. 6.)

§ 131E-114.1. Posting of information indicating number of staff on duty.

Every nursing home subject to licensure under this Part shall post in a conspicuous place in the nursing home information about required staffing that enables residents and their families to readily ascertain each day the number of direct care staff and supervisors that are required by law to be on duty for that day. (2001-85, s. 2; 2001-487, s. 85(b).)

§ 131E-114.2. Use of medication aides to perform technical aspects of medication administration.

(a)   Facilities licensed and medication administration services provided under this Part may utilize medication aides to perform the technical aspects of medication administration consistent with G.S. 90-171.20(7) and (8), and G.S. 90-171.43.

(1)   A medication aide who is employed in a facility licensed under Article 5 and Article 6, Part 1 of this Chapter shall be listed as a Nurse Aide I on the Nurse Aide I Registry in addition to being listed on the Medication Aide Registry.

(2)   Medication administration as used in Article 5 and Article 6, Part 1 of this Chapter shall not include intravenous or injectable medication services.

(b)   The Commission shall adopt rules to implement this section. Rules adopted by the Commission shall include:

(1)   Training and competency evaluation of medication aides as provided for under this section.

(2)   Requirements for listing under the Medication Aide Registry as provided for under G.S. 131E-270.

(3)   Requirements for supervision of medication aides by licensed health professionals or appropriately qualified supervisory personnel consistent with this Part. (2005-276, s. 10.40C(a); 2007-444, s. 4(a).)

§ 131E-114.3. Smoking prohibited inside long-term care facilities; penalty.

(a)   Except to the extent otherwise provided by federal law, smoking is prohibited inside long-term care facilities. As used in this section:

(1)   "Long-term care facilities" include adult care homes, nursing homes, skilled nursing facilities, facilities licensed under Chapter 122C of the General Statutes, and other licensed facilities that provide long-term care services.

(2)   "Smoking" means the use or possession of any lighted cigar, cigarette, pipe, or other lighted smoking product.

(3)   "Inside" means a fully enclosed area.

(b)   The person who owns, manages, operates, or otherwise controls a long-term care facility where smoking is prohibited under this section shall:

(1)   Conspicuously post signs clearly stating that smoking is prohibited inside the facility. The signs may include the international "No Smoking" symbol, which consists of a pictorial representation of a burning cigarette enclosed in a red circle with a red bar across it.

(2)   Direct any person who is smoking inside the facility to extinguish the lighted smoking product.

(3)   Provide written notice to individuals upon admittance that smoking is prohibited inside the facility and obtain the signature of the individual or the individual's representative acknowledging receipt of the notice.

(c)   The Department may impose an administrative penalty not to exceed two hundred dollars ($200.00) for each violation on any person who owns, manages, operates, or otherwise controls the long-term care facility and fails to comply with subsection (b) of this section. A violation of this section constitutes a civil offense only and is not a crime. (2007-459, s. 2.)

§ 131E-114.4. Examination and screening for the presence of controlled substances required for applicants for employment in nursing homes.

(a)   An offer of employment by a nursing home licensed under this Part to an applicant is conditioned on the applicant's consent to an examination and screening for controlled substances. The examination and screening shall be conducted in accordance with Article 20 of Chapter 95 of the General Statutes. A screening procedure that utilizes a single-use test device may be used for the examination and screening of applicants and may be administered on-site. If the results of the applicant's examination and screening indicate the presence of a controlled substance, the nursing home shall not employ the applicant unless and until the applicant provides to the nursing home written verification from the applicant's prescribing physician that every controlled substance identified by the examination and screening is prescribed by that physician to treat the applicant's medical or psychological condition. The verification from the physician shall include the name of the controlled substance, the prescribed dosage and frequency, and the condition for which the substance is prescribed. If the result of an applicant's or employee's examination and screening indicates the presence of a controlled substance, the nursing home may require a second examination and screening to verify the results of the prior examination and screening.

(b)   A nursing home may require random examination and screening for controlled substances as a condition of continued employment. If the nursing home has reasonable grounds to believe that an employee is an abuser of a controlled substance, the nursing home may require that employee to undergo examination and screening for controlled substances as a condition of continued employment.

(c)   A nursing home and an officer or employee of a nursing home that, in good faith, comply with this section are not liable for the failure of the nursing home to employ or continue the employment of an individual on the basis of the results of an examination and screening of the applicant or employee for controlled substances.

(d)   An entity and officers and employees of an entity that perform controlled substance examination and screening in accordance with Article 20 of Chapter 95 of the General Statutes shall be immune from civil liability for conducting or failing to conduct the examination and screening if the examination and screening are requested and received in compliance with this section and with Article 20 of Chapter 95 of the General Statutes.

(e)   The results of an examination and screening conducted at the request of a nursing home in accordance with this section are confidential and not a public record under Chapter 132 of the General Statutes. The nursing home shall maintain the confidentiality of all information related to the examination and screening of an applicant for employment or an individual currently employed by the nursing home.

(f)   The nursing home shall pay expenses related to controlled substance examination and screening pursuant to this section, except examinee-requested retests. The examinee shall pay all reasonable expenses for retests of confirmed positive results. (2013-167, s. 2.)

Part 2. Nursing Home Patients' Bill of Rights.

§ 131E-115. Legislative intent.

29

It is the intent of the General Assembly to promote the interests and well-being of the patients in nursing homes and adult care homes licensed pursuant to G.S. 131E-102, and patients in a nursing home operated by a hospital which is licensed under Article 5 of Chapter 131E of the General Statutes. It is the intent of the General Assembly that every patient's civil and religious liberties, including the right to independent personal decisions and knowledge of available choices, shall not be infringed and that the facility shall encourage and assist the patient in the fullest possible exercise of these rights. (1977, c. 897, s. 1; 1983, c. 143, s. 2; c. 775, s. 1; 1995, c. 509, s. 72; c. 535, s. 25.)

§ 131E-116. Definitions.

As used in this Part, unless otherwise specified:

(1)   "Administrator" means an administrator of a facility.

(1a)   "Commission" means the North Carolina Medical Care Commission.

(2)   "Facility" means a nursing home and a home for the aged or disabled licensed pursuant to G.S. 131E-102, and also means a nursing home operated by a hospital which is licensed under Article 5 of G.S. Chapter 131E.

(3)   "Patient" means a person who has been admitted to a facility.

(4)   "Representative payee" means a person certified by the federal government to receive and disburse benefits for a recipient of governmental assistance. (1977, c. 897, s. 1; 1983, c. 143, s. 1, c. 775, s. 1; 1993, c. 499, s. 1.)

§ 131E-117. Declaration of patient's rights.

All facilities shall treat their patients in accordance with the provisions of this Part. Every patient shall have the following rights:

(1)   To be treated with consideration, respect, and full recognition of personal dignity and individuality;

(2)   To receive care, treatment and services which are adequate, appropriate, and in compliance with relevant federal and State statutes and rules;

(3)   To receive at the time of admission and during the stay, a written statement of the services provided by the facility, including those required to be offered on an as-needed basis, and of related charges. Charges for services not covered under Medicare or Medicaid shall be specified. Upon receiving this statement, the patient shall sign a written receipt which must be on file in the facility and available for inspection;

(4)   To have on file in the patient's record a written or verbal order of the attending physician containing any information as the attending physician deems appropriate or necessary, together with the proposed schedule of medical treatment. The patient shall give prior informed consent to participation in experimental research. Written evidence of compliance with this subdivision, including signed acknowledgements by the patient, shall be retained by the facility in the patient's file;

(5)   To receive respect and privacy in the patient's medical care program. Case discussion, consultation, examination, and treatment shall remain confidential and shall be conducted discreetly. Personal and medical records shall be confidential and the written consent of the patient shall be obtained for their release to any individual, other than family members, except as needed in case of the patient's transfer to another health care institution or as required by law or third party payment contract;

(6)   To be free from mental and physical abuse and, except in emergencies, to be free from chemical and physical restraints unless authorized for a specified period of time by a physician according to clear and indicated medical need;

(7)   To receive from the administrator or staff of the facility a reasonable response to all requests;

(8)   To associate and communicate privately and without restriction with persons and groups of the patient's choice on the patient's initiative or that of the persons or groups at any reasonable hour; to send and receive mail promptly and unopened, unless the patient is unable to open and read personal mail; to have access at any reasonable hour to a telephone where the patient

31

may speak privately; and to have access to writing instruments, stationery, and postage;

(9)   To manage the patient's financial affairs unless authority has been delegated to another pursuant to a power of attorney, or written agreement, or some other person or agency has been appointed for this purpose pursuant to law. Nothing shall prevent the patient and facility from entering a written agreement for the facility to manage the patient's financial affairs. In the event that the facility manages the patient's financial affairs, it shall have an accounting available for inspection and shall furnish the patient with a quarterly statement of the patient's account. The patient shall have reasonable access to this account at reasonable hours; the patient or facility may terminate the agreement for the facility to manage the patient's financial affairs at any time upon five days' notice.

(10)   To enjoy privacy in visits by the patient's spouse, and, if both are inpatients of the facility, they shall be afforded the opportunity where feasible to share a room;

(11)   To enjoy privacy in the patient's room;

(12)   To present grievances and recommend changes in policies and services, personally or through other persons or in combination with others, on the patient's personal behalf or that of others to the facility's staff, the community advisory committee, the administrator, the Department, or other persons or groups without fear of reprisal, restraint, interference, coercion, or discrimination;

(13)   To not be required to perform services for the facility without personal consent and the written approval of the attending physician;

(14)   To retain, to secure storage for, and to use personal clothing and possessions, where reasonable;

(15)   To not be transferred or discharged from a facility except for medical reasons, the patient's own or other patients' welfare, nonpayment for the stay, or when the transfer or discharge is mandated under Title XVIII (Medicare) or Title XIX (Medicaid) of the Social Security Act. The patient shall be given at least five days' advance notice to ensure orderly transfer or discharge, unless the attending physician orders immediate transfer, and these actions, and the reasons for them, shall be documented in the patient's medical record;

(16)   To be notified within 10 days after the facility has been issued a provisional license because of violation of licensure regulations or received notice of revocation of license by the North Carolina Department of Health and Human Services and the basis on which the provisional license or notice of revocation of license was issued. The patient's responsible family member or guardian shall also be notified. (1977, c. 897, s. 1; 1983, c. 775, s. 1; 1989, c. 75; 1997-443, s. 11A.118(a).)

§ 131E-118. Transfer of management responsibilities.

The patient's representative who has been given the power in writing by the patient to manage the patient's financial affairs or the patient's legal guardian as appointed by a court or the patient's attorney-in-fact as specified in the power of attorney agreement may sign any documents required by the provisions of this Part, may perform any other act, and may receive or furnish any information required by this Part. (1977, c. 897, s. 1; 1983, c. 775, s. 1.)

§ 131E-119. No waiver of rights.

No facility may require a patient to waive the rights specified in this Part. (1977, c. 897, s. 1; 1983, c. 775, s. 1.)

§ 131E-120. Notice to patient.

(a)   A copy of G.S. 131E-115 through G.S. 131E-127 shall be posted conspicuously in a public place in all facilities. Copies of G.S. 131E-115 through G.S. 131E-127 shall be furnished to the patient upon admittance to the facility, to all patients currently residing in the facility, to the sponsoring agency, to a representative payee of the patient, or to any person designated in G.S. 131E-118, and to the patient's next of kin, if requested. Receipts for the statement signed by these persons shall be retained in the facility's files.

(b)   The address and telephone number of the section in the Department responsible for the enforcement of the provisions of this Part shall be posted and distributed with copies of the Part. The address and telephone number of

33

the county social services department shall also be posted and distributed. (1977, c. 897, s. 1; 1983, c. 775, s. 1.)

§ 131E-121. Responsibility of administrator.

Responsibility for implementing the provisions of this Part shall rest on the administrator of the facility. (1977, c. 897, s. 1; 1983, c. 775, s. 1.)

§ 131E-122. Staff training.

Each facility shall provide appropriate staff training to implement each patient's rights included in this Part. (1977, c. 897, s. 1; 1983, c. 775, s. 1.)

§ 131E-123. Civil action.

Every patient shall have the right to institute a civil action for injunctive relief to enforce the provisions of this Part. The Department, a general guardian, or any person appointed as guardian ad litem pursuant to law, may institute an action pursuant to this section on behalf of the patient or patients. Any agency or person named above may enforce the rights of the patient specified in this Part which the patient is unable to personally enforce. (1977, c. 897, s. 1; 1983, c. 775, s. 1.)

§ 131E-124. Enforcement and investigation; confidentiality.

(a)   The Department shall be responsible for the enforcement of the provisions of this Part. The Department shall investigate complaints made to it and reply within a reasonable time, not to exceed 60 days, upon receipt of a complaint.

(a1)   When the Department receives a complaint alleging a violation of the provisions of this Part pertaining to patient care or patient safety, the Department shall initiate an investigation as follows:

(1)   Immediately upon receipt of the complaint if the complaint alleges a life-threatening situation.

(2)   Within 24 hours if the complaint alleges abuse of a resident as defined by G.S. 131D-20(1).

(3)   Within 48 hours if the complaint alleges neglect of a resident as defined by G.S. 131D-20(8).

(4)   Within two weeks in all other situations.

The investigation shall be completed within 30 days. The requirements of this section are in addition to and not in lieu of any investigatory requirements for adult protective services pursuant to Article 6 of Chapter 108A of the General Statutes.

(b)   The Department is authorized to inspect patients' medical records maintained at the facility when necessary to investigate any alleged violation of this Part.

(c)   The Department shall maintain the confidentiality of all persons who register complaints with the Department and of all medical records inspected by the Department. A person who has filed a complaint shall have access to information about a complaint investigation involving a specific resident if written authorization is obtained from the resident, legal representative, or responsible party. The designation of the responsible party shall be maintained by the nursing facility in the resident's medical record.

(d)   Pursuant to 42 U.S.C. § 1395 and G.S. 131E-127, a nursing home as defined in G.S. 131E-101(6), is not in violation of any applicable statute, rule, or regulation for any action taken pursuant to a physician's order when the physician has determined that the action is medically necessary. (1977, c. 897, s. 1; 1983, c. 775, s. 1; 1999-113, s. 3; 1999-334, s. 1.9.)

§ 131E-125. Revocation of a license.

(a)   The Department shall have the authority to revoke a license issued pursuant to G.S. 131E-102 in any case where it finds that there has been a substantial failure to comply with the provisions of this Part or any failure that endangers the health, safety or welfare of patients.

A revocation shall be effected by mailing to the licensee by registered mail, or by personal service of, a notice setting forth the particular reasons for such action. Such revocation shall become effective 20 days after the mailing or service of the notice, unless the applicant or licensee, within such 20-day period, files a petition for a contested case, in which case the notice shall be deemed to be suspended. At any time at or prior to the hearing, the Department may rescind the notice of revocation upon being satisfied that the reasons for the revocation have been or will be removed.

(b)   In the case of a nursing home operated by a hospital which is licensed under Article 5 of G.S. Chapter 131E, when the Department of Health and Human Services finds that there has been a substantial failure to comply with the provisions of this Part, it may issue an order preventing the continued operation of the home.

Such order shall be effected by mailing to the hospital by registered or certified mail, or by personal service of, a notice setting forth the particular reasons for such action. Such order shall become effective 20 days after the mailing of the notice, unless the hospital, within such 20-day period, files a petition for a contested case, in which case the order shall be deemed to be suspended. At any time at or prior to the hearing, the Department of Health and Human Services may rescind the order upon being satisfied that the reasons for the order have been or will be removed. (1977, c. 897, s. 1; 1983, c. 143, s. 3; c. 775, s. 1; 1987, c. 827, s. 251; 1997-443, s. 11A.118(a).)

§ 131E-126: Repealed by Session Laws 1987, c. 600, s. 1.

§ 131E-127. No interference with practice of medicine or physician-patient relationship.

Nothing in this Part shall be construed to interfere with the practice of medicine or the physician-patient relationship. (1977, c. 897, s. 1; 1983, c. 775, s. 1.)

§ 131E-128. Nursing home advisory committees.

(a)   It is the purpose of the General Assembly that community advisory committees work to maintain the intent of this Part within the nursing homes in this State, including nursing homes operated by hospitals licensed under Article 5 of G.S. Chapter 131E. It is the further purpose of the General Assembly that the committees promote community involvement and cooperation with nursing homes and an integration of these homes into a system of care for the elderly.

(b)   (1)   A community advisory committee shall be established in each county which has a nursing home, including a nursing home operated by a hospital licensed under Article 5 of G.S. Chapter 131E, shall serve all the homes in the county, and shall work with each home in the best interest of the persons residing in each home. In a county which has one, two, or three nursing homes, the committee shall have five members. In a county with four or more nursing homes, the committee shall have one additional member for each nursing home in excess of three, and may have up to five additional members per committee at the discretion of the county commissioners.

(2)   In each county with four or more nursing homes, the committee shall establish a subcommittee of no more than five members and no fewer than three members from the committee for each nursing home in the county. Each member must serve on at least one subcommittee.

(3)   Each committee shall be appointed by the board of county commissioners. Of the members, a minority (not less than one-third, but as close to one-third as possible) must be chosen from among persons nominated by a majority of the chief administrators of nursing homes in the county and of the governing bodies of the hospitals licensed under Article 5 of G.S. Chapter 131E, which operate nursing homes. If the nursing home administrators and the governing bodies of the hospitals licensed under Article 5 of G.S. Chapter 131E, which operate nursing homes fail to make a nomination within 45 days after written notification has been sent to them by the board of county commissioners requesting a nomination, these appointments may be made by the board of county commissioners without nominations.

(c)   Each committee member shall serve an initial term of one year. Any person reappointed to a second or subsequent term in the same county shall serve a three-year term. Persons who were originally nominees of nursing home chief administrators and the governing bodies of the hospitals licensed under Article 5 of G.S. Chapter 131E, which operate nursing homes, or who were appointed by the board of county commissioners when the nursing home administrators and the governing bodies of the hospitals licensed under Article 5 of G.S. Chapter 131E, which operate nursing homes failed to make nominations, may not be reappointed without the consent of a majority of the nursing home chief administrators and the governing bodies of the hospitals licensed under Article 5 of G.S. Chapter 131E, which operate nursing homes within the county. If the nursing home chief administrators and the governing bodies of the hospitals licensed under Article 5 of G.S. Chapter 131E, which operate nursing homes fail to approve or reject the reappointment within 45 days of being requested by the board of county commissioners, the commissioners may reappoint the member if they so choose.

(d)   Any vacancy shall be filled by appointment of a person for a one-year term. Any person replacing a member nominated by the chief administrators and the governing bodies of the hospitals licensed under Article 5 of G.S. Chapter 131E, which operate nursing homes or a person appointed when the chief administrators and the governing bodies of the hospitals licensed under Article 5 of G.S. Chapter 131E, which operate nursing homes failed to make a nomination shall be selected from among persons nominated by the administrators and the governing bodies of the hospitals licensed under Article 5 of G.S. Chapter 131E, which operate nursing homes, as provided in subsection (b). If the county commissioners fail to appoint members to a committee, or fail to fill a vacancy, the appointment may be made or vacancy filled by the Secretary or the Secretary's designee no sooner than 45 days after the commissioners have been notified of the appointment or vacancy if nomination or approval of the nursing home administrators and the governing bodies of the hospitals licensed under Article 5 of G.S. Chapter 131E, which operate nursing homes is not required. If nominations or approval of the nursing home administrators and the governing bodies of the hospitals licensed under Article 5 of G.S. Chapter 131E, which operate nursing homes is required, the appointment may be made or vacancy filled by the Secretary or the Secretary's designee no sooner than 45 days after the commissioners have received the nomination or approval, or no sooner than 45 days after the 45-day period for action by the nursing home administrators and the governing bodies of the hospitals licensed under Article 5 of G.S. Chapter 131E, which operate nursing homes.

(e)   The committee shall elect from its members a chair, to serve a one-year term.

(f)   Each member must be a resident of the county which the committee serves. No person or immediate family member of a person with a financial interest in a home served by a committee, or employee or governing board member or immediate family member of an employee or governing board member of a home served by a committee, or immediate family member of a patient in a home served by a committee may be a member of a committee. Membership on a committee shall not be considered an office as defined in G.S. 128-1 or G.S. 128-1.1. Any county commissioner who is appointed to the committee shall be deemed to be serving on the committee in an ex officio capacity. Members of the committee shall serve without compensation, but may be reimbursed for the amount of actual expenses incurred by them in the performance of their duties. The names of the committee members and the date of expiration of their terms shall be filed with the Division of Aging, which shall supply a copy to the Division of Health Service Regulation.

(g)   The Division of Aging, Department of Health and Human Services, shall develop training materials which shall be distributed to each committee member and nursing home. Each committee member must receive training as specified by the Division of Aging prior to exercising any power under subsection (h) of this section. The Division of Aging, Department of Health and Human Services, shall provide the committees with information, guidelines, training, and consultation to direct them in the performance of their duties.

(h)   (1)   Each committee shall apprise itself of the general conditions under which the persons are residing in the homes, and shall work for the best interests of the persons in the homes. This may include assisting persons who have grievances with the home and facilitating the resolution of grievances at the local level.

(2)   Each committee shall quarterly visit the nursing home it serves. For each official quarterly visit, a majority of the committee members shall be present. In addition, each committee may visit the nursing home it serves whenever it deems it necessary to carry out its duties. In counties with four or more nursing homes, the subcommittee assigned to a home shall perform the duties of the committee under this subdivision, and a majority of the subcommittee members must be present for any visit.

(3)   Each member of a committee shall have the right between 10:00 A.M. and 8:00 P.M. to enter into the facility the committee serves in order to carry out the members' responsibilities. In a county where subcommittees have been

established, this right of access shall be limited to homes served by those subcommittees to which the member has been appointed.

(4)　　The committee or subcommittee may communicate through its chair with the Department or any other agency in relation to the interest of any patient. The identity of any complainant or resident involved in a complaint shall not be disclosed except as permitted under the Older Americans Act of 1965, as amended, 42 U.S.C. § 3001 et seq.

(5)　　Each home shall cooperate with the committee as it carries out its duties.

(6)　　Before entering into any nursing home, the committee, subcommittee, or member shall identify itself to the person present at the facility who is in charge of the facility at that time.

(i)　　Any written communication made by a member of a nursing home advisory committee within the course and scope of the member's duties, as specified in G.S. 131E-128, shall be privileged to the extent provided in this subsection. This privilege shall be a defense in a cause of action for libel if the member was acting in good faith and the statements or communications do not amount to intentional wrongdoing.

To the extent that any nursing home advisory committee or any member thereof is covered by liability insurance, that committee or member shall be deemed to have waived the qualified immunity herein to the extent of indemnification by insurance. (1977, c. 897, s. 2; 1977, 2nd Sess., c. 1192, s. 1; 1983, c. 143, ss. 4-9; c. 775, ss. 1, 6; 1987, c. 682, s. 1; 1995, c. 254, s. 7; 1997-176, s. 1; 1997-443, s. 11A.118(a); 2007-182, s. 1.)

§ 131E-128.1. Nursing home medication management advisory committee.

(a)　　Definitions. - As used in this section, unless the context requires otherwise, the term:

(1)　　"Advisory committee" means a medication management committee established under this section to advise the quality assurance committee.

(2)   "Medication-related error" means any preventable medication-related event that adversely affects a patient in a nursing home and that is related to professional practice, or health care products, procedures, and systems, including prescribing, prescription order communications, product labeling, packaging and nomenclature, compounding, dispensing, distribution, administration, education, monitoring, and use.

(3)   "Nursing home" means a nursing home licensed under this Chapter and includes an adult care home operated as part of a nursing home.

(4)   "Potential medication-related error" means a medication-related error that has not yet adversely affected a patient in a nursing home, but that has the potential to if not anticipated or prevented or if left unnoticed.

(5)   "Quality assurance committee" means a committee established in a nursing home in accordance with federal and State regulations to identify circumstances requiring quality assessment and assurance activities and to develop and implement appropriate plans of action to correct deficiencies in quality of care.

(b)   Purpose. - It is the purpose of the General Assembly to enhance compliance with this Part through the establishment of medication management advisory committees in nursing homes. The purpose of these committees is to assist nursing homes to identify medication-related errors, evaluate the causes of those errors, and take appropriate actions to ensure the safe prescribing, dispensing, and administration of medications to nursing home patients.

(c)   Advisory Committee Established; Membership. - Every nursing home shall establish a medication management advisory committee to advise the quality assurance committee on quality of care issues related to pharmaceutical and medication management and use in the nursing home. The nursing home shall maintain the advisory committee as part of its administrative duties. The advisory committee shall be interdisciplinary and consist of the nursing home administrator and at least the following members appointed by the nursing home administrator:

(1)   The director of nursing.

(2)   The consultant pharmacist.

(3)   A physician designated by the nursing home administrator.

41

(4)   At least three other members of the nursing home staff.

(d)   Meetings. - The advisory committee shall meet as needed but not less frequently than quarterly. The Director of Nursing or Staff Development Coordinator shall chair the advisory committee. The nursing home administrator shall ensure that a record is maintained of each meeting.

(e)   Confidentiality. - The meetings or proceedings of the advisory committee, the records and materials it produces, and the materials it considers, including analyses and reports pertaining to medication-related error reporting under G.S. 131E-128.2 and pharmacy reports on drug defects and adverse reactions under G.S. 131E-128.4, shall be confidential and not be considered public records within the meaning of G.S. 132-1. The meetings or proceedings and records and materials also shall not be subject to discovery or introduction into evidence in any civil action against a nursing home or a provider of professional health services resulting from matters that are the subject of evaluation and review by the committee. No person who was in attendance at a meeting of the committee shall testify in any civil action as to any evidence or other matters produced or presented during the meetings or proceedings of the committee or as to any findings, recommendations, evaluations, opinions, or other actions of the committee or its members. Notwithstanding the foregoing:

(1)   Information, documents, or records otherwise available, including any deficiencies found in the course of an inspection conducted under G.S. 131E-105, shall not be immune from discovery or use in a civil action merely because they were presented during meetings or proceedings of the advisory committee. A member of the advisory committee or a person who testifies before the committee may testify in a civil action but cannot be asked about that person's testimony before the committee or any opinion formed as a result of the committee meetings or proceedings.

(2)   Information that is confidential and not subject to discovery or use in civil actions under this subsection may be released to a professional standards review organization that performs any accreditation or certification function. Information released to the professional standards review organization shall be limited to information reasonably necessary and relevant to the standards review organization's determination to grant or continue accreditation or certification. Information released to the standards review organization retains its confidentiality and is not subject to discovery or use in any civil action as provided under this subsection. The standards review organization shall keep the information confidential subject to this subsection.

42

(3)   Information that is confidential and not subject to discovery or use in civil actions under this subsection may be released to the Department of Health and Human Services pursuant to its investigative authority under G.S. 131E-105. Information released to the Department shall be limited to information reasonably necessary and relevant to the Department's investigation of compliance with Part 1 of Article 6 of this Chapter. Information released to the Department retains its confidentiality and is not subject to discovery or use in any civil action as provided in this subsection. The Department shall keep the information confidential subject to this subsection.

(4)   Information that is confidential and is not subject to discovery or use in civil actions under this subsection may be released to an occupational licensing board having jurisdiction over the license of an individual involved in an incident that is under review or investigation by the advisory committee. Information released to the occupational licensing board shall be limited to information reasonably necessary and relevant to an investigation being conducted by the licensing board pertaining to the individual's involvement in the incident under review by the advisory committee. Information released to an occupational licensing board retains its confidentiality and is not subject to discovery or use in any civil action as provided in this subsection. The occupational licensing board shall keep the information confidential subject to this subsection.

(f)   Duties. - The advisory committee shall do the following:

(1)   Assess the nursing home's pharmaceutical management system, including its prescribing, distribution, administration policies, procedures, and practices and identify areas at high risk for medication-related errors.

(2)   Review the nursing home's pharmaceutical management goals and respond accordingly to ensure that these goals are being met.

(3)   Review, investigate, and respond to nursing home incident reports, deficiencies cited by licensing or credentialing agencies, and resident grievances that involve actual or potential medication-related errors.

(4)   Identify goals and recommendations to implement best practices and procedures, including risk reduction technology, to improve patient safety by reducing the risk of medication-related errors.

(5)   Develop recommendations to establish a mandatory, nonpunitive, confidential reporting system within the nursing home of actual and potential medication-related errors.

(6)   Develop specifications for drug dispensing and administration documentation procedures to ensure compliance with federal and State law, including the North Carolina Nursing Practice Act.

(7)   Develop specifications for self-administration of drugs by qualified patients in accordance with law, including recommendations for assessment procedures that identify patients who may be qualified to self-administer their medications.

(g)   Penalty. - The Department may take adverse action against the license of a nursing home upon a finding that the nursing home has failed to comply with this section, G.S. 131E-128.2, 131E-128.3, or 131E-128.4. (2003-393, s. 1; 2013-360, s. 12G.2(a), (b).)

§ 131E-128.2. Nursing home quality assurance committee; duties related to medication error prevention.

Every nursing home administrator shall ensure that the nursing home quality assurance committee develops and implements appropriate measures to minimize the risk of actual and potential medication-related errors, including the measures listed in this section. The design and implementation of the measures shall be based upon recommendations of the medication management advisory committee and shall:

(1)   Increase awareness and education of the patient and family members about all medications that the patient is using, both prescription and over-the-counter, including dietary supplements.

(2)   Increase prescription legibility.

(3)   Minimize confusion in prescription drug labeling and packaging, including unit dose packaging.

(4)   Develop a confidential and nonpunitive process for internal reporting of actual and potential medication-related errors.

(5)   To the extent practicable, implement proven medication safety practices, including the use of automated drug ordering and dispensing systems.

(6)   Educate facility staff engaged in medication administration activities on similar-sounding drug names.

(7)   Implement a system to accurately identify recipients before any drug is administered.

(8)   Implement policies and procedures designed to improve accuracy in medication administration and in documentation by properly authorized individuals, in accordance with prescribed orders and stop order policies.

(9)   Implement policies and procedures for patient self-administration of medication.

(10)   Investigate and analyze the frequency and root causes of general categories and specific types of actual or potential medication-related errors.

(11)   Develop recommendations for plans of action to correct identified deficiencies in the facility's pharmaceutical management practices. (2003-393, s. 1.)

§ 131E-128.3. Staff orientation on medication error prevention.

The nursing home administrator shall ensure that the nursing home provide a minimum of one hour of education and training in the prevention of actual or potential medication-related errors. This training shall be provided upon orientation and annually thereafter to all nonphysician personnel involved in direct patient care. The content of the training shall include at least the following:

(1)   General information relevant to the administration of medications including terminology, procedures, routes of medication administration, potential side effects, and adverse reactions.

(2)   Additional instruction on categories of medication pertaining to the specific needs of the patient receiving the medication.

(3)   The facility's policy and procedures regarding its medication administration system.

(4)   How to assist patients with safe and accurate self-administration of medication, where appropriate.

(5)   Identifying and reporting actual and potential medication-related errors. (2003-393, s. 1.)

§ 131E-128.4. Nursing home pharmacy reports; duties of consultant pharmacist.

(a)   The consultant pharmacist for a nursing home shall conduct a drug regimen review for actual and potential drug therapy problems in the nursing home and make remedial or preventive clinical recommendations into the medical record of every patient receiving medication. The consultant pharmacist shall conduct the review at least monthly in accordance with the nursing home's policies and procedures.

(b)   The consultant pharmacist shall report and document any drug irregularities and clinical recommendations promptly to the attending physician or nurse-in-charge and the nursing home administrator. The reports shall include problems identified and recommendations concerning:

(1)   Drug therapy that may be affected by biological agents, laboratory tests, special dietary requirements, and foods used or administered concomitantly with other medication to the same recipient.

(2)   Monitoring for potential adverse effects.

(3)   Allergies.

(4)   Drug interactions, including interactions between prescription drugs and over-the-counter drugs, drugs and disease, and interactions between drugs and nutrients.

(5)   Contraindications and precautions.

(6)   Potential therapeutic duplication.

46

(7)   Overextended length of treatment of certain drugs typically prescribed for a short period of time.

(8)   Beer's listed drugs that are potentially inappropriate for use by elderly persons.

(9)   Undertreatment or medical conditions that are suboptimally treated or not treated at all that warrant additional drug therapy to ensure quality of care.

(10)   Other identified problems and recommendations.

(c)   The consultant pharmacist shall report drug product defects and adverse drug reactions in accordance with the ASHSP-USP-FDA Drug Product Defect Reporting System and the USP Adverse Drug Reaction Reporting System. The term "ASHSP-USP-FDA" means American Society of Health System Pharmacists-United States Pharmacopoeia-Food and Drug Administration. Information released to the ASHSP-USP-FDA retains its confidentiality and is not subject to discovery or use in any civil action as provided under G.S. 131E-128.1.

(d)   The consultant pharmacist shall ensure that all known allergies and adverse effects are documented in plain view in the patient's medical record, including the medication administration records, and communicated to the dispensing pharmacy. The specific medications and the type of allergy or adverse reaction shall be specified in the documentation.

(e)   The consultant pharmacist shall ensure that drugs that are not specifically limited as to duration of use or number of doses shall be controlled by automatic stop orders. The consultant pharmacist shall further ensure that the prescribing provider is notified of the automatic stop order prior to the dispensing of the last dose so that the provider may decide whether to continue to use the drug.

(f)   The consultant pharmacist shall, on a quarterly basis, submit a summary of the reports submitted under subsections (a) and (b) of this section to the medication management advisory committee established under G.S. 131E-128.1. The summary shall not include any information that would identify a patient, a family member, or an employee of the nursing home. The purpose of the summary shall be to facilitate the identification and analysis of weaknesses in the nursing home's pharmaceutical care system that have an adverse impact on patient safety. (2003-393, s. 1.)

§ 131E-128.5: Repealed by Session Laws 2013-360, s. 12G.2(c), effective July 1, 2013.

§ 131E-129. Penalties; remedies.

(a)   Violation Classification and Penalties. - The Department of Health and Human Services shall impose an administrative penalty in accordance with provisions of this Article on any facility which is found to be in violation of the requirements of G.S. 131E-117 or applicable State and federal laws and regulations. Citations for violations shall be classified and penalties assessed according to the nature of the violation as follows:

(1)   "Type A1 Violation" means a violation by a facility of the regulations and requirements set forth in G.S. 131E-117, or applicable State or federal laws and regulations governing the licensure or certification of a facility which results in death or serious physical harm. The person making the findings shall do the following:

a.   Orally and immediately inform the facility of the Type A1 Violation and the specific findings.

b., c.   Repealed by Session Laws 2011-249, s. 3, effective June 23, 2011.

d.   Require a written, credible allegation regarding how the facility will immediately remove the Type A1 Violation in order to protect residents from further risk or additional harm.

e.   Within 15 working days of the investigation, send a report of the findings to the facility.

f.   Require a plan of correction to be submitted to the Department, based on the written report of the findings, that describes steps the facility will take to achieve and maintain compliance by the date specified by the Department.

The Department shall impose a civil penalty in an amount not less than one thousand dollars ($1,000) nor more than twenty thousand dollars ($20,000) for each Type A1 Violation. Where a facility has failed to correct a Type A1 Violation, the Department shall assess the facility a civil penalty in the amount of up to one thousand dollars ($1,000) for each day that the violation continues beyond the date specified for correction by the Department or its authorized

48

representative. The Department or its authorized representative shall determine whether the violation has been corrected.

(1a)   "Type A2 Violation" means a violation by a facility of the regulations, standards, and requirements set forth in G.S. 131E-117 or applicable State or federal laws and regulations governing the licensure or certification of a facility which results in substantial risk that death or serious physical harm will occur. The person making the findings shall do the following:

a.   Orally and immediately inform the facility of the Type A2 Violation and the specific findings.

b.   Require a credible allegation regarding how the facility will immediately remove the Type A2 Violation in order to protect residents from further risk or additional harm.

c.   Within 10 working days of the investigation, send a report of the findings to the facility.

d.   Require a plan of correction to be submitted to the Department, based on the written report of the findings, that describes steps the facility will take to achieve and maintain compliance by the date specified by the Department.

The violation or violations shall be corrected within the time specified for correction by the Department or its authorized representative. The Department may or may not assess a penalty taking into consideration the compliance history, preventative measures, and response to previous violations by the facility. Where a facility has failed to correct a Type A2 Violation, the Department shall assess the facility a civil penalty in the amount of up to one thousand dollars ($1,000) for each day that the deficiency continues beyond the time specified for correction by the Department or its authorized representative. The Department or its authorized representative shall determine whether the violation has been corrected.

(1b)   "Past Corrected Type A1 or Type A2 Violation" means either (i) the violation was not previously identified by the Department or its authorized representative or (ii) the violation was discovered by the facility and was self reported, but in either case the violation has been corrected. In determining whether a penalty should be assessed under this section, the Department shall consider the following factors:

a. Preventive systems in place prior to the violation.

b. Whether the violation or violations were abated immediately.

c. Whether the facility implemented corrective measures to achieve and maintain compliance.

d. Whether the facility's system to ensure compliance is maintained and continues to be implemented.

e. Whether the regulatory area remains in compliance.

(2) "Type B Violation" means a violation by a facility's licensee of the regulations, standards and requirements set forth in G.S. 131E-117 or applicable State or federal laws and regulations governing the licensure or certification of a facility which is detrimental to the health, safety, or welfare of any resident, but which does not result in substantial risk that death or serious physical harm will occur. The person making the findings shall do the following:

a. Orally and immediately inform the facility of the Type B Violation and the specific findings.

b. Require a written plan regarding how the facility will immediately remove the Type B Violation in order to protect residents from further risk or additional harm.

c. Within 10 working days of the investigation, send a report of the findings to the facility.

d. Require a plan of correction to be submitted to the Department, based on the written report of the findings, that describes steps the facility will take to achieve and maintain compliance by the date specified by the Department.

Where a facility has failed to correct a Type B Violation within the time specified for correction by the Department or its authorized representative, the Department shall assess the facility a civil penalty in the amount of up to four hundred dollars ($400.00) for each day that the violation continues beyond the date specified for correction without just reason for such failure. The Department or its authorized representative shall ensure that the violation has been corrected.

(3)   Repeat Violations. - The Department shall impose a civil penalty which is treble the amount assessed under subsection (a) of this section when a facility under the same management or ownership has received a citation during the previous 12 months for which the appeal rights are exhausted and penalty payment is expected or has occurred, and the current violation is for the same specific provision of a statute or regulation for which it received a violation during the previous 12 months. The counting of the 12-month period shall be tolled during any time when the facility is being operated by a court-appointed temporary manager pursuant to law.

(b)   Repealed by Session Laws 2011-249, s. 3, effective June 23, 2011.

(c)   Factors to be considered in determining amount of initial penalty. In determining the amount of the initial penalty to be imposed under this section, the Department shall consider the following factors:

(1)   There is substantial risk that serious physical harm, abuse, neglect, or exploitation will occur.

(2)   Serious physical harm, abuse, neglect, or exploitation, without substantial risk for resident death, did occur.

(3)   Serious physical harm, abuse, neglect, or exploitation, with substantial risk for resident death, did occur.

(4)   A resident died.

(5)   A resident died and there is substantial risk to others for serious physical harm, abuse, neglect, or exploitation.

(6)   A resident died and there is substantial risk for further resident death.

(7)   Reasonable diligence exercised by the licensee to comply with G.S. 131E-256 and G.S. 131E-265 did occur.

(8)   Efforts by the licensee to correct violations.

(9)   The number and type of previous violations committed by the licensee within the past 36 months.

(10)   The number of residents put at risk by the violations.

51

(c1)   The facts found to support the factors in subsection (c) of this section shall be the basis in determining the amount of the penalty. The Secretary shall document the findings in written record and shall make the written record available to all affected parties including:

(1)   The penalty review committee;

(2)   The local department of social services who is responsible for oversight of the facility involved;

(3)   The licensee involved;

(4)   The residents affected; and

(5)   The family member who serves as a responsible party or those who have legal authority on behalf of the affected resident.

(c2)   Local county departments of social services and Division of Health Service Regulation personnel shall submit proposed penalty recommendations to the Department within 45 days of the citation of a violation.

(d)   The Department shall impose a civil penalty of fifty dollars ($50.00) per day on any facility which refuses to allow an authorized representative of the Department to inspect the premises and records of the facility.

(e)   Any facility wishing to contest a penalty shall be entitled to an administrative hearing as provided in the Administrative Procedure Act, Chapter 150B of the General Statutes. A petition for a contested case shall be filed within 30 days after the Department mails a notice of penalty to a licensee. At least the following specific issues shall be addressed at the administrative hearing:

(1)   The reasonableness of the amount of any civil penalty assessed, and

(2)   The degree to which each factor has been evaluated pursuant to subsection (c) of this section to be considered in determining the amount of an initial penalty.

If a civil penalty is found to be unreasonable or if the evaluation of each factor is found to be incomplete, the hearing officer may recommend that the penalty be adjusted accordingly.

(e1)   Notwithstanding the notice requirements of G.S. 131E-24, any penalty imposed by the Department of Health and Human Services under this section shall commence on the day the citation is imposed.

(f)   The Secretary may bring a civil action in the superior court of the county wherein the violation occurred to recover the amount of the administrative penalty whenever a facility:

(1)   Which has not requested an administrative hearing fails to pay the penalty within 60 days after being notified of the penalty; or

(2)   Which has requested an administrative hearing fails to pay the penalty within 60 days after receipt of a written copy of the decision as provided in G.S. 150B-36.

(g)   The penalty review committee established pursuant to G.S. 131D-34(h) shall review administrative penalties assessed pursuant to this section.

(g1)   In lieu of assessing all or some of the administrative penalty, the Secretary may order a facility to provide staff training if the training is:

(1)   Specific to the violation;

(2)   Approved by the Department of Health and Human Services; and

(3)   Taught by an individual approved by the Department.

(h)   The Department shall not assess an administrative penalty against a facility under this section if a civil monetary penalty has been assessed for the same violation under federal enforcement laws and regulations.

(i)   The clear proceeds of civil penalties provided for in this section shall be remitted to the Civil Penalty and Forfeiture Fund in accordance with G.S. 115C-457.2. (1987, c. 600, s. 2; 1989, c. 556, s. 2; 1993, c. 390, s. 2; 1995, c. 396, s. 1; 1995 (Reg. Sess., 1996), c. 602, s. 2; 1997-431, s. 2; 1997-443, s. 11A.122; 1998-215, s. 78(b); 2007-182, s. 1.1; 2011-249, s. 3; 2012-194, s. 29.)

§ 131E-130. First available bed priority for certain nursing home patients.

53

(a)   If a patient is temporarily absent, for no more than 15 days, from a nursing home to obtain medical treatment at a hospital other than a State mental hospital, the nursing home; (i) shall provide the patient with the first bed available at or after the time the nursing home receives written notification of the specific date of discharge from the hospital; and (ii) shall grant the patient priority of admission over applicants for admission to the nursing home.

The duration of the temporary absence shall be calculated from the day of the patient's admission to a hospital until the date the nursing home receives written notice of the specific date of discharge.

This subsection shall not apply in instances in which the patient's treatment can no longer be provided by the nursing home upon re-admission.

(b)   If the Department finds that a nursing home has violated the provisions of subsection (a) of this section, the Department may assess a civil penalty of fifty dollars ($50.00) a day, up to a maximum of one thousand five hundred dollars ($1,500), against the nursing home, for each violation.

The clear proceeds of penalties provided for in this subsection shall be remitted to the Civil Penalty and Forfeiture Fund in accordance with G.S. 115C-457.2.

(c)   The provisions of Chapter 150B of the General Statutes that govern contested cases apply to appeals from Department action pursuant to this section. (1987 (Reg. Sess., 1988), c. 1080, s. 1; 1998-215, s. 79.)

§ 131E-131. Rule-making authority; enforcement.

The Commission shall adopt rules necessary for the implementation of this Part.

The Department shall enforce the rules adopted by the Commission to implement this Part. (1993, c. 499, s. 2.)

§ 131E-132. Reserved for future codification purposes.

§ 131E-133. Reserved for future codification purposes.

§ 131E-134. Reserved for future codification purposes.

Part 3. Home Care Agency Licensure Act.

§ 131E-135. Title; purpose.

(a)   This Part shall be known as "Home Care Agency Licensure Act."

(b)   The purpose of this Part is to establish licensing requirements for home care agencies. (1983, c. 775, s. 1; 1991, c. 59, s. 1; c. 761, s. 34.)

§ 131E-136. Definitions.

As used in this Part, unless otherwise specified:

(1)   "Commission" means the North Carolina Medical Care Commission.

(1a)   "Geographic service area" means the geographic area in which a licensed agency provides home care services.

(2)   "Home care agency" means a private or public organization that provides home care services.

(2a)   "Home care agency director" means the person having administrative responsibility for the operation of the licensed agency site.

(2b)   "Home care client" means an individual who receives home care services.

(3)   "Home care services" means any of the following services and directly related medical supplies and appliances, which are provided to an individual in a place of temporary or permanent residence used as an individual's home:

a.   Nursing care provided by or under the supervision of a registered nurse.

b.   Physical, occupational, or speech therapy, when provided to an individual who also is receiving nursing services, or any other of these therapy services, in a place of temporary or permanent residence used as the individual's home.

c.   Medical social services.

d.   In-home aide services that involve hands-on care to an individual.

e.   Infusion nursing services.

f.   Assistance with pulmonary care, pulmonary rehabilitation or ventilation.

g.   In-home companion, sitter, and respite care services provided to an individual.

h.   Homemaker services provided in combination with in-home companion, sitter, respite, or other home care services.

The term does not include: health promotion, preventative health and community health services provided by public health departments; maternal and child health services provided by public health departments, by employees of the Department of Health and Human Services under G.S. 130A-124, or by developmental evaluation centers under contract with the Department of Health and Human Services to provide services under G.S. 130A-124; hospitals licensed under Article 5 of Chapter 131E of the General Statutes when providing follow-up care initiated to patients within six months after their discharge from the hospital; facilities and programs operated under the authority of G.S. 122C and providing services within the scope of G.S. 122C; schools, when providing services pursuant to Article 9 of Chapter 115C; the practice of midwifery by a person licensed under Article 10A of Chapter 90 of the General Statutes; hospices licensed under Article 10 of Chapter 131E of the General Statutes when providing care to a hospice patient; an individual who engages solely in providing his own services to other individuals; incidental health care provided by an employee of a physician licensed to practice medicine in North Carolina in the normal course of the physician's practice; or nursing registries if the registry discloses to a client or the client's responsible party, before providing any services, that (i) it is not a licensed home care agency, and (ii) it does not make any representations or guarantees concerning the training, supervision, or competence of the personnel provided. The term sitter does not include child care facilities licensed in accordance with Chapter 110 of the General Statutes. The term respite care does not include facilities or services licensed in accordance with Chapter 122C of the General Statutes. The terms in-home companion, sitter, homemaker, and respite care services do not include (i) services certified or otherwise overseen by the Department as not providing personal care or (ii) services administered on a voluntary basis for which there is not reimbursement from the recipient or anyone acting on the recipient's behalf.

(4)   "Home health agency" means a home care agency which is certified to receive Medicare and Medicaid reimbursement for providing nursing care, therapy, medical social services, and home health aide services on a part-time, intermittent basis as set out in G.S. 131E-176(12), and is thereby also subject to Article 9 of Chapter 131E. (1971, c. 539, s. 1; 1983, c. 775, s. 1; 1983 (Reg. Sess., 1984), c. 1022, s. 4; 1987, c. 34, s. 1; 1991, c. 59, s. 1; c. 761, s. 34; 1997-443, s. 11A.90; 2005-276, s. 10.40A(m); 2008-127, s. 1.)

§ 131E-137. Services to be provided in all counties.

(a)   Every county shall provide part-time, intermittent home care nursing services, and at least one of the following home care services: part-time, intermittent physical therapy, occupational therapy, speech therapy, medical social work, or home health aide services.

(b)   Repealed by Session Laws 1991, c. 59, s. 1.

(c)   These services shall be provided by a home care agency licensed under this Part. The county may provide these services by contract with another home care agency in another county.

(d)   Repealed by Session Laws 1985, c. 8, s. 1. (1977, 2nd Sess., c. 1184; 1979, c. 754, s. 1; 1983, c. 775, s. 1; 1985, c. 8; 1991, c. 59, s. 1, c. 761, s. 34.)

§ 131E-138. Licensure requirements.

(a)   No person or governmental unit shall operate a home care agency without a license obtained from the Department. Nothing in this Part shall be construed to extend or modify the licensing of individual health professionals by the licensing boards for their professions or to create any new professional license category.

(b)   Repealed by Session Laws 1991, c. 59, s. 1.

(c)   An application for a license shall be available from the Department, and each application filed with the Department shall contain all information requested by the Department. A license shall be granted to the applicant upon a determination by the Department that the applicant has complied with the provisions of this Part and the rules promulgated by the Commission under this Part. The Department shall charge the applicant a nonrefundable annual license fee in the amount of five hundred ten dollars ($510.00).

(d)   The Department shall renew the license in accordance with the rules of the Commission.

(e)   Each license shall be issued only for the premises and persons named in the license and shall not be transferable or assignable except with the written approval of the Department.

(f)   The license shall be posted in a conspicuous place on the licensed premises.

(g)   The Commission shall adopt rules to ensure that a home care agency shall be deemed to meet the licensure requirements and issued a license without further review or inspection if: (i) the agency is already certified or accredited by the Joint Commission on Accreditation of Health Care Organizations, National League for Nursing, National Home Caring Council, North Carolina Accreditation Commission for In-Home Aide Services, or other entities recognized by the Commission and (ii) the agency is certified or accredited for all of the home care services that it provides; or (iii) in the case of continuing care retirement communities licensed by the North Carolina Department of Insurance under Article 64 of Chapter 58 which also have nursing beds licensed by the Department of Health and Human Services under Article 6 of Chapter 131E, the Department certifies, as part of its licensure review or survey of the nursing beds, that the facility also meets all of the rules and regulations adopted by the Commission pursuant to this Part. The Department may, at its discretion, determine the frequency and extent of the review and inspection of home health agencies already certified as meeting federal requirements, but not more frequently than on an annual basis for routine reviews. (1971, c. 539, s. 1; 1973, c. 476, s. 128; 1983, c. 775, s. 1; 1991, c. 59, s. 1; c. 761, s. 34; 1997-443, s. 11A.118(a); 2003-284, s. 34.4(a); 2005-276, s. 41.2(d); 2008-127, s. 2; 2009-451, s. 10.76(d).)

§ 131E-138.1. Licensure fees for nursing beds and adult care home beds in continuing care retirement communities.

The Department shall charge continuing care retirement communities licensed under Article 64 of Chapter 58 of the General Statutes that have nursing home beds or adult care home beds licensed by the Department a nonrefundable annual base license fee in the amount of four hundred fifty dollars ($450.00) plus a nonrefundable annual per-bed fee in the amount of twelve dollars and fifty cents ($12.50). (2003-284, s. 34.9(a); 2005-276, s. 41.2(i).)

§ 131E-139. Adverse action on a license.

(a)   The Department may suspend, revoke, annul, withdraw, recall, cancel or amend a license when there has been a substantial failure to comply with the provisions of this Part or the rules promulgated under this Part.

(b)   The provisions of Chapter 150B of the General Statutes, The Administrative Procedure Act, shall govern all administrative action and judicial review in cases where the Department has taken the action described in subsection (a). (1971, c. 539, s. 1; 1973, c. 476, s. 128; 1983, c. 775, s. 1; 1987, c. 827, s. 1; 1991, c. 59, s. 1, c. 761, s. 34.)

§ 131E-140. Rules and enforcement.

(a)   The Commission may adopt, amend and repeal all rules necessary for the implementation of this Part and Part 3A of Article 6 of this Chapter. Provided, these rules shall not extend, modify, or limit the licensing of individual health professionals by their respective licensing boards; nor shall these rules in any way be construed to extend the appropriate scope of practice of any individual health care provider. Rules authorized under this section include rules:

(1)   That recognize the different types of home care services and shall adopt specific requirements for the provision of each type of home care service.

(2)   To establish staff qualifications, including professional requirements for home care agency staff. The rules may require that one or more staff of an agency be either licensed or certified. The rules may establish minimum training and education qualifications for staff and may include the recognition of professional certification boards for those professions not licensed or certified

59

under other provisions of the North Carolina General Statutes provided that the professional board evaluates applicants on a basis that protects the public health, safety, or welfare.

(3)   For the purpose of ensuring effective supervision of in-home aide staff and timely provision of services, the Commission shall adopt rules defining geographic service areas for in-home aide services and staffing qualifications for licensed home care agencies.

(4)   Prohibiting licensed home care agencies from hiring individuals listed on the Health Care Personnel Registry in accordance with G.S. 131E-256(a)(1).

(5)   Requiring applicants for home care licensure to receive training in the requirements for licensure, the licensure process, and the rules pertaining to the operation of a home care agency.

(a1)   The Commission shall adopt rules defining the scope of permissible advertising and promotional practice by home care agencies.

(b)   The Department shall enforce the rules adopted or amended by the Commission with respect to home care agencies and shall conduct an inspection of each agency at least every three years. (1971, c. 539, s. 1; 1973, c. 476, s. 128; 1983, c. 775, s. 1; 1991, c. 59, s. 1; c. 761, s. 34; 2005-276, ss. 10.40A(a), 10.40A(o).)

§ 131E-141. Inspection.

(a)   The Department shall inspect home care agencies in accordance with rules adopted by the Commission to determine compliance with the provisions of this Part and the rules established by the Commission.

(b)   Notwithstanding the provisions of G.S. 8-53, "Communications between physician and patient," or any other provision of law relating to the confidentiality of communications between physician and patient, the representatives of the Department who make these inspections may review any writing or other record in any recording medium which pertains to the admission, discharge, medication, treatment, medical condition, or history of persons who are or have been clients of the agency being inspected unless that client objects in writing to review of that client's records. Physicians, psychiatrists, nurses, and anyone else involved in giving treatment at or through an agency who may be interviewed by representatives of the Department may disclose to these representatives information related to any inquiry, notwithstanding the existence of the physician-patient privilege in G.S. 8-53, "Communication between physician and patient," or any other rule of law; provided the client has not made written objection to this disclosure. The agency, its employees, and any person interviewed during these inspections shall be immune from liability for damages resulting from the disclosure of any information to the Department. Any confidential or privileged information received from review of records or interviews, except as noted in G.S. 131E-124(c), shall be kept confidential by the Department and not disclosed without written authorization of the client or legal representative, or unless disclosure is ordered by a court of competent jurisdiction. The Department shall institute appropriate policies and procedures to ensure that this information shall not be disclosed without authorization or court order. The Department shall not disclose the name of anyone who has furnished information concerning an agency without the consent of that person. Neither the names of persons furnishing information nor any confidential or privileged information obtained from records or interviews shall be considered "public records" within the meaning of G.S. 132-1, " 'Public records' defined." Prior to releasing any information or allowing any inspections referred to in this section, the client must be advised in writing by the licensed agency that the client has the right to object in writing to release of information or review of the client's records and that by an objection in writing the client may prohibit the inspection or release of the records.

(c)   An agency must provide each client with a written notice of the Division of Health Service Regulation hotline number in advance of furnishing care to the client or during the initial evaluation visit before the initiation of services. (1971, c. 539, s. 1; 1973, c. 476, s. 128; 1981, c. 586, s. 2; 1983, c. 775, s. 1; 1991, c. 59, s. 1; c. 761, s. 34; 1999-113, s. 4; 2005-276, s. 10.40A(b); 2007-182, s. 1.)

§ 131E-141.1. Penalties for violation.

Any person who knowingly and willfully establishes, conducts, manages or operates any home care agency without a license is guilty of a Class 3 misdemeanor and upon conviction is liable only for a fine of not more than five hundred dollars ($500.00) for the first offense and not more than five hundred dollars ($500.00) for each subsequent offense. (1991, c. 59, s. 1, c. 761, s. 34; 1993, c. 539, s. 961; 1994, Ex. Sess., c. 24, s. 14(c).)

61

§ 131E-142. Injunction.

(a)   Notwithstanding the existence or pursuit of any other remedy, the Department shall, in the manner provided by law, maintain an action in the name of the State for injunction or other process against any person or governmental unit to restrain or prevent the establishment, conduct, management or operation of a home care agency without a license.

(b)   If any person shall hinder the proper performance of duty of the Secretary or a representative in carrying out the provisions of this Part, the Secretary may institute an action in the superior court of the county in which the hindrance occurred for injunctive relief against the continued hindrance irrespective of all other remedies at law.

(c)   Actions under this section shall be in accordance with Article 37 of Chapter 1 of the General Statutes and Rule 65 of the Rules of Civil Procedure. (1983, c. 775, s. 1; 1991, c. 59, s. 1, c. 761, s. 34.)

§ 131E-143. Smoking prohibited; penalty.

(a)   A home care agency shall prohibit its employees from smoking while providing services to an individual in the individual's home. The home care agency shall inform its clients that employees of the agency are prohibited from smoking in a client's home. As used in this section:

(1)   "Employee" includes an individual under contract with the home care agency to provide home care services.

(2)   "Smoking" means the use or possession of any lighted cigar, cigarette, pipe, or other lighted smoking product.

(b)   The Department may impose an administrative penalty not to exceed two hundred dollars ($200.00) for each violation on any person who owns, manages, operates, or otherwise controls the home care agency and fails to comply with this section. A violation of this section constitutes a civil offense only and is not a crime. (2007-459, s. 4.)

§ 131E-144. Reserved for future codification purposes.

Part 3A. Home Care Clients' Bill of Rights.

§ 131E-144.1. Legislative intent.

It is the intent of the General Assembly to support an individual's desire to live at home and receive home care services. (2005-276, s. 10.40A(n).)

§ 131E-144.2. Definitions.

Unless otherwise specified, the definitions that are provided in Part 3 of Article 6 of this Chapter apply in this Part. (2005-276, s. 10.40A(n).)

§ 131E-144.3. Declaration of home care clients' rights.

Each client of a home care agency shall have the following rights:

(1)   To be informed and participate in his or her plan of care.

(2)   To be treated with respect, consideration, dignity, and full recognition of his or her individuality and right to privacy.

(3)   To receive care and services that are adequate, appropriate, and in compliance with relevant federal and State laws and rules and regulations.

(4)   To voice grievances about care and not be subjected to discrimination or reprisal for doing so.

(5)   To have his or her personal and medical records kept confidential and not be disclosed except as permitted or required by applicable State or federal law.

(6)   To be free of mental and physical abuse, neglect, and exploitation.

(7)   To receive a written statement of services provided by the agency and the charges the client is liable for paying.

(8)   To be informed of the process for acceptance and continuance of service and eligibility determination.

(9)   To accept or refuse services.

(10)   To be informed of the agency's on-call service.

(11)   To be informed of supervisory accessibility and availability.

(12)   To be advised of the agency's procedures for discharge.

(13)   To receive a reasonable response to his or her requests of the agency.

(14)   To be notified within 10 days when the agency's license has been revoked, suspended, canceled, annulled, withdrawn, recalled, or amended.

(15)   To be advised of the agency's policies regarding patient responsibilities. (2005-276, s. 10.40A(n); 2011-314, s. 6.)

§ 131E-144.4. Notice to client.

(a)   During the agency's initial evaluation visit or before furnishing services, a home care agency shall provide each client with the following:

(1)   A copy of the declaration of home care clients' rights.

(2)   A copy of the agency's policies regarding client responsibilities as it relates to safety and care plan compliance.

(3)   The address and telephone number for information, questions, or complaints about services provided by the agency.

(4)   The address and telephone number of the section of the Department of Health and Human Services responsible for the enforcement of the provisions of this Part.

(b)   Receipts for the declaration of home care clients' rights and contact information required in this section shall be signed by the client and shall be retained in the agency's files. (2005-276, s. 10.40A(n).)

§ 131E-144.5. Implementation.

Responsibility for implementing the provisions of this Part shall rest with the home care agency director. Each agency shall provide appropriate training to implement this Part. (2005-276, s. 10.40A(n).)

§ 131E-144.6. Enforcement and investigation.

(a)   The Department of Health and Human Services shall be responsible for enforcing the provisions of this Part. The Department shall investigate complaints made to it and reply within a reasonable period of time, not to exceed 60 days.

(a1)   When the Department of Health and Human Services receives a complaint alleging a violation of the provisions of this Part pertaining to client care or client safety, the Department shall initiate an investigation as follows:

(1)   Immediately upon receipt of the complaint if the complaint alleges a life-threatening situation.

(2)   Within 24 hours if the complaint alleges abuse of a client as defined by G.S. 131D-20(1).

(3)   Within 48 hours if the complaint alleges neglect of a client as defined by G.S. 131D-20(8).

(4)   Within two weeks in all other situations.

The investigation shall be completed within 30 days. The requirements of this section are in addition to and not in lieu of any investigatory and reporting requirements for health care personnel pursuant to Article 15 of this Chapter, or for adult protective services pursuant to Article 6 of Chapter 108A of the General Statutes.

(b)   A home care agency shall investigate, within 72 hours, complaints made to the agency by a home care client or the client's family and must document both the existence of the complaint and the resolution of the complaint. (2005-276, s. 10.40A(n).)

§ 131E-144.7. Confidentiality.

(a)   The Department of Health and Human Services may inspect home care clients' medical records maintained at the agency when necessary to investigate any alleged violation of this Part.

(b)   The Department shall maintain the confidentiality of all persons who register complaints with the Department and of all medical records inspected by the Department. A person who has filed a complaint shall have access to information about a complaint investigation involving a specific home care client if written authorization is obtained from the client or legal representative. (2005-276, s. 10.40A(n).)

Part 4. Ambulatory Surgical Facility Licensure.

§ 131E-145. Title; purpose.

(a)   This Part shall be known as the "Ambulatory Surgical Facility Licensure Act."

(b)   The purpose of this Part is to provide for the development, establishment and enforcement of basic standards:

(1)   For the care and treatment of individuals in ambulatory surgical facilities; and

(2)   For the maintenance and operation of ambulatory surgical facilities so as to ensure safe and adequate treatment of such individuals in ambulatory surgical facilities. (1977, 2nd Sess., c. 1214, s. 1; 1983, c. 775, s. 1.)

§ 131E-146. Definitions.

As used in this Part, unless otherwise specified:

(1)   "Ambulatory surgical facility" means a facility designed for the provision of a specialty ambulatory surgical program or a multispecialty ambulatory surgical program. An ambulatory surgical facility serves patients who require local, regional or general anesthesia and a period of post-operative observation. An ambulatory surgical facility may only admit patients for a period of less than 24 hours and must provide at least one designated operating room as defined in subdivision (1c) of this section or at least one gastrointestinal endoscopy room as defined in subdivision (1b) of this section and at least one designated recovery room, have available the necessary equipment and trained personnel to handle emergencies, provide adequate quality assurance and assessment by an evaluation and review committee, and maintain adequate medical records for each patient. An ambulatory surgical facility may be operated as a part of a physician or dentist's office, provided the facility is licensed under G.S. Chapter 131E, Article 6, Part 4, but the performance of incidental, limited ambulatory surgical procedures which do not constitute an ambulatory surgical program as defined in subdivision (1a) and which are performed in a physician or dentist's office does not make that office an ambulatory surgical facility.

(1a)   "Ambulatory surgical program" means a formal program for providing on a same-day basis those surgical procedures which require local, regional or general anesthesia and a period of post-operative observation to patients whose admission for more than 24 hours is determined, prior to surgery or gastrointestinal endoscopy, to be medically unnecessary.

(1b)   "Gastrointestinal endoscopy room" means a room used for the performance of procedures that require the insertion of a flexible endoscope into a gastrointestinal orifice to visualize the gastrointestinal lining and adjacent organs for diagnostic or therapeutic purposes.

(1c)   "Operating room" means a room used for the performance of surgical procedures requiring one or more incisions and that is required to comply with all applicable licensure codes and standards for an operating room.

(2)   "Commission" means the North Carolina Medical Care Commission. (1977, 2nd Sess., c. 1214, s. 1; 1983, c. 775, s. 1; 1983 (Reg. Sess., 1984), c. 1064, s. 1; 1997-456, s. 49(a); 2001-242, s. 1; 2005-346, s. 4.)

§ 131E-147. Licensure requirement.

(a)   No person shall operate an ambulatory surgical facility without a license obtained from the Department.

(b)   Applications shall be available from the Department, and each application filed with the Department shall contain all necessary and reasonable information that the Department may by rule require. A license shall be granted to the applicant upon a determination by the Department that the applicant has complied with the provisions of this Part and the rules promulgated by the Commission under this Part. The Department shall charge the applicant a nonrefundable annual base license fee in the amount of eight hundred fifty dollars ($850.00) plus a nonrefundable annual per-operating room fee in the amount of seventy-five dollars ($75.00).

(c)   A license to operate an ambulatory surgical facility shall be annually renewed upon the filing and the department's approval of a renewal application. The renewal application shall be available from the Department and shall contain all necessary and reasonable information that the Department may by rule require.

(d)   Each license shall be issued only for the premises and persons named in the application and shall not be transferable or assignable except with the written approval of the Department.

(e)   Licenses shall be posted in a conspicuous place on the licensed premises. (1977, 2nd Sess., c. 1214, s. 1; 1983, c. 775, s. 1; 2003-284, s. 34.5(a); 2005-276, s. 41.2(e); 2009-451, s. 10.76(b).)

§ 131E-147.1. Fair billing and collections practices for ambulatory surgical facilities.

All ambulatory surgical facilities licensed under this Part shall be subject to the fair billing and collections practices set out in G.S. 131E-91. (2013-382, s. 13.3.)

§ 131E-148. Adverse action on a license.

68

(a)   Subject to subsection (b), the Department is authorized to deny a new or renewal application for a license, and to amend, recall, suspend or revoke an existing license upon a determination that there has been a substantial failure to comply with the provisions of this Part or the rules promulgated under this Part.

(b)   The provisions of Chapter 150A of the General Statutes, the Administrative Procedure Act, shall govern all administrative action and judicial review in cases where the Department has taken the action described in subsection (a). (1977, 2nd Sess., c. 1214, s. 1; 1983, c. 775, s. 1.)

§ 131E-149. Rules and enforcement.

(a)   The Commission is authorized to adopt, amend and repeal all rules necessary for the implementation of this Part. These rules shall be no stricter than those issued by the Commission under G.S. 131E-79 of the Hospital Licensing Act.

(b)   The Department shall enforce the rules adopted or amended by the Commission with respect to ambulatory surgical facilities. (1977, 2nd Sess., c. 1214, s. 1; 1983, c. 775, s. 1.)

§ 131E-150. Inspections.

(a)   The Department shall make or cause to be made inspections of ambulatory surgical facilities as necessary. The Department is authorized to delegate to a State officer, agent, board, bureau or division of State government the authority to make inspections according to the rules adopted by the Commission. The Department may revoke this delegated authority in its discretion.

(b)   Notwithstanding the provisions of G.S. 8-53, "Communications between physician and patient," or any other provision of law relating to the confidentiality of communications between physician and patient, the representatives of the Department who make these inspections may review any writing or other record in any recording medium which pertains to the admission, discharge, medication, treatment, medical condition, or history of persons who are or have been patients of the facility being inspected unless that patient objects in writing

69

to review of that patient's records. Physicians, psychologists, psychiatrists, nurses, and anyone else involved in giving treatment at or through a facility who may be interviewed by representatives of the Department may disclose to these representatives information related to an inquiry, notwithstanding the existence of the physician-patient privilege in G.S. 8-53, "Communication between physician and patient," or any other rule of law; Provided the patient has not made written objection to this disclosure. The facility, its employees, and any person interviewed during these inspections shall be immune from liability for damages resulting from the disclosure of any information to the Department. Any confidential or privileged information received from review of records or interviews shall be kept confidential by the Department and not disclosed without written authorization of the patient or legal representative, or unless disclosure is ordered by a court of competent jurisdiction. The Department shall institute appropriate policies and procedures to ensure that this information shall not be disclosed without authorization or court order. The Department shall not disclose the name of anyone who has furnished information concerning a facility without the consent of that person. Neither the names of persons furnishing information nor any confidential or privileged information obtained from records or interviews shall be considered "public records" within the meaning of G.S. 132-1, "'Public records' defined." Prior to releasing any information or allowing any inspections referred to in this section, the patient must be advised in writing by the facility that the patient has the right to object in writing to this release of information or review of the records and that by objecting in writing, the patient may prohibit the inspection or release of the records. (1977, 2nd Sess., c. 1214, s. 1; 1981, c. 586, s. 5; 1983, c. 775, s. 1.)

§ 131E-151. Penalties.

A person who owns in whole or in part or operates an ambulatory surgical facility without a license is guilty of a Class 3 misdemeanor, and upon conviction will be subject only to a fine of not more than fifty dollars ($50.00) for the first offense and not more than five hundred dollars ($500.00) for each subsequent offense. Each day of continuing violation after conviction is considered a separate offense. (1977, 2nd Sess., c. 1214, s. 1; 1983, c. 775, s. 1; 1993, c. 539, s. 962; 1994, Ex. Sess., c. 24, s. 14(c).)

§ 131E-152. Injunction.

(a)   Notwithstanding the existence or pursuit of any other remedy, the Department may, in the manner provided by law, maintain an action in the name of the State for injunction or other process against any person or governmental unit to restrain or prevent the establishment, conduct, management or operation of an ambulatory surgical facility without a license.

(b)   If any person shall hinder the proper performance of duty of the Secretary or a representative in carrying out the provisions of this Part, the Secretary may institute an action in the superior court of the county in which the hindrance occurred for injunctive relief against the continued hindrance, irrespective of all other remedies at law.

(c)   Actions under this section shall be in accordance with Article 37 of Chapter 1 of the General Statutes and Rule 65 of the Rules of Civil Procedure. (1977, 2nd Sess., c. 1214, s. 1; 1983, c. 775, s. 1.)

§ 131E-153. Reserved for future codification purposes.

§ 131E-154. Reserved for future codification purposes.

Part 5. Nursing Pool Licensure Act.

§ 131E-154.1. Title; purpose.

(a)   This Part shall be known as "Nursing Pool Licensure Act".

(b)   The purpose of this Part is to establish licensing requirements for nursing pools. (1989, c. 744, s. 1.)

§ 131E-154.2. Definitions.

As used in this Part, unless the context clearly implies otherwise:

(1)   "Commission" means the North Carolina Medical Care Commission.

(2)   "Department" means the Department of Health and Human Services.

(3)   "Health Care Facility" means a hospital, psychiatric facility; rehabilitation facility; long-term care facility; home health agency; intermediate care facility for the mentally retarded; chemical dependency treatment facility; and ambulatory surgical facility.

(4)   "Nursing pool" means any person, firm, corporation, partnership, or association engaged for hire in the business of providing or procuring temporary employment in health care facilities for nursing personnel, including nurses, nursing assistants, nurses aides, and orderlies. "Nursing pool" does not include an individual who engages solely in providing his own services on a temporary basis to health care facilities.

(5)   "Trauma" means acute physical injury to the human body that is judged, by the use of standardized field triage criteria (anatomic, physiologic, or mechanism of injury), to create a significant risk of mortality or major morbidity. (1989, c. 744, s. 1; 1993, c. 336, s. 2; 1997-443, s. 11A.118(a).)

§ 131E-154.3. Licensing.

(a)   No person shall operate or represent himself to the public as operating a nursing pool without obtaining a license from the Department.

(b)   The Department shall provide applications for nursing pool licensure. Each application filed with the Department shall contain all information requested. A license shall be granted to the applicant upon a determination by the Department that the applicant has complied with the provisions of this Part and with the rules adopted by the Commission. Each license shall be issued only for the premises and persons named, shall not be transferrable or assignable except with the written approval of the Department, and shall be posted in a conspicuous place on the licensed premises.

(c)   The Department shall renew the license in accordance with this Part and with rules adopted pursuant to it.

(d)   Nursing pools administered by health care facilities and agencies licensed under Article 5 or 6 of Chapter 131E of the General Statutes shall not be required to be separately licensed under this Article. However, any facility or agency exempted from licensure as a nursing pool under this subsection shall be subject to rules adopted pursuant to this Article. (1989, c. 744, s. 1.)

§ 131E-154.4. Rules and enforcement.

(a)   The Commission shall adopt, amend, and repeal all rules necessary for the implementation of this Part. These rules shall include the following requirements:

(1)   The nursing pool shall document that each employee who provides care meets the minimum licensing, training, and continuing education standards for the position in which the employee will be working;

(2)   The nursing pool shall comply with all other pertinent regulations relating to the health and other qualifications of personnel;

(3)   The nursing pool shall carry general and professional liability insurance to insure against the loss, damage, or expense incident to a claim arising out of the death or injury of any person as the result of negligence or malpractice in the provision of health care services by the nursing pool or its employees;

(4)   The nursing pool shall have written administrative and personnel policies to govern the services that it provides. These policies shall include those concerning patient care, personnel, training and orientation, supervision, employee evaluation, and organizational structure; and

(5)   Any other aspects of nursing pool services that may need to be regulated to protect the public.

(b)   The Commission shall adopt no rules pertaining to the regulation of charges by the nursing pool or to wages paid by the nursing pool. (1989, c. 744, s. 1.)

§ 131E-154.5. Inspections.

The Department shall inspect all nursing pools that are subject to rules adopted pursuant to this Part in order to determine compliance with the provisions of this Part and with rules adopted pursuant to it. Inspections shall be conducted in accordance with rules adopted by the Commission. (1989, c. 744, s. 1.)

§ 131E-154.6. Adverse action on a license; appeal procedures.

(a)   The Department may suspend, revoke, annul, withdraw, recall, cancel, or amend a license when there has been a substantial failure to comply with the provisions of this Part or with the rules adopted pursuant to it.

(b)   The provisions of Chapter 150B of the General Statutes, the Administrative Procedure Act, shall govern all administrative action and judicial review in cases in which the Department has taken the action described in subsection (a) of this section. (1989, c. 744, s. 1.)

§ 131E-154.7. Injunction.

(a)   Notwithstanding the existence or pursuit of any other remedy, the Department may maintain an action in the name of the State for injunctive relief or other process against any person to restrain or prevent the establishment, conduct, management, or operation of a nursing pool without a license or to restrain or prevent substantial noncompliance with this Part or the rules adopted pursuant to it.

(b)   If any person hinders the proper performance of duty of the Department in carrying out the provisions of this Part, the Department may institute an action in the superior court of the county in which the hindrance occurred for injunctive relief against the continued hindrance. (1989, c. 744, s. 1.)

§ 131E-154.8. Confidentiality.

(a)   Notwithstanding G.S. 8-53 or any other law pertaining to confidentiality of communications between physician and patient, in the course of an inspection conducted pursuant to G.S. 131E-154.5:

(1)   Department representatives may review any writing or other record concerning the admission, discharge, medication, treatment, medical condition, or history of any person who is or has been a nursing pool patient; and

(2)   Any person involved in treating a patient at or through a nursing pool may disclose information to a Department representative unless the patient

objects in writing to review of his records or disclosure of the information. A nursing pool shall not release any information or allow any inspections under this section without first informing each affected patient in writing of his right to object to and thus prohibit release of information or review of records pertaining to him.

A nursing pool, its employees, and any other person interviewed in the course of an inspection shall be immune from liability for damages resulting from disclosure of the information to the Department.

(b)   The Department shall not disclose:

(1)   Any confidential or privileged information obtained under this section unless the patient or his legal representative authorizes disclosure in writing or unless a court of competent jurisdiction orders disclosure; or

(2)   The name of anyone who has furnished information concerning a nursing pool without that person's consent.

The Department shall institute appropriate policies and procedures to ensure that unauthorized disclosure does not occur. Any Department employee who willfully discloses this information without appropriate authorization or court order shall be guilty of a Class 3 misdemeanor and, upon conviction, only fined at the discretion of the court but not in excess of five hundred dollars ($500.00).

(c)   All confidential or privileged information obtained under this section and the names of all persons providing this information are exempt from Chapter 132 of the General Statutes. (1989, c. 744, s. 1; 1993, c. 539, s. 963; 1994, Ex. Sess., c. 24, s. 14(c).)

§ 131E-154.9. Reserved for future codification purposes.

§ 131E-154.10. Reserved for future codification purposes.

§ 131E-154.11. Reserved for future codification purposes.

Part 6. North Carolina New Organizational Vision Award (NC NOVA) Special Licensure Designation.

§ 131E-154.12. Title; purpose.

(a)   This Part shall be known as the "North Carolina New Organizational Vision Award (NC NOVA) Special Licensure Designation."

(b)   The purpose of this Part is to establish special licensure designation requirements for nursing homes and home care agencies licensed pursuant to this Chapter and adult care homes licensed pursuant to Article 1 of Chapter 131D of the General Statutes. Application for the Special Licensure Designation is voluntary. (2006-104, s. 1.)

§ 131E-154.13. Definitions.

The following definitions apply in this Part, unless otherwise specified:

(1)   Independent Review Organization. - The organization responsible for the application, review, and determination process for NC NOVA designation.

(2)   North Carolina New Organizational Vision Award (NC NOVA). - A special licensure designation for home care agencies and nursing homes licensed pursuant to this Chapter, and adult care homes licensed pursuant to Article 1 of Chapter 131D of the General Statutes, that have been determined through written and on-site review by an independent review organization to have met a comprehensive set of workplace related interventions intended to improve the recruitment and retention, quality, and job satisfaction of direct care staff and the care provided to long-term care clients and residents.

(3)   NC NOVA Partner Team. - The entity responsible for developing the criteria and protocols for the NC NOVA special licensure designation. The Partner Team is inclusive of representatives from the following organizations: Association for Home and Hospice Care of North Carolina, Direct Care Workers Association of North Carolina, Duke University Gerontological Nursing Program, Friends of Residents in Long Term Care, North Carolina Assisted Living Association, North Carolina Association of Long Term Care Facilities, North Carolina Association of Non-Profit Homes for the Aging, North Carolina Department of Health and Human Services, North Carolina Foundation for Advanced Health Programs, North Carolina Health Care Facilities Association, The Carolinas Center for Medical Excellence, and the University of North Carolina at Chapel Hill - Institute on Aging.

(4)   NC NOVA Provider Information Manual. - The document developed by
the NC NOVA Partner Team that specifies the scope of criteria for NC NOVA
designation as well as information and procedures pertaining to the application,
review, determination, and termination process. (2006-104, s. 1.)

§ 131E-154.14. NC NOVA program established.

(a)   The Department of Health and Human Services shall establish the NC
NOVA program.

(b)   The Department shall adopt rules to implement the NC NOVA program
in accordance with the criteria and protocols established by the NC NOVA
Partner Team and detailed in the NC NOVA Provider Information Manual.

(c)   Any information submitted by applicants or obtained by the independent
review organization related to NC NOVA, as well as annual turnover data
voluntarily submitted by home care agencies, adult care homes, and nursing
facilities for the purposes of assessing statewide turnover trends, shall not be
considered a public record under G.S. 132-1.

(d)   Any licensed home care agency, adult care home, or nursing home that
is determined not to have met the criteria for NC NOVA designation may reapply
at intervals specified by the NC NOVA Partner Team and detailed in the NC
NOVA Provider Information Manual.

(e)   The Department of Health and Human Services, Division of Health
Service Regulation, shall issue a NC NOVA special licensure designation
document to any licensed home care agency, adult care home, or nursing home
that is determined by the independent review organization to have met the
criteria for NC NOVA designation. The special licensure designation document
shall be in addition to the operating license issued by the Division.

(f)   The Division of Health Service Regulation shall issue the NC NOVA
special licensure document to successful applicants within 30 days of
notification by the independent review organization.

(g)   The NC NOVA special licensure designation shall be in effect for a two-
year period unless the provider has a change in ownership.

(1)   Upon a change in ownership, if the new owner wishes to continue the NC NOVA designation, the new owner must communicate the desire in writing to the independent review organization within 30 days of the effective date of the change of ownership and proceed with an expedited review in accordance with procedures detailed by the NC NOVA Partner Team and included in the NC NOVA Provider Information Manual.

a.   If the new owner continues to meet the NC NOVA criteria, based upon the expedited review, the special licensure designation will remain in effect for the remainder of the two-year period.

b.   If the new owner fails to meet NC NOVA criteria, the special designation document shall be immediately returned to the Division of Health Service Regulation. The new owner may reapply for NC NOVA designation under subsection (e) of this section.

(2)   Within 30 days of the effective date of the change of ownership, if the new owner fails to notify the independent review organization in writing of the desire to retain the special licensure designation by undergoing an expedited review, the designation will become null and void, and the special designation document must be immediately returned to the Division of Health Service Regulation. (2006-104, s. 1; 2007-182, s. 1.)

Article 7.

Regulation of Emergency Medical Services.

§ 131E-155. Definitions.

As used in this Article, unless otherwise specified:

(1)   "Ambulance" means any privately or publicly owned motor vehicle, aircraft, or vessel that is specially designed, constructed, or modified and equipped and is intended to be used for and is maintained or operated for the transportation of patients on the streets or highways, waterways or airways of this State.

(2)   Repealed by Session Laws 1997-443, s. 11A.129C.

(3)   Redesignated as subdivision (13a).

(4)   "Commission" means the North Carolina Medical Care Commission.

(5)   "Emergency medical dispatcher" means an emergency telecommunicator who has completed an educational program approved by the Department and has been credentialed as an emergency medical dispatcher by the Department.

(6)   "Emergency medical services" means services rendered by emergency medical services personnel in responding to improve the health and wellness of the community and to address the individual's need for emergency medical care within the scope of practice as defined by the North Carolina Medical Board in accordance with G.S. 143-514 in order to prevent loss of life or further aggravation of physiological or psychological illness or injury.

(6a)   "Emergency medical services instructor" means an individual who has completed educational requirements approved by the Department and has been credentialed as an emergency medical services instructor by the Department.

(6b)   "Emergency Medical Services Peer Review Committee" means a panel composed of EMS program representatives to be responsible for analyzing patient care data and outcome measures to evaluate the ongoing quality of patient care, system performance, and medical direction within the EMS system. The committee membership shall include physicians, nurses, EMS personnel, medical facility personnel, and county government officials. Review of medical records by the EMS Peer Review Committee is confidential and protected under G.S. 143-518. An EMS Peer Review Committee, its members, proceedings, records and materials produced, and materials considered shall be afforded the same protections afforded Medical Review Committees, their members, proceedings, records, and materials under G.S. 131E-95.

(7)   "Emergency medical services personnel" means all the personnel defined in subdivisions (5), (6a), (8), (9), (10), (12), (13), (14), and (15) of this section.

(8)   "Emergency medical services-nurse practitioner" means a registered nurse who is licensed to practice nursing in North Carolina and approved to perform medical acts by the North Carolina Medical Board and the North

Carolina Board of Nursing. Upon successful completion of an orientation program conducted under the authority of the medical director and approved by the Department, emergency medical services-nurse practitioners shall be approved by the medical director to issue instructions to EMS personnel. These instructions shall be in accordance with protocols approved by the EMS system and Office of Emergency Medical Services and under the direction of the medical director.

(9)   "Emergency medical services-physician assistant" means a physician assistant who is licensed by the North Carolina Medical Board. Upon successful completion of an orientation program conducted under the authority of the medical director and approved by the Department, emergency medical services-physician assistants shall be approved by the medical director to issue instructions to EMS personnel. These instructions shall be in accordance with protocols approved by the EMS system and Office of Emergency Medical Services and under the direction of the medical director.

(10)   "Emergency medical technician" means an individual who has completed an educational program in emergency medical care approved by the Department and has been credentialed as an emergency medical technician by the Department.

(11)   Repealed by Session Laws 2003-392, s. 2(a), effective August 7, 2003.

(12)   "Emergency medical technician-intermediate" means an individual who has completed an educational program in emergency medical care approved by the Department and has been credentialed as an emergency medical technician-intermediate by the Department.

(13)   "Emergency medical technician-paramedic" means an individual who has completed an educational program in emergency medical care approved by the Department and has been credentialed as an emergency medical technician-paramedic by the Department.

(13a)   "EMS provider" means a firm, corporation or association which engages in or professes to provide emergency medical services.

(14)   "Medical responder" means an individual who has completed an educational program in emergency medical care and first aid approved by the Department and has been credentialed as a medical responder by the Department.

(15)   "Mobile intensive care nurse" means a registered nurse who is licensed to practice nursing in North Carolina and is approved by the medical director, following successful completion of an orientation program conducted under the authority of the medical director and approved by the Department, to issue instructions to EMS personnel. These instructions shall be in accordance with protocols approved by the EMS system and Office of Emergency Medical Services and under the direction of the medical director.

(16)   "Patient" means an individual who is sick, injured, wounded, or otherwise incapacitated or helpless such that the need for some medical assistance might be anticipated.

(17)   "Practical examination" means a test where an applicant for credentialing as an emergency medical technician, medical responder, emergency medical technician-intermediate, or emergency medical technician-paramedic demonstrates the ability to perform specified emergency medical care skills. (1983, c. 775, s. 1; 1997-443, s. 11A.129C; 2001-210, s. 1; 2003-392, s. 2(a).)

§ 131E-155.1. EMS Provider License required.

(a)   No firm, corporation, or association shall furnish, operate, conduct, maintain, advertise, or otherwise engage in or profess to provide emergency medical services or transport patients upon the streets or highways, waterways, or airways in North Carolina unless a valid EMS Provider License has been issued by the Department.

(b)   Before an EMS Provider License may be issued, the firm, corporation, or association seeking the license shall apply to the Department for this license. Application shall be made upon forms and according to procedures established by the Department. Prior to issuing an original or renewal EMS Provider License, the Department shall determine that the applicant meets all requirements for this license as set forth in this Article and in the rules adopted under this Article. EMS Provider Licenses shall be valid for a period specified by the Department, provided that the period shall be a minimum of four years unless action is taken under subsection (d) of this section.

(c)   The Commission shall adopt rules setting forth the qualifications required for obtaining or renewing an EMS Provider License.

(d)   The Department may deny, suspend, amend, or revoke an EMS Provider License in any case where the Department finds that there has been a substantial failure to comply with the provisions of this Article or the rules adopted under this Article. The Department's decision to deny, suspend, amend, or revoke an EMS Provider License may be appealed by the applicant or licensee pursuant to the provisions of Article 3 of Chapter 150B of the General Statutes, the Administrative Procedure Act.

(e)   Operating as an EMS provider without a valid EMS Provider License is a Class 3 misdemeanor. Each day's operation as an EMS provider without a license is a separate offense. (1995, c. 413, s. 1; 2001-210, s. 1.)

§ 131E-156. Permit required to operate ambulance.

(a)   No person, firm, corporation, or association, either as owner, agent, provider, or otherwise, shall furnish, operate, conduct, maintain, advertise, or otherwise engage in or profess to be engaged in the business or service of transporting patients upon the streets or highways, waterways or airways in North Carolina unless a valid permit from the Department has been issued for each ambulance used in the business or service.

(b)   Before a permit may be issued for a vehicle to be operated as an ambulance, the EMS provider shall apply to the Department for an ambulance permit. Application shall be made upon forms and according to procedures established by the Department. Prior to issuing an original or renewal permit for an ambulance, the Department shall determine that the vehicle for which the permit is issued meets all requirements as to equipment, design, supplies and sanitation as set forth in this Article and in the rules of the Commission and that the EMS provider has the credentialed personnel necessary to operate the ambulance in accordance with this Article. Permits issued for ambulances shall be valid for a period specified by the Department, not to exceed four years.

(c)   Duly authorized representatives of the Department may issue temporary permits for vehicles not meeting required standards for a period not to exceed 60 days, when it determines the public interest will be served.

(d)   When a permit has been issued for an ambulance as specified by this Article, the vehicle and records relating to the maintenance and operation of the vehicle shall be open to inspection by duly authorized representatives of the

Department at all reasonable times. (1967, c. 343, s. 3; 1973, c. 476, s. 128; c. 1224, s. 1; 1983, c. 775, s. 1; 2001-210, s. 1.)

§ 131E-157. Standards for equipment; inspection of equipment and supplies required for ambulances.

(a)   The Commission shall adopt rules specifying equipment, sanitation, supply and design requirements for ambulances.

(b)   The Department shall inspect each ambulance for compliance with the requirements set forth by the Commission and this Article when it deems an inspection is necessary. The Department shall maintain a record of the inspection.

(c)   Upon a determination, based upon an inspection, that an ambulance fails to meet the requirements of this Article or rules adopted under this Article, the Department may deny, suspend, or revoke the permit for the ambulance concerned until these requirements are met. (1967, c. 343, s. 3; 1973, c. 476, s. 128; c. 1224, s. 1; 1983, c. 775, s. 1; 2001-210, s. 1.)

§ 131E-158. Credentialed personnel required.

(a)   Every ambulance when transporting a patient shall be occupied at a minimum by all of the following:

(1)   At least one emergency medical technician who shall be responsible for the medical aspects of the mission prior to arrival at the medical facility, assuming no other individual with higher credentials is available.

(2)   One medical responder who is responsible for the operation of the vehicle and rendering assistance to the emergency medical technician.

An ambulance owned and operated by a licensed health care facility that is used solely to transport sick or infirm patients with known nonemergency medical conditions between facilities or between a residence and a facility for scheduled medical appointments is exempt from the requirements of this subsection.

(b)   The Commission shall adopt rules setting forth exemptions to the requirements stated in (a) of this section applicable to situations where exemptions are considered by the Commission to be in the public interest. (1967, c. 343, s. 3; 1973, c. 476, s. 128; c. 725; c. 1224, s. 1; 1975, c. 612; 1983, c. 775, s. 1; 1989, c. 300; 1997-443, s. 11A.129D; 2001-210, s. 1.)

§ 131E-159. Credentialing requirements.

(a)   Individuals seeking credentials as an emergency medical technician, emergency medical technician-intermediate, emergency medical technician-paramedic, medical responder, emergency medical dispatcher, or emergency medical services instructor shall apply to the Department using forms prescribed by that agency. The Department's representatives shall examine the applicant by either written, practical, or written and practical examination. The Department shall issue appropriate credentials to the applicant who meets all the requirements set forth in this Article and the rules adopted for this Article and who successfully completes the examinations required for credentialing. Emergency medical technician, medical responder, emergency medical dispatcher, emergency medical technician-intermediate, emergency medical technician-paramedic, and emergency medical services instructor credentials shall be valid for a period not to exceed four years and may be renewed if the holder meets the requirements set forth in the rules of the Commission. The Department is authorized to revoke or suspend these credentials at any time it determines that the holder no longer meets the qualifications prescribed.

(b)   The Commission shall adopt rules setting forth the qualifications required for credentialing of medical responders, emergency medical technicians, emergency medical technician-intermediates, emergency medical technician-paramedics, emergency medical dispatchers, and emergency medical services instructors.

(c)   Individuals currently credentialed as an emergency medical technician, emergency medical technician intermediate, emergency medical technician paramedic, medical responder, and emergency medical services instructor by the National Registry of Emergency Medical Technicians or by another state where the education/credentialing requirements have been approved for legal recognition by the Department of Health and Human Services, in accordance with rules promulgated by the Medical Care Commission, and who is either currently residing in North Carolina or affiliated with a permitted EMS provider

84

offering service within North Carolina, may be eligible for credentialing as an emergency medical technician, emergency medical technician-intermediate, emergency medical technician-paramedic, medical responder, and emergency medical services instructor without examination. This credentialing shall be valid for a period not to exceed the length of the applicant's original credentialing or four years, whichever is less.

(d)   An individual currently credentialed as an emergency medical dispatcher by a national credentialing agency, or by another state where the education/credentialing requirements have been approved for legal recognition by the Department of Health and Human Services, in accordance with rules issued by the Medical Care Commission, and who is either currently residing in North Carolina or affiliated with an emergency medical dispatcher program approved by the Department of Health and Human Services offering service within North Carolina, may be eligible for credentialing as an emergency medical dispatcher without examination. This credentialing shall be valid for a period not to exceed the length of the applicant's original credentialing or four years, whichever is less.

(e)   Duly authorized representatives of the Department may issue temporary credentials with or without examination upon finding that this action will be in the public interest. Temporary credentials shall be valid for a period not exceeding 90 days.

(f)   The Department may deny, suspend, amend, or revoke the credentials of a medical responder, emergency medical technician, emergency medical technician-intermediate, emergency medical technician-paramedic, emergency medical dispatcher, or emergency medical services instructor in any case in which the Department finds that there has been a substantial failure to comply with the provisions of this Article or the rules issued under this Article. Prior to implementation of any of the above disciplinary actions, the Department shall consider the recommendations of the EMS Disciplinary Committee pursuant to G.S. 143-519. The Department's decision to deny, suspend, amend, or revoke credentials may be appealed by the applicant or credentialed personnel pursuant to the provisions of Article 3 of Chapter 150B of the General Statutes, the Administrative Procedure Act.

(g)   An individual who applies for EMS credentials, seeks to renew EMS credentials, or holds EMS credentials is subject to a criminal background review by the Department. At the request of the Department, the Emergency Medical Services Disciplinary Committee, established by G.S. 143-519, shall review criminal background information and make a recommendation regarding the eligibility of an individual to obtain initial EMS credentials, renew EMS credentials, or maintain EMS credentials. The Department and the Emergency Medical Services Disciplinary Committee shall keep all information obtained pursuant to this subsection confidential. The Medical Care Commission shall adopt rules to implement the provisions of this subsection, including rules to establish a reasonable fee to offset the actual costs of criminal history information obtained pursuant to G.S. 114-19.21.

(h)   A person who is required to register as a sex offender under Article 27A of Chapter 14 of the General Statutes, or who was convicted of an offense which would have required registration if committed at a time when such registration would have been required by law, shall not be granted EMS credentials. The Department shall not renew the credentials of any person who would be ineligible for EMS credentials under this subsection. (1967, c. 343, s. 3; 1973, c. 476, s. 128; c. 725; c. 1224, s. 1; 1975, c. 612; 1983, c. 775, s. 1; 1987, c. 495, s. 2; 1993, c. 135, s. 1; 1997-443, ss. 11A.118(a), 11A.129E; 2001-210, s. 1; 2003-392, s. 2(b); 2007-411, s. 1; 2011-37, s. 1.)

§ 131E-160. Exemptions.

All of the following vehicles are exempt from the provisions of this Article:

(1)   Privately owned vehicles not used in the business of transporting patients.

(2)   A vehicle rendering service as an ambulance in case of a major catastrophe or emergency, when the permitted ambulances based in the locality of the catastrophe or emergency are insufficient to render the services required.

(3)   Any ambulance based outside this State, except that an ambulance which receives a patient within this State for transportation to a location within this State shall comply with the provisions of this Article.

(4)   Ambulances owned and operated by an agency of the United States government.

(5)   Vehicles owned and operated by rescue squads chartered by the State of North Carolina as nonprofit corporations or associations which are not

regularly used to transport sick, injured, wounded or otherwise incapacitated or helpless persons except as a part of rescue operations. (1967, c. 343, s. 3; c. 1257, s. 2; 1983, c. 775, s. 1; 2001-210, s. 1.)

§ 131E-161. Violation declared misdemeanor.

It shall be the responsibility of the EMS provider to ensure that the ambulance operation complies with the provisions of this Article and all rules adopted for this Article. Upon the violation of any part of this Article or any rule adopted under authority of this Article, the Department shall have the power to deny, revoke, or suspend the permits of all vehicles owned or operated by the violator. The operation of an ambulance without a valid permit or after a permit has been denied, suspended, or revoked or without appropriate credentialed staffing as required by G.S. 131E-158, shall constitute a Class 1 misdemeanor. (1967, c. 343, s. 3; 1973, c. 476, s. 128; 1983, c. 775, s. 1; 1993, c. 539, s. 964; 1994, Ex. Sess., c. 24, s. 14(c); 1997-443, s. 11A.129F; 2001-210, s. 1.)

Article 7A.

Statewide Trauma System Act of 1993.

§ 131E-162. Statewide trauma system.

The Department shall establish and maintain a program for the development of a statewide trauma system. The Department shall consolidate all State functions relating to trauma systems, both regulatory and developmental, under the auspices of this program.

The Commission shall adopt rules to carry out the purpose of this Article. These rules shall be adopted with the advice of the State Emergency Medical Services Advisory Council and shall include the operation of a statewide trauma registry, statewide educational requirements fundamental to the implementation of the trauma system. The rules adopted by the Commission shall establish guidelines for monitoring and evaluating the system including standards and criteria for the denial, suspension, voluntary withdrawal, or revocation of credentials for trauma center designation, and the establishment of regional trauma peer review committees. Each regional trauma peer review committee shall be responsible

87

for analyzing trauma patient care data and outcome measures to evaluate the ongoing quality of patient care, system performance, and medical direction within the regional trauma system. The committee membership shall include physicians, nurses, EMS personnel, trauma registrars, and hospital administrators. Review of medical records by the Trauma Peer Review Committee is confidential and protected under G.S. 143-518. A Trauma Peer Review Committee, its members, proceedings, records and materials produced, and materials considered shall be afforded the same protections afforded Medical Review Committees, their members, proceedings, records, and materials under G.S. 131E-95. The rules adopted by the Commission shall avoid duplication of reporting and minimize the cost to hospitals or other persons reporting under this section. The Office of Emergency Medical Services shall be the agency responsible for monitoring system development, ensuring compliance with rules, and overseeing system effectiveness.

With respect to collection of data and educational requirements regarding trauma, rules adopted by the Medical Care Commission shall limit the authority of the Department to hospitals and Emergency Medical Services providers. Nothing in this Article shall be interpreted so as to grant the Department authority to require private physicians, schools, or universities, except those participating in the trauma system, to provide information or data or to conduct educational programs regarding trauma. (1993, c. 336, s. 1; 2001-210, s. 2; 2003-392, s. 2(c).)

§ 131E-163. Reserved for future codification purposes.

§ 131E-164. Reserved for future codification purposes.

Article 8.

Cardiac Rehabilitation Certification Program.

§ 131E-165. Title; purpose.

(a)   This Article shall be known as the "Cardiac Rehabilitation Certification Program."

(b)   The purpose of this Article is to provide for the development, establishment, and enforcement of rules and certification:

(1)   For the care and treatment of individuals in outpatient cardiac rehabilitation programs; and

(2)   For the maintenance and operation of cardiac rehabilitation programs to ensure safe and adequate treatment of individuals in cardiac rehabilitation programs. (1983, c. 775, s. 1; 1995, c. 182, s. 1.)

§ 131E-166. Definitions.

As used in this Article, unless otherwise specified:

(1)   "Cardiac Rehabilitation Program" means a program certified under this Article for the delivery of cardiac rehabilitation services to outpatients and includes, but shall not be limited to, coordinated, physician-directed, individualized programs of therapeutic activity and adaption designed to assist the cardiac patient in attaining the highest rehabilitative potential.

(2)   "Certification" means the issuance of a certificate by the Department upon determination that cardiac rehabilitation services offered at a given program site meet all cardiac rehabilitation program rules. (1983, c. 775, s. 1; 1995, c. 182, s. 2.)

§ 131E-167. Certificate requirement.

(a)   Applications for certification shall be available from the Department, and each application filed with the Department shall contain all necessary and reasonable information that the Department may by rule require. A certificate shall be granted to the applicant for a period not to exceed one year upon a determination by the Department that the applicant has substantially complied with the provisions of this Article and the rules promulgated by the Department under this Article. The Department shall charge the applicant a nonrefundable annual certification fee in the amount of three hundred eighty-five dollars ($385.00).

(b)   A provisional certificate may be issued for a period not to exceed six months to a program:

(1)   That does not substantially comply with the rules, when failure to comply does not endanger the health, safety, or welfare of the clients being served by the program;

(2)   During the initial stages of operation if determined appropriate by the Department.

(c)   Prior to offering a cardiac rehabilitation program as defined in this Article, such a program must be inspected, evaluated, and certified as having substantially met the rules adopted by the Department under this Article.

(d)   A certificate to operate a Cardiac Rehabilitation Program shall be renewed upon the successful re-evaluation of the program as stated in the rules adopted pursuant to this Article.

(e)   Each certificate shall be issued only for the premises and persons named in the application and shall not be transferable or assignable except with the written approval of the Department.

(f)   A certificate shall be posted in a conspicuous place on the certified premises. (1983, c. 775, s. 1; 2003-284, s. 34.6(a); 2005-276, s. 41.2(f); 2009-451, s. 10.76(c).)

§ 131E-168. Adverse action on a certificate.

(a)   Subject to subsection (b), the Department is authorized to deny a new or renewal certificate and to suspend or revoke an existing certificate upon determination that there has been a substantial failure to comply with the provisions of this Article or the rules promulgated under this Article.

(b)   The provisions of Chapter 150A of the General Statutes, the Administrative Procedure Act, shall govern all administrative action and judicial review in cases where the Department has taken the action described in subsection (a). (1983, c. 775, s. 1.)

§ 131E-169. Rules and enforcement.

(a)   The Department is authorized to adopt, amend, and repeal all rules as may be designed to further the accomplishment of this Article.

(b)   The Department shall enforce the rules adopted for the certification of cardiac rehabilitation programs. (1983, c. 775, s. 1.)

§ 131E-170. Inspections.

(a)   The Department shall make or cause to be made inspections of Cardiac Rehabilitation Programs as it deems necessary. The Department is empowered to delegate to a State officer, agent, board, bureau or division of State government the authority to make these inspections according to the rules promulgated by the Department. In addition, an individual who is not a State officer or agent and who is delegated the authority to make these inspections must be approved by the Department. The Department may revoke this delegated authority in its discretion.

(b)   Notwithstanding the provisions of G.S. 8-53, "Communications between physician and patient," or any other provision of law relating to the confidentiality of communications between physician and patient, the representatives of the Department who make these inspections may review any writing or other record in any recording medium which pertains to the admission, discharge, medication, treatment, medical condition, or history of persons who are or have been patients of the program being inspected unless that patient objects in writing to review of that patient's records. Physicians, psychiatrists, nurses, and anyone else involved in giving treatment at or through a program who may be interviewed by representatives of the Department may disclose to these representatives information related to any inquiry, notwithstanding the existence of the physician-patient privilege in G.S. 8-53, "Communication between physician and patient," or any other rule of law, provided the patient has not made written objection to this disclosure. The program, its employees, and any person interviewed during these inspections shall be immune from liability for damages resulting from the disclosure of any information to the Department. Any confidential or privileged information received from review of records or interviews shall be kept confidential by the Department and not disclosed without written authorization of the patient or legal representative, or unless disclosure is ordered by a court of competent jurisdiction. The Department shall institute appropriate policies and procedures to ensure that this information shall not be disclosed without authorization or court order. The Department shall not

91

disclose the name of anyone who has furnished information concerning a facility without the consent of that person. Neither the names of persons furnishing information nor any confidential or privileged information obtained from records or interviews shall be considered "public records" within the meaning of G.S. 132-1, "'Public records' defined." Prior to releasing any information or allowing any inspections referred to in this section, the patient must be advised in writing by the program that the patient has the right to object in writing to the release of information or review of the records and that by an objection in writing the patient may prohibit the inspection or release of the records. (1983, c. 775, s. 1.)

§§ 131E-171 through 131E-174. Reserved for future codification purposes.

Article 9.

Certificate of Need.

§ 131E-175. Findings of fact.

The General Assembly of North Carolina makes the following findings:

(1)   That the financing of health care, particularly the reimbursement of health services rendered by health service facilities, limits the effect of free market competition and government regulation is therefore necessary to control costs, utilization, and distribution of new health service facilities and the bed complements of these health service facilities.

(2)   That the increasing cost of health care services offered through health service facilities threatens the health and welfare of the citizens of this State in that citizens need assurance of economical and readily available health care.

(3)   That, if left to the market place to allocate health service facilities and health care services, geographical maldistribution of these facilities and services would occur and, further, less than equal access to all population groups, especially those that have traditionally been medically underserved, would result.

(3a)   That access to health care services and health care facilities is critical to the welfare of rural North Carolinians, and to the continued viability of rural communities, and that the needs of rural North Carolinians should be considered in the certificate of need review process.

(4)   That the proliferation of unnecessary health service facilities results in costly duplication and underuse of facilities, with the availability of excess capacity leading to unnecessary use of expensive resources and overutilization of health care services.

(5)   Repealed by Session Laws 1987, c. 511, s. 1.

(6)   That excess capacity of health service facilities places an enormous economic burden on the public who pay for the construction and operation of these facilities as patients, health insurance subscribers, health plan contributors, and taxpayers.

(7)   That the general welfare and protection of lives, health, and property of the people of this State require that new institutional health services to be offered within this State be subject to review and evaluation as to need, cost of service, accessibility to services, quality of care, feasibility, and other criteria as determined by provisions of this Article or by the North Carolina Department of Health and Human Services pursuant to provisions of this Article prior to such services being offered or developed in order that only appropriate and needed institutional health services are made available in the area to be served.

(8)   That because persons who have received exemptions under Section 11.9(a) of S.L. 2000-67, as amended, and under Section 11.69(b) of S.L. 1997-443, as amended by Section 12.16C(a) of S.L. 1998-212, and as amended by Section 1 of S.L. 1999-135, have had sufficient time to complete development plans and initiate construction of beds in adult care homes.

(9)   That because with the enactment of this legislation, beds allowed under the exemptions noted above and pending development will count in the inventory of adult care home beds available to provide care to residents in the State Medical Facilities Plan.

(10)   That because State and county expenditures provide support for nearly three-quarters of the residents in adult care homes through the State County Special Assistance program, and excess bed capacity increases costs per resident day, it is in the public interest to promote efficiencies in delivering care

93

in those facilities by controlling and directing their growth in an effort to prevent underutilization and higher costs and provide appropriate geographical distribution.

(11)   That physicians providing gastrointestinal endoscopy services in unlicensed settings should be given an opportunity to obtain a license to provide those services to ensure the safety of patients and the provision of quality care.

(12)   That demand for gastrointestinal endoscopy services is increasing at a substantially faster rate than the general population given the procedure is recognized as a highly effective means to diagnose and prevent cancer. (1977, 2nd Sess., c. 1182, s. 2; 1981, c. 651, s. 1; 1983, c. 775, s. 1; 1987, c. 511, s. 1; 1993, c. 7, s. 1; 1997-443, s. 11A.118(a); 2001-234, s. 1; 2005-346, s. 5.)

§ 131E-176. Definitions.

As used in this Article, unless the context clearly requires otherwise, the following terms have the meanings specified:

(1)   "Adult care home" means a facility with seven or more beds licensed under Part 1 of Article 1 of Chapter 131D of the General Statutes or Chapter 131E of the General Statutes that provides residential care for aged or disabled persons whose principal need is a home which provides the supervision and personal care appropriate to their age and disability and for whom medical care is only occasional or incidental.

(1a)   (See note) "Air ambulance" means aircraft used to provide air transport of sick or injured persons between destinations within the State.

(1b)   "Ambulatory surgical facility" means a facility designed for the provision of a specialty ambulatory surgical program or a multispecialty ambulatory surgical program. An ambulatory surgical facility serves patients who require local, regional or general anesthesia and a period of post-operative observation. An ambulatory surgical facility may only admit patients for a period of less than 24 hours and must provide at least one designated operating room or gastrointestinal endoscopy room, as defined in Article 5 Part 1 and Article 6, Part 4 of this Chapter, and at least one designated recovery room, have available the necessary equipment and trained personnel to handle emergencies, provide adequate quality assurance and assessment by an evaluation and review committee, and maintain adequate medical records for each patient. An ambulatory surgical facility may be operated as a part of a physician or dentist's office, provided the facility is licensed under G.S. Chapter 131E, Article 6, Part D, but the performance of incidental, limited ambulatory surgical procedures which do not constitute an ambulatory surgical program as defined in subdivision (1c) of this section and which are performed in a physician's or dentist's office does not make that office an ambulatory surgical facility.

(1c)   "Ambulatory surgical program" means a formal program for providing on a same-day basis those surgical procedures which require local, regional or general anesthesia and a period of post-operative observation to patients whose admission for more than 24 hours is determined, prior to surgery or gastrointestinal endoscopy, to be medically unnecessary.

(2)   "Bed capacity" means space used exclusively for inpatient care, including space designed or remodeled for licensed inpatient beds even though temporarily not used for such purposes. The number of beds to be counted in any patient room shall be the maximum number for which adequate square footage is provided as established by rules of the Department except that single beds in single rooms are counted even if the room contains inadequate square footage. The term "bed capacity" also refers to the number of dialysis stations in kidney disease treatment centers, including freestanding dialysis units.

(2a)   "Bone marrow transplantation services" means the process of infusing bone marrow into persons with diseases to stimulate the production of blood cells.

(2b)   "Burn intensive care services" means services provided in a unit designed to care for patients who have been severely burned.

(2c)   "Campus" means the adjacent grounds and buildings, or grounds and buildings not separated by more than a public right-of-way, of a health service facility and related health care entities.

(2d)   "Capital expenditure" means an expenditure for a project, including but not limited to the cost of construction, engineering, and equipment which under generally accepted accounting principles is not properly chargeable as an expense of operation and maintenance. Capital expenditure includes, in addition, the fair market value of an acquisition made by donation, lease, or comparable arrangement by which a person obtains equipment, the expenditure for which would have been considered a capital expenditure under this Article if the person had acquired it by purchase.

95

(2e)   Repealed by Session Laws 2005-325, s. 1, effective for hospices and hospice offices December 31, 2005.

(2f)   "Cardiac catheterization equipment" means the equipment used to provide cardiac catheterization services.

(2g)   "Cardiac catheterization services" means those procedures, excluding pulmonary angiography procedures, in which a catheter is introduced into a vein or artery and threaded through the circulatory system into the heart specifically to diagnose abnormalities in the motion, contraction, and blood flow of the moving heart or to perform surgical therapeutic interventions to restore, repair, or reconstruct the coronary blood vessels of the heart.

(3)   "Certificate of need" means a written order which affords the person so designated as the legal proponent of the proposed project the opportunity to proceed with the development of such project.

(4)   Repealed by Session Laws 1993, c. 7, s. 2.

(5)   "Change in bed capacity" means (i) any relocation of health service facility beds, or dialysis stations from one licensed facility or campus to another, or (ii) any redistribution of health service facility bed capacity among the categories of health service facility bed as defined in G.S. 131E-176(9c), or (iii) any increase in the number of health service facility beds, or dialysis stations in kidney disease treatment centers, including freestanding dialysis units.

(5a)   "Chemical dependency treatment facility" means a public or private facility, or unit in a facility, which is engaged in providing 24-hour a day treatment for chemical dependency or substance abuse. This treatment may include detoxification, administration of a therapeutic regimen for the treatment of chemically dependent or substance abusing persons and related services. The facility or unit may be:

a.   A unit within a general hospital or an attached or freestanding unit of a general hospital licensed under Article 5, Chapter 131E, of the General Statutes,

b.   A unit within a psychiatric hospital or an attached or freestanding unit of a psychiatric hospital licensed under Article 1A of General Statutes Chapter 122 or Article 2 of General Statutes Chapter 122C,

c.   A freestanding facility specializing in treatment of persons who are substance abusers or chemically dependent licensed under Article 1A of General Statutes Chapter 122 or Article 2 of General Statutes Chapter 122C; and may be identified as "chemical dependency, substance abuse, alcoholism, or drug abuse treatment units," "residential chemical dependency, substance abuse, alcoholism or drug abuse facilities," or by other names if the purpose is to provide treatment of chemically dependent or substance abusing persons, but shall not include social setting detoxification facilities, medical detoxification facilities, halfway houses or recovery farms.

(5b)   "Chemical dependency treatment beds" means beds that are licensed for the inpatient treatment of chemical dependency. Residential treatment beds for the treatment of chemical dependency or substance abuse are chemical dependency treatment beds. Chemical dependency treatment beds shall not include beds licensed for detoxification.

(6)   "Department" means the North Carolina Department of Health and Human Services.

(7)   To "develop" when used in connection with health services, means to undertake those activities which will result in the offering of institutional health service or the incurring of a financial obligation in relation to the offering of such a service.

(7a)   "Diagnostic center" means a freestanding facility, program, or provider, including but not limited to, physicians' offices, clinical laboratories, radiology centers, and mobile diagnostic programs, in which the total cost of all the medical diagnostic equipment utilized by the facility which cost ten thousand dollars ($10,000) or more exceeds five hundred thousand dollars ($500,000). In determining whether the medical diagnostic equipment in a diagnostic center costs more than five hundred thousand dollars ($500,000), the costs of the equipment, studies, surveys, designs, plans, working drawings, specifications, construction, installation, and other activities essential to acquiring and making operational the equipment shall be included. The capital expenditure for the equipment shall be deemed to be the fair market value of the equipment or the cost of the equipment, whichever is greater.

(7b)   "Expedited review" means the status given to an application's review process when the applicant petitions for the review and the Department approves the request based on findings that all of the following are met:

97

a.   The review is not competitive.

b.   The proposed capital expenditure is less than five million dollars ($5,000,000).

c.   A request for a public hearing is not received within the time frame defined in G.S. 131E-185.

d.   The agency has not determined that a public hearing is in the public interest.

(7c)   "Gamma knife" means equipment which emits photon beams from a stationary radioactive cobalt source to treat lesions deep within the brain and is one type of stereotactic radiosurgery.

(7d)   "Gastrointestinal endoscopy room" means a room used for the performance of procedures that require the insertion of a flexible endoscope into a gastrointestinal orifice to visualize the gastrointestinal lining and adjacent organs for diagnostic or therapeutic purposes.

(8),   (9) Repealed by Session Laws 1987, c. 511, s. 1.

(9a)   "Health service" means an organized, interrelated medical, diagnostic, therapeutic, and/or rehabilitative activity that is integral to the prevention of disease or the clinical management of a sick, injured, or disabled person. "Health service" does not include administrative and other activities that are not integral to clinical management.

(9b)   "Health service facility" means a hospital; long-term care hospital; psychiatric facility; rehabilitation facility; nursing home facility; adult care home; kidney disease treatment center, including freestanding hemodialysis units; intermediate care facility for the mentally retarded; home health agency office; chemical dependency treatment facility; diagnostic center; hospice office, hospice inpatient facility, hospice residential care facility; and ambulatory surgical facility.

(9c)   "Health service facility bed" means a bed licensed for use in a health service facility in the categories of (i) acute care beds; (ii) psychiatric beds; (iii) rehabilitation beds; (iv) nursing home beds; (v) intermediate care beds for the mentally retarded; (vi) chemical dependency treatment beds; (vii) hospice inpatient facility beds; (viii) hospice residential care facility beds; (ix) adult care home beds; and (x) long-term care hospital beds.

(10)   "Health maintenance organization (HMO)" means a public or private organization which has received its certificate of authority under Article 67 of Chapter 58 of the General Statutes and which either is a qualified health maintenance organization under Section 1310(d) of the Public Health Service Act or:

a.   Provides or otherwise makes available to enrolled participants health care services, including at least the following basic health care services: usual physician services, hospitalization, laboratory, X ray, emergency and preventive services, and out-of-area coverage;

b.   Is compensated, except for copayments, for the provision of the basic health care services listed above to enrolled participants by a payment which is paid on a periodic basis without regard to the date the health care services are provided and which is fixed without regard to the frequency, extent, or kind of health service actually provided; and

c.   Provides physicians' services primarily (i) directly through physicians who are either employees or partners of such organizations, or (ii) through arrangements with individual physicians or one or more groups of physicians organized on a group practice or individual practice basis.

(10a)   "Heart-lung bypass machine" means the equipment used to perform extra-corporeal circulation and oxygenation during surgical procedures.

(11)   Repealed by Session Laws 1991, c. 692, s. 1.

(12)   "Home health agency" means a private organization or public agency, whether owned or operated by one or more persons or legal entities, which furnishes or offers to furnish home health services.

"Home health services" means items and services furnished to an individual by a home health agency, or by others under arrangements with such others made by the agency, on a visiting basis, and except for paragraph e. of this subdivision, in a place of temporary or permanent residence used as the individual's home as follows:

a. Part-time or intermittent nursing care provided by or under the supervision of a registered nurse;

b. Physical, occupational or speech therapy;

c. Medical social services, home health aid services, and other therapeutic services;

d. Medical supplies, other than drugs and biologicals and the use of medical appliances;

e. Any of the foregoing items and services which are provided on an outpatient basis under arrangements made by the home health agency at a hospital or nursing home facility or rehabilitation center and the furnishing of which involves the use of equipment of such a nature that the items and services cannot readily be made available to the individual in his home, or which are furnished at such facility while he is there to receive any such item or service, but not including transportation of the individual in connection with any such item or service.

(13) "Hospital" means a public or private institution which is primarily engaged in providing to inpatients, by or under supervision of physicians, diagnostic services and therapeutic services for medical diagnosis, treatment, and care of injured, disabled, or sick persons, or rehabilitation services for the rehabilitation of injured, disabled, or sick persons. The term includes all facilities licensed pursuant to G.S. 131E-77 of the General Statutes, except long-term care hospitals.

(13a) "Hospice" means any coordinated program of home care with provision for inpatient care for terminally ill patients and their families. This care is provided by a medically directed interdisciplinary team, directly or through an agreement under the direction of an identifiable hospice administration. A hospice program of care provides palliative and supportive medical and other health services to meet the physical, psychological, social, spiritual and special needs of patients and their families, which are experienced during the final stages of terminal illness and during dying and bereavement.

(13b) "Hospice inpatient facility" means a freestanding licensed hospice facility or a designated inpatient unit in an existing health service facility which provides palliative and supportive medical and other health services to meet the physical, psychological, social, spiritual, and special needs of terminally ill patients and

100

their families in an inpatient setting. For purposes of this Article only, a hospital which has a contractual agreement with a licensed hospice to provide inpatient services to a hospice patient as defined in G.S. 131E-201(4) and provides those services in a licensed acute care bed is not a hospice inpatient facility and is not subject to the requirements in G.S. 131E-176(5)(ii) for hospice inpatient beds.

(13c) "Hospice residential care facility" means a freestanding licensed hospice facility which provides palliative and supportive medical and other health services to meet the physical, psychological, social, spiritual, and special needs of terminally ill patients and their families in a group residential setting.

(14) Repealed by Session Laws 1987, c. 511, s. 1.

(14a) "Intermediate care facility for the mentally retarded" means facilities licensed pursuant to Article 2 of Chapter 122C of the General Statutes for the purpose of providing health and habilitative services based on the developmental model and principles of normalization for persons with mental retardation, autism, cerebral palsy, epilepsy or related conditions.

(14b) Repealed by Session Laws 1991, c. 692, s. 1.

(14c) Reserved for future codification.

(14d) Repealed by Session Laws 2001-234, s. 2, effective January 1, 2002.

(14e) "Kidney disease treatment center" means a facility that is certified as an end-stage renal disease facility by the Centers for Medicare and Medicaid Services, Department of Health and Human Services, pursuant to 42 C.F.R. § 405.

(14f) Reserved for future codification.

(14g) "Linear accelerator" means a machine used to produce ionizing radiation in excess of 1,000,000 electron volts in the form of a beam of electrons or photons to treat cancer patients.

(14h) Reserved for future codification.

(14i) "Lithotriptor" means extra-corporeal shock wave technology used to treat persons with kidney stones and gallstones.

101

(14j)   Reserved for future codification.

(14k)   "Long-term care hospital" means a hospital that has been classified and designated as a long-term care hospital by the Centers for Medicare and Medicaid Services, Department of Health and Human Services, pursuant to 42 C.F.R. § 412.

(14l)   Reserved for future codification.

(14m)   "Magnetic resonance imaging scanner" means medical imaging equipment that uses nuclear magnetic resonance.

(14n)   "Main campus" means all of the following for the purposes of G.S. 131E-184(f) and (g) only:

a.   The site of the main building from which a licensed health service facility provides clinical patient services and exercises financial and administrative control over the entire facility, including the buildings and grounds adjacent to that main building.

b.   Other areas and structures that are not strictly contiguous to the main building but are located within 250 yards of the main building.

(14o)   "Major medical equipment" means a single unit or single system of components with related functions which is used to provide medical and other health services and which costs more than seven hundred fifty thousand dollars ($750,000). In determining whether the major medical equipment costs more than seven hundred fifty thousand dollars ($750,000), the costs of the equipment, studies, surveys, designs, plans, working drawings, specifications, construction, installation, and other activities essential to acquiring and making operational the major medical equipment shall be included. The capital expenditure for the equipment shall be deemed to be the fair market value of the equipment or the cost of the equipment, whichever is greater. Major medical equipment does not include replacement equipment as defined in this section.

(15)   Repealed by Session Laws 1987, c. 511, s. 1.

(15a)   "Multispecialty ambulatory surgical program" means a formal program for providing on a same-day basis surgical procedures for at least three of the following specialty areas: gynecology, otolaryngology, plastic surgery, general surgery, ophthalmology, orthopedic, or oral surgery.

(15b)   "Neonatal intensive care services" means those services provided by a health service facility to high-risk newborn infants who require constant nursing care, including but not limited to continuous cardiopulmonary and other supportive care.

(16)   "New institutional health services" means any of the following:

a.   The construction, development, or other establishment of a new health service facility.

b.   Except as otherwise provided in G.S. 131E-184(e), the obligation by any person of a capital expenditure exceeding two million dollars ($2,000,000) to develop or expand a health service or a health service facility, or which relates to the provision of a health service. The cost of any studies, surveys, designs, plans, working drawings, specifications, and other activities, including staff effort and consulting and other services, essential to the acquisition, improvement, expansion, or replacement of any plant or equipment with respect to which an expenditure is made shall be included in determining if the expenditure exceeds two million dollars ($2,000,000).

c.   Any change in bed capacity as defined in G.S. 131E-176(5).

d.   The offering of dialysis services or home health services by or on behalf of a health service facility if those services were not offered within the previous 12 months by or on behalf of the facility.

e.   A change in a project that was subject to certificate of need review and for which a certificate of need was issued, if the change is proposed during the development of the project or within one year after the project was completed. For purposes of this subdivision, a change in a project is a change of more than fifteen percent (15%) of the approved capital expenditure amount or the addition of a health service that is to be located in the facility, or portion thereof, that was constructed or developed in the project.

f.   The development or offering of a health service as listed in this subdivision by or on behalf of any person:

1.   Bone marrow transplantation services.

2.   Burn intensive care services.

103

2a.   Cardiac catheterization services, except cardiac catheterization services provided on equipment furnished by a person authorized to operate such equipment in North Carolina pursuant to either a certificate of need issued for mobile cardiac catheterization equipment or a settlement agreement executed by the Department for provision of cardiac catheterization services.

3.   Neonatal intensive care services.

4.   Open-heart surgery services.

5.   Solid organ transplantation services.

f1.   The acquisition by purchase, donation, lease, transfer, or comparable arrangement of any of the following equipment by or on behalf of any person:

1.   Air ambulance.

2.   Repealed by Session Laws 2005-325, s. 1, effective for hospices and hospice offices December 31, 2005.

3.   Cardiac catheterization equipment.

4.   Gamma knife.

5.   Heart-lung bypass machine.

5a.   Linear accelerator.

6.   Lithotriptor.

7.   Magnetic resonance imaging scanner.

8.   Positron emission tomography scanner.

9.   Simulator.

g.   to k. Repealed by Session Laws 1987, c. 511, s. 1.

l.   The purchase, lease, or acquisition of any health service facility, or portion thereof, or a controlling interest in the health service facility or portion thereof, if the health service facility was developed under a certificate of need issued pursuant to G.S. 131E-180.

m.   Any conversion of nonhealth service facility beds to health service facility beds.

n.   The construction, development or other establishment of a hospice, hospice inpatient facility, or hospice residential care facility;

o.   The opening of an additional office by an existing home health agency or hospice within its service area as defined by rules adopted by the Department; or the opening of any office by an existing home health agency or hospice outside its service area as defined by rules adopted by the Department.

p.   The acquisition by purchase, donation, lease, transfer, or comparable arrangement by any person of major medical equipment.

q.   The relocation of a health service facility from one service area to another.

r.   The conversion of a specialty ambulatory surgical program to a multispecialty ambulatory surgical program or the addition of a specialty to a specialty ambulatory surgical program.

s.   The furnishing of mobile medical equipment to any person to provide health services in North Carolina, which was not in use in North Carolina prior to the adoption of this provision, if such equipment would otherwise be subject to review in accordance with G.S. 131E-176(16)(f1.) or G.S. 131E-176(16)(p) if it had been acquired in North Carolina.

t.   Repealed by Session Laws 2001-242, s. 4, effective June 23, 2001.

u.   The construction, development, establishment, increase in the number, or relocation of an operating room or gastrointestinal endoscopy room in a licensed health service facility, other than the relocation of an operating room or gastrointestinal endoscopy room within the same building or on the same grounds or to grounds not separated by more than a public right-of-way adjacent to the grounds where the operating room or gastrointestinal endoscopy room is currently located.

105

v.   The change in designation, in a licensed health service facility, of an operating room to a gastrointestinal endoscopy room or change in designation of a gastrointestinal endoscopy room to an operating room that results in a different number of each type of room than is reflected on the health service facility's license in effect as of January 1, 2005.

(17)   "North Carolina State Health Coordinating Council" means the Council that prepares, with the Department of Health and Human Services, the State Medical Facilities Plan.

(17a)   "Nursing care" means:

a.   Skilled nursing care and related services for residents who require medical or nursing care;

b.   Rehabilitation services for the rehabilitation of injured, disabled, or sick persons; or

c.   Health-related care and services provided on a regular basis to individuals who because of their mental or physical condition require care and services above the level of room and board, which can be made available to them only through institutional facilities.

These are services which are not primarily for the care and treatment of mental diseases.

(17b)   "Nursing home facility" means a health service facility whose bed complement of health service facility beds is composed principally of nursing home facility beds.

(18)   To "offer," when used in connection with health services, means that the person holds himself out as capable of providing, or as having the means for the provision of, specified health services.

(18a)   Repealed by Session Laws 2005-325, s. 1, effective for hospices and hospice offices December 31, 2005.

(18b)   "Open-heart surgery services" means the provision of surgical procedures that utilize a heart-lung bypass machine during surgery to correct cardiac and coronary artery disease or defects.

106

(18c)   "Operating room" means a room used for the performance of surgical procedures requiring one or more incisions and that is required to comply with all applicable licensure codes and standards for an operating room.

(19)   "Person" means an individual, a trust or estate, a partnership, a corporation, including associations, joint stock companies, and insurance companies; the State, or a political subdivision or agency or instrumentality of the State.

(19a)   "Positron emission tomography scanner" means equipment that utilizes a computerized radiographic technique that employs radioactive substances to examine the metabolic activity of various body structures.

(20)   "Project" or "capital expenditure project" means a proposal to undertake a capital expenditure that results in the offering of a new institutional health service as defined by this Article. A project, or capital expenditure project, or proposed project may refer to the project from its earliest planning stages up through the point at which the specified new institutional health service may be offered. In the case of facility construction, the point at which the new institutional health service may be offered must take place after the facility is capable of being fully licensed and operated for its intended use, and at that time it shall be considered a health service facility.

(21)   "Psychiatric facility" means a public or private facility licensed pursuant to Article 2 of Chapter 122C of the General Statutes and which is primarily engaged in providing to inpatients, by or under the supervision of a physician, psychiatric services for the diagnosis and treatment of mentally ill persons.

(22)   "Rehabilitation facility" means a public or private inpatient facility which is operated for the primary purpose of assisting in the rehabilitation of disabled persons through an integrated program of medical and other services which are provided under competent, professional supervision.

(22a)   "Replacement equipment" means equipment that costs less than two million dollars ($2,000,000) and is purchased for the sole purpose of replacing comparable medical equipment currently in use which will be sold or otherwise disposed of when replaced. In determining whether the replacement equipment costs less than two million dollars ($2,000,000), the costs of equipment, studies, surveys, designs, plans, working drawings, specifications, construction, installation, and other activities essential to acquiring and making operational the replacement equipment shall be included. The capital expenditure for the

107

equipment shall be deemed to be the fair market value of the equipment or the cost of the equipment, whichever is greater.

(23)   Repealed by Session Laws 1991, c. 692, s. 1.

(24)   Repealed by Session Laws 1993, c. 7, s. 2.

(24a)   "Service area" means the area of the State, as defined in the State Medical Facilities Plan or in rules adopted by the Department, which receives services from a health service facility.

(24b)   "Simulator" means a machine that produces high quality diagnostic radiographs and precisely reproduces the geometric relationships of megavoltage radiation therapy equipment to the patient.

(24c)   Reserved for future codification.

(24d)   "Solid organ transplantation services" means the provision of surgical procedures and the interrelated medical services that accompany the surgery to remove an organ from a patient and surgically implant an organ from a donor.

(24e)   Reserved for future codification.

(24f)   "Specialty ambulatory surgical program" means a formal program for providing on a same-day basis surgical procedures for only the specialty areas identified on the ambulatory surgical facility's 1993 Application for Licensure as an Ambulatory Surgical Center and authorized by its certificate of need.

(25)   "State Medical Facilities Plan" means the plan prepared by the Department of Health and Human Services and the North Carolina State Health Coordinating Council, and approved by the Governor. In preparing the Plan, the Department and the State Health Coordinating Council shall maintain a mailing list of persons who have requested notice of public hearings regarding the Plan. Not less than 15 days prior to a scheduled public hearing, the Department shall notify persons on its mailing list of the date, time, and location of the hearing. The Department shall hold at least one public hearing prior to the adoption of the proposed Plan and at least six public hearings after the adoption of the proposed Plan by the State Health Coordinating Council. The Council shall accept oral and written comments from the public concerning the Plan.

(26)   Repealed by Session Laws 1983 (Regular Session, 1984), c. 1002, s. 9.

(27)   Repealed by Session Laws 1987, c. 511, s. 1. (1977, 2nd Sess., c. 1182, s. 2; 1981, c. 651, ss. 1, 2; c. 1127, ss. 24-29; 1983, c. 775, s. 1; 1983 (Reg. Sess., 1984), c. 1002, ss. 1-9; c. 1022, ss. 2, 3; c. 1064, s. 1; c. 1110, ss. 1, 2; 1985, c. 589, ss. 42, 43(a); c. 740, ss. 1, 2, 6; 1985 (Reg. Sess., 1986), c. 1001, s. 2; 1987, c. 34; c. 511, s. 1; 1991, c. 692, s. 1; c. 701, s. 1; 1993, c. 7, s. 2; c. 376, ss. 1-4; 1997-443, s. 11A.118(a); 2000-135, ss. 1, 2; 2001-234, s. 2; 2001-242, ss. 2, 4; 2003-229, s. 13; 2003-390, ss. 1, 2; 2005-325, s. 1; 2005-346, s. 6(a)-(d); 2009-145, s. 2; 2009-462, s. 4(k); 2013-360, s. 12G.3(a).)

§ 131E-177. Department of Health and Human Services is designated State Health Planning and Development Agency; powers and duties.

The Department of Health and Human Services is designated as the State Health Planning and Development Agency for the State of North Carolina, and is empowered to exercise the following powers and duties:

(1)   To establish standards and criteria or plans required to carry out the provisions and purposes of this Article and to adopt rules pursuant to Chapter 150B of the General Statutes, to carry out the purposes and provisions of this Article;

(2)   Adopt, amend, and repeal such rules and regulations, consistent with the laws of this State, as may be required by the federal government for grants-in-aid for health service facilities and health planning which may be made available by the federal government. This section shall be liberally construed in order that the State and its citizens may benefit from such grants-in-aid;

(3)   Define, by rule, procedures for submission of periodic reports by persons or health service facilities subject to agency review under this Article;

(4)   Develop policy, criteria, and standards for health service facilities planning; shall conduct statewide registration and inventories of and make determinations of need for health service facilities, health services as specified in G.S. 131E-176(16)f., and equipment as specified in G.S. 131E-176(16)f1., which shall include consideration of adequate geographic location of equipment and services; and develop a State Medical Facilities Plan;

(5)   Implement, by rule, criteria for project review;

109

(6)   Have the power to grant, deny, or withdraw a certificate of need and to impose such sanctions as are provided for by this Article;

(7)   Solicit, accept, hold and administer on behalf of the State any grants or devises of money, securities or property to the Department for use by the Department in the administration of this Article; and

(8)   Repealed by Session Laws 1987, c. 511, s. 1.

(9)   Collect fees for submitting applications for certificates of need.

(10)   The authority to review all records in any recording medium of any person or health service facility subject to agency review under this Article which pertain to construction and acquisition activities, staffing or costs and charges for patient care, including but not limited to, construction contracts, architectural contracts, consultant contracts, purchase orders, cancelled checks, accounting and financial records, debt instruments, loan and security agreements, staffing records, utilization statistics and any other records the Department deems to be reasonably necessary to determine compliance with this Article.

The Secretary of Health and Human Services shall have final decision-making authority with regard to all functions described in this section. (1977, 2nd Sess., c. 1182, s. 2; 1981, c. 651, s. 1; 1983, c. 713, s. 96; c. 775, ss. 1, 6; 1987, c. 511, s. 1; 1991, c. 692, s. 2; 1993, c. 7, s. 3; c. 383, ss. 2, 3; 1997-443, s. 11A.118(a); 2007-323, s. 30.4(a); 2011-284, s. 90.)

§ 131E-178. Activities requiring certificate of need.

(a)   No person shall offer or develop a new institutional health service without first obtaining a certificate of need from the Department; provided, however, no person who provides gastrointestinal endoscopy procedures in one or more gastrointestinal endoscopy rooms located in a nonlicensed setting, shall be required to obtain a certificate of need to license that setting as an ambulatory surgical facility with the existing number of gastrointestinal endoscopy rooms, provided that:

(1)   The license application is postmarked for delivery to the Division of Health Service Regulation by December 31, 2006;

(2)   The applicant verifies, by affidavit submitted to the Division of Health Service Regulation within 60 days of the effective date of this act, that the facility is in operation as of the effective date of this act or that the completed application for the building permit for the facility was submitted by the effective date of this act;

(3)   The facility has been accredited by The Accreditation Association for Ambulatory Health Care, The Joint Commission on Accreditation of Healthcare Organizations, or The American Association for Accreditation of Ambulatory Surgical Facilities by the time the license application is postmarked for delivery to the Division of Health Service Regulation of the Department; and

(4)   The license application includes a commitment and plan for serving indigent and medically underserved populations.

All other persons proposing to obtain a license to establish an ambulatory surgical facility for the provision of gastrointestinal endoscopy procedures shall be required to obtain a certificate of need. The annual State Medical Facilities Plan shall not include policies or need determinations that limit the number of gastrointestinal endoscopy rooms that may be approved.

(b)   No person shall make an acquisition by donation, lease, transfer, or comparable arrangement without first obtaining a certificate of need from the Department, if the acquisition would have been a new institutional health service if it had been made by purchase. In determining whether an acquisition would have been a new institutional health service, the capital expenditure for the asset shall be deemed to be the fair market value of the asset or the cost of the asset, whichever is greater.

(c)   No person shall incur an obligation for a capital expenditure which is a new institutional health service without first obtaining a certificate of need from the Department. An obligation for a capital expenditure is incurred when:

(1)   An enforceable contract, excepting contracts which are expressly contingent upon issuance of a certificate of need, is entered into by a person for the construction, acquisition, lease or financing of a capital asset;

(2)   A person takes formal action to commit funds for a construction project undertaken as his own contractor; or

(3)   In the case of donated property, the date on which the gift is completed.

111

(d)   Where the estimated cost of a proposed capital expenditure, including the fair market value of equipment acquired by purchase, lease, transfer, or other comparable arrangement, is certified by a licensed architect or engineer to be equal to or less than the expenditure minimum for capital expenditure for new institutional health services, such expenditure shall be deemed not to exceed the amount for new institutional health services regardless of the actual amount expended, provided that the following conditions are met:

(1)   The certified estimated cost is prepared in writing 60 days or more before the obligation for the capital expenditure is incurred. Certified cost estimates shall be available for inspection at the facility and sent to the Department upon its request.

(2)   The facility on whose behalf the expenditure was made notifies the Department in writing within 30 days of the date on which such expenditure is made if the expenditure exceeds the expenditure minimum for capital expenditures. The notice shall include a copy of the certified cost estimate.

(e)   The Department may grant certificates of need which permit capital expenditures only for predevelopment activities. Predevelopment activities include the preparation of architectural designs, plans, working drawings, or specifications, the preparation of studies and surveys, and the acquisition of a potential site. (1977, 2nd Sess., c. 1182, s. 2; 1979, c. 876, s. 2; 1981, c. 651, s. 3; 1983, c. 775, s. 1; 1983 (Reg. Sess., 1984), c. 1110, s. 3; 1985, c. 740, s. 3; 1985 (Reg. Sess., 1986), c. 1001, s. 1; 1987, c. 511, s. 1; c. 768; 1991, c. 692, s. 3; 1993, c. 7, s. 4; 2005-346, s. 7; 2007-182, s. 1.)

§ 131E-179. Research activities.

(a)   Notwithstanding any other provisions of this Article, a health service facility may offer new institutional health services to be used solely for research, or incur the obligation of a capital expenditure solely for research, without a certificate of need, if the Department grants an exemption. The Department shall grant an exemption if the health service facility files a notice of intent with the Department in accordance with rules promulgated by the Department and if the Department finds that the offering or obligation will not:

(1)   Affect the charges of the health service facility for the provision of medical or other patient care services other than services which are included in the research;

(2)   Substantially change the bed capacity of the facility; or

(3)   Substantially change the medical or other patient care services of the facility.

(b)   After a health service facility has received an exemption pursuant to subsection (a) of this section, it shall not offer the new institutional health services, or use a facility acquired through the capital expenditure, in a manner which affects the charges of the facility for the provision of medical or other patient care services, other than the services which are included in the research and shall not charge patients for the use of the service for which an exemption has been granted, without first obtaining a certificate of need from the Department; provided, however, that any facility or service acquired or developed under the exemption provided by this section shall not be subject to the foregoing restrictions on its use if the facility or service could otherwise be offered or developed without a certificate of need.

(c)   Any of the activities described in subsection (a) of this section shall be deemed to be solely for research even if they include patient care provided on an occasional and irregular basis and not as a part of the research program. (1983, c. 775, s. 1; 1987, c. 511, s. 1; 1991, c. 692, s. 4.)

§ 131E-180: Repealed by Session Laws 2005-325, s. 2, effective August 26, 2005.

§ 131E-180.1: Expired.

§ 131E-181. Nature of certificate of need.

(a)   A certificate of need shall be valid only for the defined scope, physical location, and person named in the application. A certificate of need shall not be transferred or assigned except as provided in G.S. 131E-189(c).

(b)   A recipient of a certificate of need, or any person who may subsequently acquire, in any manner whatsoever permitted by law, the service for which that

113

certificate of need was issued, is required to materially comply with the representations made in its application for that certificate of need. The Department shall require any recipient of a certificate of need, or its successor, whose service is in operation to submit to the Department evidence that the recipient, or its successor, is in material compliance with the representations made in its application for the certificate of need which granted the recipient the right to operate that service. In determining whether the recipient of a certificate of need, or its successor, is operating a service which materially differs from the representations made in its application for that certificate of need, the Department shall consider cost increases to the recipient, or its successor, including, but not limited to, the following:

(1)   Any increase in the consumer price index;

(2)   Any increased cost incurred because of Government requirements, including federal, State, or any political subdivision thereof; and

(3)   Any increase in cost due to professional fees or the purchase of services and supplies.

(c)   Whenever a certificate of need is issued more than 12 months after the application for the certificate of need began review, the Department shall adjust the capital expenditure amount proposed by increasing it to reflect any inflation in the Department of Commerce's Construction Cost Index that has occurred since the date when the application began review; and the Department shall use this recalculated capital expenditure amount in the certificate of need issued for the project.

(d)   A project authorized by a certificate of need is complete when the health service or the health service facility for which the certificate of need was issued is licensed and certified and is in material compliance with the representations made in the certificate of need application. (1977, 2nd Sess., c. 1182, s. 2; 1981, c. 651, s. 5; 1983, c. 775, s. 1; 1985, c. 521, s. 1; 1985 (Reg. Sess., 1986), c. 968, s. 1; 1987, c. 511, s. 1; 1989, c. 233, c. 751, s. 9(c); 1991, c. 692, s. 5; 1991 (Reg. Sess., 1992), c. 959, s. 85; 1993, c. 7, s. 5.)

§ 131E-182. Application.

(a)	The Department in its rules shall establish schedules for submission and review of completed applications. The schedules shall provide that applications for similar proposals in the same service area will be reviewed together.

(b)	An application for a certificate of need shall be made on forms provided by the Department. The application forms, which may vary according to the type of proposal, shall require such information as the Department, by its rules deems necessary to conduct the review. An applicant shall be required to furnish only that information necessary to determine whether the proposed new institutional health service is consistent with the review criteria implemented under G.S. 131E-183 and with duly adopted standards, plans and criteria.

(c)	An application fee is imposed on an applicant for a certificate of need. An applicant must submit the fee with the application. The fee is not refundable, regardless of whether a certificate of need is issued. Fees collected under this section shall be credited to the General Fund as nontax revenue. The application fee is five thousand dollars ($5,000) plus an amount equal to three-tenths of one percent (.3%) of the amount of the capital expenditure proposed in the application that exceeds one million dollars ($1,000,000). In no event may the fee exceed fifty thousand dollars ($50,000). (1977, 2nd Sess., c. 1182, s. 2; 1981, c. 651, s. 6; 1983, c. 713, s. 97; c. 775, ss. 1, 6; 1987, c. 511, s. 1; 2005-325, s. 3; 2005-346, s. 8; 2007-323, s. 30.4(b).)

§ 131E-183. Review criteria.

(a)	The Department shall review all applications utilizing the criteria outlined in this subsection and shall determine that an application is either consistent with or not in conflict with these criteria before a certificate of need for the proposed project shall be issued.

(1)	(See note) The proposed project shall be consistent with applicable policies and need determinations in the State Medical Facilities Plan, the need determination of which constitutes a determinative limitation on the provision of any health service, health service facility, health service facility beds, dialysis stations, operating rooms, or home health offices that may be approved.

(2)	Repealed by Session Laws 1987, c. 511, s. 1.

(3)   The applicant shall identify the population to be served by the proposed project, and shall demonstrate the need that this population has for the services proposed, and the extent to which all residents of the area, and, in particular, low income persons, racial and ethnic minorities, women, handicapped persons, the elderly, and other underserved groups are likely to have access to the services proposed.

(3a)   In the case of a reduction or elimination of a service, including the relocation of a facility or a service, the applicant shall demonstrate that the needs of the population presently served will be met adequately by the proposed relocation or by alternative arrangements, and the effect of the reduction, elimination or relocation of the service on the ability of low income persons, racial and ethnic minorities, women, handicapped persons, and other underserved groups and the elderly to obtain needed health care.

(4)   Where alternative methods of meeting the needs for the proposed project exist, the applicant shall demonstrate that the least costly or most effective alternative has been proposed.

(5)   Financial and operational projections for the project shall demonstrate the availability of funds for capital and operating needs as well as the immediate and long-term financial feasibility of the proposal, based upon reasonable projections of the costs of and charges for providing health services by the person proposing the service.

(6)   The applicant shall demonstrate that the proposed project will not result in unnecessary duplication of existing or approved health service capabilities or facilities.

(7)   The applicant shall show evidence of the availability of resources, including health manpower and management personnel, for the provision of the services proposed to be provided.

(8)   The applicant shall demonstrate that the provider of the proposed services will make available, or otherwise make arrangements for, the provision of the necessary ancillary and support services. The applicant shall also demonstrate that the proposed service will be coordinated with the existing health care system.

(9)   An applicant proposing to provide a substantial portion of the project's services to individuals not residing in the health service area in which the project

116

is located, or in adjacent health service areas, shall document the special needs and circumstances that warrant service to these individuals.

(10)   When applicable, the applicant shall show that the special needs of health maintenance organizations will be fulfilled by the project. Specifically, the applicant shall show that the project accommodates:

a.   The needs of enrolled members and reasonably anticipated new members of the HMO for the health service to be provided by the organization; and

b.   The availability of new health services from non-HMO providers or other HMOs in a reasonable and cost-effective manner which is consistent with the basic method of operation of the HMO. In assessing the availability of these health services from these providers, the applicant shall consider only whether the services from these providers:

1.   Would be available under a contract of at least five years' duration;

2.   Would be available and conveniently accessible through physicians and other health professionals associated with the HMO;

3.   Would cost no more than if the services were provided by the HMO; and

4.   Would be available in a manner which is administratively feasible to the HMO.

(11)   Repealed by Session Laws 1987, c. 511, s. 1.

(12)   Applications involving construction shall demonstrate that the cost, design, and means of construction proposed represent the most reasonable alternative, and that the construction project will not unduly increase the costs of providing health services by the person proposing the construction project or the costs and charges to the public of providing health services by other persons, and that applicable energy saving features have been incorporated into the construction plans.

(13)   The applicant shall demonstrate the contribution of the proposed service in meeting the health-related needs of the elderly and of members of medically underserved groups, such as medically indigent or low income persons, Medicaid and Medicare recipients, racial and ethnic minorities, women, and

117

handicapped persons, which have traditionally experienced difficulties in obtaining equal access to the proposed services, particularly those needs identified in the State Health Plan as deserving of priority. For the purpose of determining the extent to which the proposed service will be accessible, the applicant shall show:

a.   The extent to which medically underserved populations currently use the applicant's existing services in comparison to the percentage of the population in the applicant's service area which is medically underserved;

b.   Its past performance in meeting its obligation, if any, under any applicable regulations requiring provision of uncompensated care, community service, or access by minorities and handicapped persons to programs receiving federal assistance, including the existence of any civil rights access complaints against the applicant;

c.   That the elderly and the medically underserved groups identified in this subdivision will be served by the applicant's proposed services and the extent to which each of these groups is expected to utilize the proposed services; and

d.   That the applicant offers a range of means by which a person will have access to its services. Examples of a range of means are outpatient services, admission by house staff, and admission by personal physicians.

(14)   The applicant shall demonstrate that the proposed health services accommodate the clinical needs of health professional training programs in the area, as applicable.

(15)   through (18) Repealed by Session Laws 1987, c. 511, s. 1.

(18a)   The applicant shall demonstrate the expected effects of the proposed services on competition in the proposed service area, including how any enhanced competition will have a positive impact upon the cost effectiveness, quality, and access to the services proposed; and in the case of applications for services where competition between providers will not have a favorable impact on cost effectiveness, quality, and access to the services proposed, the applicant shall demonstrate that its application is for a service on which competition will not have a favorable impact.

(19)   Repealed by Session Laws 1987, c. 511, s. 1.

118

(20)   An applicant already involved in the provision of health services shall provide evidence that quality care has been provided in the past.

(21)   Repealed by Session Laws 1987, c. 511, s. 1.

(b)   The Department is authorized to adopt rules for the review of particular types of applications that will be used in addition to those criteria outlined in subsection (a) of this section and may vary according to the purpose for which a particular review is being conducted or the type of health service reviewed. No such rule adopted by the Department shall require an academic medical center teaching hospital, as defined by the State Medical Facilities Plan, to demonstrate that any facility or service at another hospital is being appropriately utilized in order for that academic medical center teaching hospital to be approved for the issuance of a certificate of need to develop any similar facility or service.

(c)   Repealed by Session Laws 1987, c. 511, s. 1. (1977, 2nd Sess., c. 1182, s. 2; 1981, c. 651, s. 7; 1983, c. 775, s. 1; c. 920, s. 2; 1983 (Reg. Sess., 1984), c. 1002, s. 10; 1985, c. 445, s. 1; 1987, c. 511, s. 1; 1991, c. 692, s. 6; c. 701, s. 2; 1993, c. 7, s. 6; 2001-242, s. 3.)

§ 131E-184. Exemptions from review.

(a)   Except as provided in subsection (b), the Department shall exempt from certificate of need review a new institutional health service if it receives prior written notice from the entity proposing the new institutional health service, which notice includes an explanation of why the new institutional health service is required, for any of the following:

(1)   To eliminate or prevent imminent safety hazards as defined in federal, State, or local fire, building, or life safety codes or regulations.

(1a)   To comply with State licensure standards.

(1b)   To comply with accreditation or certification standards which must be met to receive reimbursement under Title XVIII of the Social Security Act or payments under a State plan for medical assistance approved under Title XIX of that act.

(2)   Repealed by Session Laws 1987, c. 511, s. 1.

(3)   To provide data processing equipment.

(4)   To provide parking, heating or cooling systems, elevators, or other basic plant or mechanical improvements, unless these activities are integral portions of a project that involves the construction of a new health service facility or portion thereof and that is subject to certificate of need review.

(5)   To replace or repair facilities destroyed or damaged by accident or natural disaster.

(6)   To provide any nonhealth service facility or service.

(7)   To provide replacement equipment.

(8)   To acquire an existing health service facility, including equipment owned by the health service facility at the time of acquisition.

(9)   To develop or acquire a physician office building regardless of cost, unless a new institutional health service other than defined in G.S. 131E-176(16)b. is offered or developed in the building.

(b)   Those portions of a proposed project which are not proposed for one or more of the purposes under subsection (a) of this section are subject to certificate of need review, if these non-exempt portions of the project are new institutional health services under G.S. 131E-176(16).

(c)   The Department shall exempt from certificate of need review any conversion of existing acute care beds to psychiatric beds provided:

(1)   The hospital proposing the conversion has executed a contract with the Department's Division of Mental Health, Developmental Disabilities, and Substance Abuse Services and/or one or more of the Area Mental Health, Developmental Disabilities, and Substance Abuse Authorities to provide psychiatric beds to patients referred by the contracting agency or agencies; and

(2)   The total number of beds to be converted shall not be more than twice the number of beds for which the contract pursuant to subdivision (1) of this subsection shall provide.

(d)   In accordance with, and subject to the limitations of G.S. 148-19.1, the Department shall exempt from certificate of need review the construction and operation of a new chemical dependency or substance abuse facility for the purpose of providing inpatient chemical dependency or substance abuse services solely to inmates of the Division of Adult Correction of the Department of Public Safety. If an inpatient chemical dependency or substance abuse facility provides services both to inmates of the Division of Adult Correction of the Department of Public Safety and to members of the general public, only the portion of the facility that serves inmates shall be exempt from certificate of need review.

(e)   The Department shall exempt from certificate of need review a capital expenditure that exceeds the two million dollar ($2,000,000) threshold set forth in G.S. 131E-176(16)b. if all of the following conditions are met:

(1)   The proposed capital expenditure would:

a.   Be used solely for the purpose of renovating, replacing on the same site, or expanding an existing:

1.   Nursing home facility,

2.   Adult care home facility, or

3.   Intermediate care facility for the mentally retarded; and

b.   Not result in a change in bed capacity, as defined in G.S. 131E-176(5), or the addition of a health service facility or any other new institutional health service other than that allowed in G.S. 131E-176(16)b.

(2)   The entity proposing to incur the capital expenditure provides prior written notice to the Department, which notice includes documentation that demonstrates that the proposed capital expenditure would be used for one or more of the following purposes:

a.   Conversion of semiprivate resident rooms to private rooms.

b.   Providing innovative, homelike residential dining spaces, such as cafes, kitchenettes, or private dining areas to accommodate residents and their families or visitors.

c.   Renovating, replacing, or expanding residential living or common areas to improve the quality of life of residents.

(f)   The Department shall exempt from certificate of need review the purchase of any replacement equipment that exceeds the two million dollar ($2,000,000) threshold set forth in G.S. 131E-176(22) if all of the following conditions are met:

(1)   The equipment being replaced is located on the main campus.

(2)   The Department has previously issued a certificate of need for the equipment being replaced. This subdivision does not apply if a certificate of need was not required at the time the equipment being replaced was initially purchased by the licensed health service facility.

(3)   The licensed health service facility proposing to purchase the replacement equipment shall provide prior written notice to the Department, along with supporting documentation to demonstrate that it meets the exemption criteria of this subsection.

(g)   The Department shall exempt from certificate of need review any capital expenditure that exceeds the two million dollar ($2,000,000) threshold set forth in G.S. 131E-176(16)b. if all of the following conditions are met:

(1)   The sole purpose of the capital expenditure is to renovate, replace on the same site, or expand the entirety or a portion of an existing health service facility that is located on the main campus.

(2)   The capital expenditure does not result in (i) a change in bed capacity as defined in G.S. 131E-176(5) or (ii) the addition of a health service facility or any other new institutional health service other than that allowed in G.S. 131E-176(16)b.

(3)   The licensed health service facility proposing to incur the capital expenditure shall provide prior written notice to the Department, along with supporting documentation to demonstrate that it meets the exemption criteria of this subsection. (1983, c. 775, s. 1; 1987, c. 511, s. 1; 1991 (Reg. Sess., 1992), c. 1030, s. 37; 1993, c. 7, s. 7; 2001-424, s. 25.19(c); 2002-159, s. 41; 2009-145, s. 1; 2009-487, s. 3; 2011-145, s. 19.1(h); 2013-360, s. 12G.3(b); 2013-363, s. 4.6.)

§ 131E-185. Review process.

(a)   Repealed by Session Laws 1987, c. 511, s. 1.

(a1)   Except as provided in subsection (c) of this section, there shall be a time limit of 90 days for review of the applications, beginning on the day established by rule as the day on which applications for the particular service in the service area shall begin review.

(1)   Any person may file written comments and exhibits concerning a proposal under review with the Department, not later than 30 days after the date on which the application begins review. These written comments may include:

a.   Facts relating to the service area proposed in the application;

b.   Facts relating to the representations made by the applicant in its application, and its ability to perform or fulfill the representations made;

c.   Discussion and argument regarding whether, in light of the material contained in the application and other relevant factual material, the application complies with relevant review criteria, plans, and standards.

(2)   No more than 20 days from the conclusion of the written comment period, the Department shall ensure that a public hearing is conducted at a place within the appropriate service area if one or more of the following circumstances apply; the review to be conducted is competitive; the proponent proposes to spend five million dollars ($5,000,000) or more; a written request for a public hearing is received before the end of the written comment period from an affected party as defined in G.S. 131E-188(c); or the agency determines that a hearing is in the public interest. At such public hearing oral arguments may be made regarding the application or applications under review; and this public hearing shall include the following:

a.   An opportunity for the proponent of each application under review to respond to the written comments submitted to the Department about its application;

b.   An opportunity for any person, except one of the proponents, to comment on the applications under review;

123

c.   An opportunity for a representative of the Department, or such other person or persons who are designated by the Department to conduct the hearing, to question each proponent of applications under review with regard to the contents of the application;

The Department shall maintain a recording of any required public hearing on an application until such time as the Department's final decision is issued, or until a final agency decision is issued pursuant to a contested case hearing, whichever is later; and any person may submit a written synopsis or verbatim statement that contains the oral presentation made at the hearing.

(3)   The Department may contract or make arrangements with a person or persons located within each service area for the conduct of such public hearings as may be necessary. The Department shall publish, in each service area, notice of the contracts that it executes for the conduct of those hearings.

(4)   Within 15 days from the beginning of the review of an application or applications proposing the same service within the same service area, the Department shall publish notice of the deadline for receipt of written comments, of the time and place scheduled for the public hearing regarding the application or applications under review, and of the name and address of the person or agency that will preside.

(5)   The Department shall maintain all written comments submitted to it during the written comment stage and any written submissions received at the public hearing as part of the Department's file respecting each application or group of applications under review by it. The application, written comments, and public hearing comments, together with all documents that the Department used in arriving at its decision, from whatever source, and any documents that reflect or set out the Department's final analysis of the application or applications under review, shall constitute the Department's record for the application or applications under review.

(a2)   When an expedited review has been approved by the Department, no public hearing shall be held. The Department may contact the applicant and request additional or clarifying information, amendments to, or substitutions for portions of the application. The Department may negotiate conditions to be imposed on the certificate of need with the applicant.

(b)   Repealed by Session Laws 1991 (Reg. Sess., 1992), c. 900, s. 137(a).

(c)   The Department may extend the review period for a period not to exceed 60 days and provide notice of such extension to all applicants. For expedited reviews, the Department may extend the review period only if it has requested additional substantive information from the applicant. (1977, 2nd Sess., c. 1182, s. 2; 1981, c. 651, ss. 9, 10; 1983, c. 775, s. 1; 1987, c. 511, s. 1; 1991, c. 692, s. 7; 1991 (Reg. Sess., 1992), c. 900, s. 137(a), (b); 1993, c. 7, s. 8; 2005-325, s. 4.)

§ 131E-186. Decision.

(a)   Within the prescribed time limits in G.S. 131E-185, the Department shall issue a decision to "approve," "approve with conditions," or "deny," an application for a new institutional health service. Approvals involving new or expanded nursing care or intermediate care for the mentally retarded bed capacity shall include a condition that specifies the earliest possible date the new institutional health service may be certified for participation in the Medicaid program. The date shall be set far enough in advance to allow the Department to identify funds to pay for care in the new or expanded facility in its existing Medicaid budget or to include these funds in its State Medicaid budget request for the year in which Medicaid certification is expected.

(b)   Within five business days after it makes a decision on an application, the Department shall provide written notice of all the findings and conclusions upon which it based its decision, including the criteria used by the Department in making its decision, to the applicant. (1977, 2nd Sess., c. 1182, s. 2; 1983, c. 775, s. 1; 1987, c. 511, s. 1; 1991 (Reg. Sess., 1992), c. 900, s. 137(c).)

§ 131E-187. Issuance of a certificate of need.

(a),(b) Repealed by Session Laws 2009-373, s. 1, effective July 31, 2009.

(c)   The Department shall issue a certificate of need in accordance with the time line requirements of this section but only after all applicable conditions of approval that can be satisfied before issuance of the certificate of need have been met. The Department shall issue a certificate of need within:

125

(1)   Thirty-five days of the date of the decision referenced in G.S. 131E-186, when no request for a contested case hearing has been filed in accordance with G.S. 131E-188.

(2)   Five business days after it receives a file-stamped copy of the notice of voluntary dismissal, unless the voluntary dismissal is a stipulation of dismissal without prejudice.

(3)   Thirty-five days of the date of the written notice of the final agency decision affirming or approving the issuance, unless a notice of appeal to the North Carolina Court of Appeals is timely filed.

(4)   Twenty days after a mandate is issued by the North Carolina Court of Appeals affirming the issuance of a certificate of need, unless a notice of appeal or petition for discretionary review to the North Carolina Supreme Court is timely filed.

(5)   Five business days after the North Carolina Supreme Court issues a mandate affirming the issuance of a certificate of need or an order declining to certify the case for discretionary review if the order declining to certify the case disposes of the appeal in its entirety. (1977, 2nd Sess., c. 1182, s. 2; 1983, c. 775, s. 1; 1987, c. 511, s. 1; 2009-373, s. 1.)

§ 131E-188. Administrative and judicial review.

(a)   After a decision of the Department to issue, deny or withdraw a certificate of need or exemption or to issue a certificate of need pursuant to a settlement agreement with an applicant to the extent permitted by law, any affected person, as defined in subsection (c) of this section, shall be entitled to a contested case hearing under Article 3 of Chapter 150B of the General Statutes. A petition for a contested case shall be filed within 30 days after the Department makes its decision. When a petition is filed, the Department shall send notification of the petition to the proponent of each application that was reviewed with the application for a certificate of need that is the subject of the petition. Any affected person shall be entitled to intervene in a contested case.

A contested case shall be conducted in accordance with the following timetable:

(1)   An administrative law judge or a hearing officer, as appropriate, shall be assigned within 15 days after a petition is filed.

(2)   The parties shall complete discovery within 90 days after the assignment of the administrative law judge or hearing officer.

(3)   The hearing at which sworn testimony is taken and evidence is presented shall be held within 45 days after the end of the discovery period.

(4)   The administrative law judge or hearing officer shall make a final decision within 75 days after the hearing.

(5)   Repealed by Session Laws 2011-398, s. 46, as amended by Session Laws 2011-326, s. 23, effective January 1, 2012, and applicable to contested cases commenced on or after that date.

The administrative law judge or hearing officer assigned to a case may extend the deadlines in subdivisions (2) through (4) so long as the administrative law judge or hearing officer makes a final decision in the case within 270 days after the petition is filed.

(a1)   On or before the date of filing a petition for a contested case hearing on the approval of an applicant for a certificate of need, the petitioner shall deposit a bond with the clerk of superior court where the new institutional health service that is the subject of the petition is proposed to be located. The bond shall be secured by cash or its equivalent in an amount equal to five percent (5%) of the cost of the proposed new institutional health service that is the subject of the petition, but may not be less than five thousand dollars ($5,000) and may not exceed fifty thousand dollars ($50,000). A petitioner who received approval for a certificate of need and is contesting only a condition in the certificate is not required to file a bond under this subsection.

The applicant who received approval for the new institutional health service that is the subject of the petition may bring an action against a bond filed under this subsection in the superior court of the county where the bond was filed. Upon finding that the petition for a contested case was frivolous or filed to delay the applicant, the court may award the applicant part or all of the bond filed under this subsection. At the conclusion of the contested case, if the court does not find that the petition for a contested case was frivolous or filed to delay the applicant, the petitioner shall be entitled to the return of the bond deposited with the superior court upon demonstrating to the clerk of superior court where the bond was filed that the contested case hearing is concluded.

(b)   Any affected person who was a party in a contested case hearing shall be entitled to judicial review of all or any portion of any final decision in the following manner. The appeal shall be to the Court of Appeals as provided in G.S. 7A-29(a). The procedure for the appeal shall be as provided by the rules of appellate procedure. The appeal of the final decision shall be taken within 30 days of the receipt of the written notice of final decision, and notice of appeal shall be filed with the Office of Administrative Hearings and served on the Department and all other affected persons who were parties to the contested hearing.

(b1)   Before filing an appeal of a final decision granting a certificate of need, the affected person shall deposit a bond with the Clerk of the Court of Appeals. The bond requirements of this subsection shall not apply to any appeal filed by the Department.

(1)   The bond shall be secured by cash or its equivalent in an amount equal to five percent (5%) of the cost of the proposed new institutional health service that is the subject of the appeal, but may not be less than five thousand dollars ($5,000) and may not exceed fifty thousand dollars ($50,000); provided that the applicant who received approval of the certificate of need may petition the Court of Appeals for a higher bond amount for the payment of such costs and damages as may be awarded pursuant to subdivision (2) of this subsection. This amount shall be determined by the Court in its discretion, not to exceed three hundred thousand dollars ($300,000). A holder of a certificate of need who is appealing only a condition in the certificate is not required to file a bond under this subsection.

(2)   If the Court of Appeals finds that the appeal was frivolous or filed to delay the applicant, the court shall remand the case to the superior court of the county where a bond was filed for the contested case hearing on the certificate of need. The superior court may award the holder of the certificate of need part or all of the bond. The court shall award the holder of the certificate of need reasonable attorney fees and costs incurred in the appeal to the Court of Appeals. If the Court of Appeals does not find that the appeal was frivolous or filed to delay the applicant and does not remand the case to superior court for a possible award of all or part of the bond to the holder of the certificate of need, the person originally filing the bond shall be entitled to a return of the bond.

128

(c)   The term "affected persons" includes: the applicant; any individual residing within the service area or the geographic area served or to be served by the applicant; any individual who regularly uses health service facilities within that geographic area or the service area; any person who provides services, similar to the services under review, to individuals residing within the service area or the geographic area proposed to be served by the applicant; any person who, prior to receipt by the agency of the proposal being reviewed, has provided written notice to the agency of an intention to provide similar services in the future to individuals residing within the service area or the geographic area to be served by the applicant; third party payers who reimburse health service facilities for services in the service area in which the project is proposed to be located; and any agency which establishes rates for health service facilities or HMOs located in the service area in which the project is proposed to be located. (1977, 2nd Sess., c. 1182, s. 2; 1981, c. 651, s. 11; 1983, c. 775, s. 1; 1983 (Reg. Sess., 1984), c. 1000, s. 1; 1987, c. 511, s. 1; 1991, c. 692, s. 8; c. 701, s. 3; 1993, c. 7, s. 9; 1997-443, s. 11A.118(a); 2005-325, s. 5; 2007-182, s. 1; 2009-373, s. 2; 2011-326, s. 23; 2011-398, s. 46.)

§ 131E-189. Withdrawal of a certificate of need.

(a)   The Department shall specify in each certificate of need the time the holder has to make the service or equipment available or to complete the project and the timetable to be followed. The timetable shall be the one proposed by the holder of the certificate of need unless the Department specifies a different timetable in its decision letter. The holder of the certificate shall submit such periodic reports on his progress in meeting the timetable as may be required by the Department. If no progress report is provided or, after reviewing the progress, the Department determines that the holder of the certificate is not meeting the timetable and the holder cannot demonstrate that it is making good faith efforts to meet the timetable, the Department may withdraw the certificate. If the Department determines that the holder of the certificate is making a good faith effort to meet the timetable, the Department may, at the request of the holder, extend the timetable for a specified period.

(b)   The Department may withdraw any certificate of need, if the holder of the certificate fails to develop the service in a manner consistent with the representations made in the application or with any condition or conditions the Department placed on the certificate of need.

(c)   The Department may immediately withdraw any certificate of need if the holder of the certificate, before completion of the project or operation of the facility, transfers ownership or control of the facility, the project, or the certificate of need. Any transfer after that time will be subject to the requirement that the service be provided consistent with the representations made in the application and any applicable conditions the Department placed on the certificate of need. Transfers resulting from death or personal illness or other good cause, as determined by the Department, shall not result in withdrawal if the Department receives prior written notice of the transfer and finds good cause. Transfers resulting from death shall not result in withdrawal. (1977, 2nd Sess., c. 1182, s. 2; 1981, c. 651, s. 12; 1983, c. 775, s. 1; 1987, c. 511, s. 1; 1993, c. 7, s. 10.)

§ 131E-190. Enforcement and sanctions.

(a)   Only those new institutional health services which are found by the Department to be needed as provided in this Article and granted certificates of need shall be offered or developed within the State.

(b)   No formal commitments made for financing, construction, or acquisition regarding the offering or development of a new institutional health service shall be made by any person unless a certificate of need for such service or activities has been granted.

(c)   Repealed by Session Laws 1993, c. 7, s. 11.

(d)   If any person proceeds to offer or develop a new institutional health service without having first obtained a certificate of need for such services, the penalty for such violation of this Article and rules hereunder may include the withholding of federal and State funds under Titles V, XVIII, and XIX of the Social Security Act for reimbursement of capital and operating expenses related to the provision of the new institutional health service.

(e)   The Department may revoke or suspend the license of any person who proceeds to offer or develop a new institutional health service without having first obtained a certificate of need for such services.

(f)   The Department may assess a civil penalty of not more than twenty thousand dollars ($20,000) against any person who knowingly offers or develops any new institutional health service within the meaning of this Article without a certificate of need issued under this Article and the rules pertaining thereto, or in violation of the terms or conditions of such a certificate, whenever it determines a violation has occurred and each time the service is provided in violation of this provision. In determining the amount of the penalty the Department shall consider the degree and extent of harm caused by the violation and the cost of rectifying the damage. A person who is assessed a penalty shall be notified of the penalty by registered or certified mail. The notice shall state the reasons for the penalty. If a person fails to pay a penalty, the Department shall refer the matter to the Attorney General for collection. For the purpose of this subsection, the word "person" shall not include an individual in his capacity as an officer, director, or employee of a person as otherwise defined in this Article.

The clear proceeds of penalties provided for in this subsection shall be remitted to the Civil Penalty and Forfeiture Fund in accordance with G.S. 115C-457.2.

(g)   No agency of the State or any of its political subdivisions may appropriate or grant funds or financially assist in any way a person, applicant, or facility which is or whose project is in violation of this Article.

(h)   If any person proceeds to offer or develop a new institutional health service without having first obtained a certificate of need for such services, the Secretary of Health and Human Services or any person aggrieved, as defined by G.S. 150B-2(6), may bring a civil action for injunctive relief, temporary or permanent, against the person offering, developing or operating any new institutional health service. The action may be brought in the superior court of any county in which the health service facility is located or in the superior court of Wake County.

(i)   If the Department determines that the recipient of a certificate of need, or its successor, is operating a service which materially differs from the representations made in its application for that certificate of need, the Department may bring an action in Wake County Superior Court or the superior court of any county in which the certificate of need is to be utilized for injunctive relief, temporary or permanent, requiring the recipient, or its successor, to materially comply with the representations in its application. The Department may also bring an action in Wake County Superior Court or the superior court of any county in which the certificate of need is to be utilized to enforce the provisions of this subsection and G.S. 131E-181(b) and the rules adopted in accordance with this subsection and G.S. 131E-181(b). (1977, 2nd Sess., c. 1182, s. 2; 1981, c. 651, s. 13; 1983, c. 775, s. 1; 1985 (Reg. Sess., 1986), c.

131

968, s. 2; 1987, c. 511, s. 1; 1991, c. 692, s. 9; 1993, c. 7, s. 11; 1997-443, s. 11A.118(a); 1998-215, s. 80.)

§ 131E-191. Repealed by Session Laws 1987, c. 511, s. 1.

§ 131E-191.1. Lobbyists prohibited from serving on the North Carolina State Health Coordinating Council.

No person registered as a lobbyist under Chapter 120C of the General Statutes shall be appointed to or serve on the North Carolina State Health Coordinating Council. No person previously registered as a lobbyist under Chapter 120C of the General Statutes shall be appointed to or serve on the North Carolina State Health Coordinating Council within 120 days after the expiration of the lobbyist's registration. (2009-477, s. 2.)

§ 131E-192. Reserved for future codification purposes.

Article 9A.

Certificate of Public Advantage.

§ 131E-192.1. Findings.

The General Assembly of North Carolina makes the following findings:

(1)   That technological and scientific developments in hospital care have enhanced the prospects for further improvement in the quality of care provided by North Carolina hospitals to North Carolina citizens.

(2)   That the cost of improved technology and improved scientific methods for the provision of hospital care contributes substantially to the increasing cost of hospital care. Cost increases make it increasingly difficult for hospitals in rural areas of North Carolina to offer care.

(3)   That changes in federal and State regulations governing hospital operation and reimbursement have constrained the ability of hospitals to acquire and develop new and improved machinery and methods for the provision of hospital-related care.

132

(4)   That cooperative agreements among hospitals and between hospitals and others for the provision of health care services may foster improvements in the quality of health care for North Carolina citizens, moderate increases in cost, improve access to needed services in rural areas of North Carolina, and enhance the likelihood that smaller hospitals in North Carolina will remain open in beneficial service to their communities.

(5)   That hospitals are often in the best position to identify and structure cooperative arrangements that enhance quality of care, improve access, and achieve cost-efficiency in the provision of care.

(6)   That federal and State antitrust laws may prohibit or discourage cooperative arrangements that are beneficial to North Carolina citizens despite their potential for or actual reduction in competition and that such agreements should be permitted and encouraged.

(7)   That competition as currently mandated by federal and State antitrust laws should be supplanted by a regulatory program to permit and encourage cooperative agreements between hospitals, or between hospitals and others, that are beneficial to North Carolina citizens when the benefits of cooperative agreements outweigh their disadvantages caused by their potential or actual adverse effects on competition.

(8)   That regulatory as well as judicial oversight of cooperative agreements should be provided to ensure that the benefits of cooperative agreements permitted and encouraged in North Carolina outweigh any disadvantages attributable to any reduction in competition likely to result from the agreements. (1993, c. 529, s. 5.2.)

§ 131E-192.2. Definitions.

The following definitions apply in this Article:

(1)   "Attorney General" means the Attorney General of the State of North Carolina or any attorney on his or her staff to whom the Attorney General delegates authority and responsibility to act pursuant to this Article.

(2)   "Cooperative agreement" means an agreement among two or more hospitals, between a hospital and any other person, or between a person who

133

controls a hospital and another hospital or person who controls a hospital for any of the following:

a.   The sharing, allocation, or referral of patients, personnel, instructional programs, support services and facilities, or medical, diagnostic, or laboratory facilities or equipment, or procedures or other services traditionally offered by hospitals.

b.   A purchase of assets pursuant to a merger or sale, a partnership, a joint venture, or any other affiliation by which ownership or control over all or substantially all of the stock, assets, or activities of one or more hospitals or persons who control hospitals are transferred to another hospital or person who controls a hospital.

"Cooperative agreement" shall not include any agreement that would permit self-referrals of patients by a health care provider that is otherwise prohibited by law.

(3)   "Department" means the Department of Health and Human Services.

(4)   "Federal or State antitrust laws" means any and all federal or State laws prohibiting monopolies or agreements in restraint of trade, including the federal Sherman Act, Clayton Act, Federal Trade Commission Act, and North Carolina laws codified in Chapter 75 of the General Statutes that prohibit restraints on competition.

(5)   "Hospital" means any hospital required to be licensed under Chapters 131E or 122C of the General Statutes.

(6)   "Person" means any individual, firm, partnership, corporation, association, public or private institution, political subdivision, or government agency. (1993, c. 529, s. 5.2; 1995, c. 205, s. 1; 1997-443, s. 11A.118(a).)

§ 131E-192.3. Certificate of public advantage; application.

(a)   A hospital and any person who is a party to a cooperative agreement with a hospital may negotiate, enter into, and conduct business pursuant to a cooperative agreement without being subject to damages, liability, or scrutiny under any State antitrust law if a certificate of public advantage is issued for the cooperative agreement, or in the case of activities to negotiate or enter into a cooperative agreement, if an application for a certificate of public advantage is filed in good faith. It is the intention of the General Assembly that immunity from federal antitrust laws shall also be conferred by this statute and the State regulatory program that it establishes.

(b)   Parties to a cooperative agreement may apply to the Department for a certificate of public advantage governing that cooperative agreement. The application must include an executed written copy of the cooperative agreement or letter of intent with respect to the agreement, a description of the nature and scope of the activities and cooperation in the agreement, any consideration passing to any party under the agreement, and any additional materials necessary to fully explain the agreement and its likely effects. A copy of the application and all additional related materials shall be submitted to the Attorney General at the same time the application is submitted to the Department. (1993, c. 529, s. 5.2.)

§ 131E-192.4. Procedure for review; standards for review.

(a)   The Department shall review an application in accordance with the standards set forth in subsection (b) of this section and shall hold a public hearing with the opportunity for the submission of oral and written public comments in accordance with rules adopted by the Department. The Department shall determine whether the application should be granted or denied within 90 days of the date the application is filed. The Department may extend the review period for a specified period of time upon notice to the parties.

(b)   The Department shall determine that a certificate of public advantage should be issued for a cooperative agreement if it determines that an applicant has demonstrated by clear and convincing evidence that the benefits likely to result from the agreement outweigh the disadvantages likely to result from a reduction in competition from the agreement.

(1)   In evaluating the potential benefits of a cooperative agreement, the Department shall consider whether one or more of the following benefits may result from the cooperative agreement:

a.   Enhancement of the quality of hospital and hospital-related care provided to North Carolina citizens.

135

b.   Preservation of hospital facilities in geographical proximity to the communities traditionally served by those facilities.

c.   Lower costs of, or gains in, the efficiency of delivering hospital services.

d.   Improvements in the utilization of hospital resources and equipment.

e.   Avoidance of duplication of hospital resources.

f.   The extent to which medically underserved populations are expected to utilize the proposed services.

(2)   In evaluating the potential disadvantages of a cooperative agreement, the Department shall consider whether one or more of the following disadvantages may result from the cooperative agreements:

a.   The extent to which the agreement may increase the costs or prices of health care at a hospital which is party to the cooperative agreement.

b.   The extent to which the agreement may have an adverse impact on patients in the quality, availability, and price of health care services.

c.   The extent to which the agreement may reduce competition among the parties to the agreement and the likely effects thereof.

d.   The extent to which the agreement may have an adverse impact on the ability of health maintenance organizations, preferred provider organizations, managed health care service agents, or other health care payors to negotiate optimal payment and service arrangements with hospitals, physicians, allied health care professionals, or other health care providers.

e.   The extent to which the agreement may result in a reduction in competition among physicians, allied health professionals, other health care providers, or other persons furnishing goods or services to, or in competition with, hospitals.

f.   The availability of arrangements that are less restrictive to competition and achieve the same benefits or a more favorable balance of benefits over disadvantages attributable to any reduction in competition.

(3)   In making its determination, the Department may consider other benefits or disadvantages that may be identified. (1993, c. 529, s. 5.2; 1997-456, s. 27.)

§ 131E-192.5. Issuance of a certificate.

If the Department determines that the likely benefits of a cooperative agreement outweigh the likely disadvantages attributable to reduction of competition as a result of the agreement by clear and convincing evidence, and the Attorney General has not stated any objection to issuance of a certificate during the review period, the Department shall issue a certificate of public advantage for the cooperative agreement at the conclusion of the review period. The certificate shall include any conditions of operation under the agreement that the Department, in consultation with the Attorney General, determines to be appropriate in order to ensure that the cooperative agreement and the activities engaged under it are consistent with this Article and its purpose to limit health care costs. The Department shall include conditions to control prices of health care services provided under the cooperative agreement. Consideration shall be given to assure that access to health care is provided to all areas of the State. The Department shall publish its decisions on applications for certificates of public advantage in the North Carolina Register. (1993, c. 529, s. 5.2.)

§ 131E-192.6. Objection by Attorney General.

If the Attorney General is not persuaded that an applicant has demonstrated by clear and convincing evidence that the benefits likely to result from the agreement outweigh the likely disadvantages of any reduction of competition to result from the agreement as set forth in G.S. 131E-192.4, the Attorney General may, within the review period, state an objection to the issuance of a certificate of public advantage and may extend the review period for a specified period of time. Notice of the objection and any extension of the review period shall be provided in writing to the applicant, together with a general explanation of the concerns of the Attorney General. The parties may attempt to reach an agreement with the Attorney General on modifications to the agreement or to conditions in the certificate so that the Attorney General no longer objects to issuance of a certificate. If the Attorney General withdraws the objection and the Department maintains its determination that a certificate should be issued, the Department shall issue a certificate of public advantage with any appropriate conditions as soon as practicable following the withdrawal of the objection. If the Attorney General does not withdraw the objection, a certificate shall not be issued. (1993, c. 529, s. 5.2.)

§ 131E-192.7. Record keeping.

The Department shall maintain on file all cooperative agreements for which certificates of public advantage are in effect and a copy of the certificate, including any conditions imposed in it. Any party to a cooperative agreement who terminates an agreement shall file a notice of termination with the Department within 30 days after termination. These files shall be public records as set forth in Chapter 132 of the General Statutes. (1993, c. 529, s. 5.2.)

§ 131E-192.8. Review after issuance of certificate.

If at any time following the issuance of a certificate of public advantage, the Department or the Attorney General has questions concerning whether the parties to the cooperative agreement have complied with any condition of the certificate or whether the benefits or likely benefits resulting from a cooperative agreement may no longer outweigh the disadvantages or likely disadvantages attributable to a reduction in competition resulting from the agreement, the Department or the Attorney General shall advise the parties to the agreement, and either the Department or the Attorney General shall request any information necessary to complete a review of the matter. (1993, c. 529, s. 5.2.)

§ 131E-192.9. Periodic reports.

(a)   During the time that a certificate is in effect, a report of activities pursuant to the cooperative agreement must be filed every two years with the Department on or before the anniversary date on which the certificate was issued. A copy of the periodic report shall be submitted to the Attorney General at the same time that it is filed with the Department. A report shall include all of the following:

(1)   A description of the activities conducted pursuant to the agreement.

(2)   Price and cost information.

(3)   The nature and scope of the activities pursuant to the agreement anticipated for the next two years, the likely effect of those activities.

(4)   A signed certificate by each party to the agreement that the benefits or likely benefits of the cooperative agreement as conditioned continue to outweigh the disadvantages or likely disadvantages of any reduction in competition from the agreement as conditioned.

(5)   Any additional information requested by the Department or the Attorney General.

The Department shall give public notice in the North Carolina Register that a report has been received. After notice is given, the public shall have 30 days to file written comments on the report and on the benefits and disadvantages of continuing the certificate of public advantage. Periodic reports, public comments, and information submitted in response to a request shall be public records as set forth in Chapter 132 of the General Statutes.

(b)   Failure to file a periodic report required by this section after notice of default or failure to provide information requested pursuant to a review under G.S. 131E-192.8 is grounds for the revocation of the certificate by the Attorney General or the Department.

(c)   The Department shall review each periodic report, public comments, and information submitted in response to a request under G.S. 131E-192.8 to determine whether the advantages or likely advantages of the cooperative agreement continue to outweigh the disadvantages or likely disadvantages of any reduction in competition from the agreement, and to determine what, if any, changes in the conditions of the certificate should be made. In the review the Department shall consider the benefits and disadvantages set forth in G.S. 131E-192.4. Within 60 days of the filing of a periodic report, the Department shall determine whether the certificate should remain in effect and whether any changes to the conditions in the certificate should be made. The Department may extend the review period an additional 30 days. If either the Department or the Attorney General determines that the parties to a cooperative agreement have not complied with any condition of the certificate, the Department or the Attorney General shall revoke the certificate and the parties shall be notified. If the certificate is revoked, the parties shall be entitled to no benefits under this Article, beginning on the date of revocation. If the Department determines that the certificate should remain in effect and the Attorney General has not stated any objection to the certificate remaining in effect during the review period, the certificate shall remain in effect subject to any changes in the conditions of the certificate imposed by the Department. The parties shall be notified in writing of the Department's decision and of any changes in the conditions of the certificate. The Department shall publish its decision and any changes in the conditions in the North Carolina Register.

If the Department determines that the benefits or likely benefits of the agreement and the unavoidable costs of terminating the agreement do not continue to outweigh the disadvantages or likely disadvantages of any reduction in competition from the agreement, or if the Attorney General objects to the certificate remaining in effect based upon a review of the benefits and disadvantages set forth in G.S. 131E-192.4, the Department shall notify the parties to the agreement in writing of its determination or the objections of the Attorney General and shall provide a summary of any concerns of the Department or Attorney General to the parties. (1993, c. 529, s. 5.2.)

§ 131E-192.10. Right to judicial action.

(a)   Any applicant or other person aggrieved by a decision to issue or not issue a certificate of public advantage is entitled to judicial review of the action or inaction in superior court. Suit for judicial review under this subsection shall be filed within 30 days of public notice of the decision to issue or deny issuance of the certificate. To prevail in any action for judicial review brought under this subsection, the plaintiff or petitioner must establish that the determination by the Department or the Attorney General was arbitrary or capricious.

(b)   Any party or other person aggrieved by a decision to allow a certificate to remain in effect or to make changes in the conditions of a certificate is entitled to judicial review of the decision in superior court. Suit for judicial review under this subsection shall be filed within 30 days of public notice of the decision to allow the certificate to remain in effect or to make changes in the conditions of the certificate. To prevail in any action for judicial review brought under this subsection, the plaintiff or petitioner must establish that the determination by the Department or the Attorney General was arbitrary or capricious.

(c)   If the Department or the Attorney General determines that the certificate should not remain in effect, the Attorney General may bring suit in the Superior

140

Court of Wake County on behalf of the Department, or on its own behalf, to seek an order to authorize the cancellation of the certificate. To prevail in the action, the Attorney General must establish that the benefits resulting from the agreement are outweighed by the disadvantages attributable to a reduction in competition resulting from the agreement.

(d) In any action instituted under this section, the work product of the Department, the Attorney General or his staff, is not a public record under Chapter 132, and shall not be discoverable or admissable, nor shall the Attorney General or any member of his staff be compelled to be a witness, whether in discovery or at any hearing or trial. (1993, c. 529, s. 5.2.)

§ 131E-192.11. Fees for applications and periodic reports.

(a)   The Department and the Attorney General shall establish a schedule of fees for filing an application for a certificate of public advantage and for filing a periodic report based on the total cost of the project for which the application or periodic report is made. The fee for filing an application may not exceed fifteen thousand dollars ($15,000). The fee for filing a periodic report may not exceed two thousand five hundred dollars ($2,500). The fee schedule established should generate sufficient revenue to offset the costs of the program. An application filing fee must be paid to the Department at the time an application for a certificate of public advantage is submitted to it pursuant to G.S. 131E-192.3. A periodic report filing fee must be paid to the Department at the time a periodic report is submitted to it pursuant to G.S. 131E-192.9.

(b)   If the Department or the Attorney General determines that consultants are needed to complete a review of an application, an additional application fee may be established by prior agreement with the applicants before the application is considered. The amount of the additional fee may not exceed the costs of contracting with the necessary consultants. The additional fee shall not be considered in determining whether an application fee exceeds the maximum application fee amount set in subsection (a) of this section. (1993, c. 529, s. 5.2; 1995, c. 205, s. 2.)

§ 131E-192.12. Department and Attorney General authority.

The Department and Attorney General shall have the necessary powers to adopt rules to conduct a review of applications for certificates of public advantage and of periodic reports filed in connection therewith and to bring actions in the Superior Court of Wake County as required under G.S. 131E-192.10. This Article shall not limit the authority of the Attorney General under federal or State antitrust laws. (1993, c. 529, s. 5.2.)

§ 131E-192.13. Effects of certificate of public advantage; other laws.

(a)   Activities conducted pursuant to a cooperative agreement for which a certificate of public advantage has been issued are immunized from challenge or scrutiny under State antitrust laws. In addition, conduct in negotiating and entering into a cooperative agreement for which an application for a certificate of public advantage is filed in good faith shall be immune from challenge or scrutiny under State antitrust laws, regardless of whether a certificate is issued. It is the intention of the General Assembly that this Article shall also immunize covered activities from challenge or scrutiny under federal antitrust law.

(b)   Nothing in this Article shall exempt hospitals or other health care providers from compliance with State or federal laws governing certificate of need, licensure, or other regulatory requirements.

(c)   Any dispute among the parties to a cooperative agreement concerning its meaning or terms is governed by normal principles of contract law. (1993, c. 529, s. 5.2.)

§§ 131E-193 through 131E-199. Reserved for future codification purposes.

Article 10.

Hospice Licensure Act.

§ 131E-200. Title; purpose.

This Article shall be known as the "Hospice Licensure Act." The purpose of this Article is to establish licensing requirements for hospices. (1983 (Reg. Sess., 1984), c. 1022, s. 1; 1987, c. 34.)

§ 131E-201. Definitions.

As used in this Article, unless a different meaning or construction is clearly required by the context:

(1)   "Commission" means the North Carolina Medical Care Commission.

(2)   "Department" means the Department of Health and Human Services.

(3)   "Hospice" means any coordinated program of home care with provision for inpatient care for terminally ill patients and their families. This care is provided by a medically directed interdisciplinary team, directly or through an agreement under the direction of an identifiable hospice administration. A hospice program of care provides palliative and supportive medical and other health services to meet the physical, psychological, social, spiritual, and special needs of patients and their families, which are experienced during the final stages of terminal illness and during dying and bereavement.

(3a)   "Hospice inpatient facility" means a freestanding licensed hospice facility or a designated inpatient unit in an existing health service facility which provides palliative and supportive medical and other health services to meet the physical, psychological, social, spiritual, and special needs of terminally ill patients and their families in an inpatient setting.

(4)   "Hospice patient" means a patient diagnosed as terminally ill by a physician licensed to practice medicine in North Carolina, who the physician anticipates to have a life expectancy of weeks or months, generally not to exceed six months, and who alone, or in conjunction with designated family members, has voluntarily requested and been accepted into a licensed hospice program.

(5)   "Hospice patient's family" means the hospice patient's immediate kin, including a spouse, brother, sister, child, or parent. Other relations and individuals with significant personal ties to the hospice patient may be

143

designated as members of the hospice patient's family by mutual agreement among the hospice patient, the relation or individual and the hospice team.

(5a)   "Hospice residential care facility" means a freestanding licensed hospice facility which provides palliative and supportive medical and other health services to meet the physical, psychological, social, spiritual, and special needs of terminally ill patients and their families in a group residential setting.

(5b)   "Hospice services" means the provision of palliative and supportive medical and other health services to meet the physical, psychological, social, spiritual, and special needs of patients and their families, which are experienced during the final stages of terminal illness and during dying and bereavement.

(6)   "Hospice team" or "Interdisciplinary team" means the following hospice personnel: physician licensed to practice medicine in North Carolina; nurse holding a valid, current license as required by North Carolina law; social worker; clergy member; and trained hospice volunteer. Other health care practitioners may be included on the team as the needs of the patient dictate or at the request of the physician. Other providers of special services may also be included as the needs of the patient dictate.

(7)   "Identifiable hospice administration" means an administrative group, individual, or legal entity that has an identifiable organizational structure, accountable to a governing board directly or through a chief executive officer. This administration shall be responsible for the management of all aspects of the program.

(8)   "Palliative care" means treatment directed at controlling pain, relieving other symptoms, and focusing on the special needs of the patient and family as they experience the stress of the dying process, rather than the treatment aimed at investigation and intervention for the purpose of cure or prolongation of life. (1983 (Reg. Sess., 1984), c. 1022, s. 1; 1993, c. 376, s. 5; 1997-443, s. 11A.118(a).)

§ 131E-202. Licensing.

(a)   The Commission shall adopt rules for the licensing and regulation of hospices, hospice inpatient facilities, and hospice residential care facilities pursuant to this Article for the purpose of providing care, treatment, health, safety, welfare, and comfort of hospice patients. These rules shall include, but not be limited to:

(1)   The qualifications and supervision of licensed and nonlicensed personnel;

(2)   The provision and coordination of home and inpatient care, including the development of a written care plan;

(3)   The management, operation, staffing, and equipping of the hospice program;

(4)   Clinical and business records kept by the hospice, hospice inpatient care facility, and hospice residential care facility; and

(5)   Procedures for the review of utilization and quality of care.

(b)   The Department shall provide applications for hospice licensure. Each application filed with the Department shall contain all information requested therein. A license shall be granted to the applicant upon determination by the Department that the applicant has complied with the provisions of this Article and with the rules adopted by the Commission thereunder. Each license shall be issued only for the premises and persons named therein, shall not be transferable or assignable except with the written approval of the Department, and shall be posted in a conspicuous place on the licensed premises. The Department shall charge the applicant a nonrefundable annual license fee in the amount of four hundred dollars ($400.00).

(c)   The Department shall renew the license in accordance with this Article and with rules adopted thereunder. (1983 (Reg. Sess., 1984), c. 1022, s. 1; 1993, c. 376, s. 6; 2009-451, s. 10.76(h).)

§ 131E-203. Coverage.

(a)   Except as provided in subsection (b) of this section, no person or other entity shall operate or represent himself or itself to the public as operating a hospice, a hospice inpatient facility, or a hospice residential care facility, or offer or represent himself or itself to the public as offering hospice services without obtaining a license from the Department pursuant to this Article.

145

(b)   Hospices administered by local health departments established under Article 2 of Chapter 130A of the General Statutes shall not be required to be licensed under this Article. Additionally, health care facilities and agencies licensed under Article 5 or 6 of Chapter 131E of the General Statutes shall not be required to be separately licensed under this Article. However, any facility or agency exempted from licensure under this subsection which operates a hospice, a hospice inpatient facility, or a hospice residential care facility, or offers hospice services shall be subject to rules adopted pursuant to this Article.

(c)   Hospice care shall be available 24 hours a day, seven days a week. (1983 (Reg. Sess., 1984), c. 1022, s. 1; 1993, c. 376, s. 7.)

§ 131E-204. Inspections.

The Department shall inspect all hospices that are subject to rules adopted pursuant to this Article in order to determine compliance with the provisions of this Article and with rules adopted thereunder. Inspections shall be conducted in accordance with rules adopted by the Commission. (1983 (Reg. Sess., 1984), c. 1022, s. 1.)

§ 131E-205. Adverse action on a license; appeal procedures.

(a)   The Department may suspend, revoke, cancel, or amend a license when there has been a substantial failure to comply with this Article or with rules and regulations adopted thereunder.

(b)   Chapter 150A of the General Statutes, the Administrative Procedure Act, shall govern all administrative action pursuant to subsection (a) and all judicial review arising therefrom. (1983 (Reg. Sess., 1984), c. 1022, s. 1.)

§ 131E-206. Injunction.

(a)   Notwithstanding the existence or pursuit of any other remedy, the Department may maintain an action in the name of the State for injunctive relief or other process against any person to restrain or prevent the establishment, conduct, management, or operation of a hospice without a license.

(b)   Notwithstanding the provisions of G.S. 131E-203(b) or the existence of any other remedy, the Department may maintain an action in the name of the State for injunctive relief or other process against any person to restrain or prevent substantial noncompliance with this Article or the rules adopted thereunder.

(c)   If any person shall hinder the proper performance of duty of the Department in carrying out the provisions of this Article, the Department may institute an action in the superior court of the county in which the hindrance occurred for injunctive relief against the continued hindrance. (1983 (Reg. Sess., 1984), c. 1022, s. 1.)

§ 131E-207. Confidentiality.

(a)   Notwithstanding G.S. 8-53 or any other law relating to confidentiality of communications between physician and patient, in the course of an inspection conducted under G.S. 131E-204:

(1)   Department representatives may review any writing or other record concerning the admission, discharge, medication, treatment, medical condition, or history of any person who is or has been a hospice patient; and

(2)   Any person involved in treating a patient at or through a hospice may disclose information to a Department representative unless the patient objects in writing to review of his records or disclosure of the information. A hospice shall not release any information or allow any inspections under this section without first informing each affected patient in writing of his right to object to and thereby prohibit release of information or review of records pertaining to him.

A hospice, its employees and any other person interviewed in the course of an inspection shall be immune from liability for damages resulting from disclosure of any information to the Department.

(b)   The Department shall not disclose:

147

(1)   Any confidential or privileged information obtained under this section unless the patient or his legal representative authorizes disclosure in writing or unless a court of competent jurisdiction orders disclosure; or

(2)   The name of anyone who has furnished information concerning a hospice without that person's consent.

The Department shall institute appropriate policies and procedures to ensure that unauthorized disclosure does not occur. Any Department employee who willfully discloses this information without appropriate authorization or court order shall be guilty of a Class 3 misdemeanor and upon conviction only fined at the discretion of the court but not to exceed five hundred dollars ($500.00).

(c)   All confidential or privileged information obtained under this section and the names of persons providing this information shall be exempt from Chapter 132 of the General Statutes. (1983 (Reg. Sess., 1984), c. 1022, s. 1; 1993, c. 539, s. 965; 1994, Ex. Sess., c. 24, s. 14(c).)

§ 131E-208. Reserved for future codification purposes.

§ 131E-209. Reserved for future codification purposes.

Article 11.

North Carolina Medical Database Commission.

§§ 131E-210 through 131E-213: Repealed by Session Laws 1995, c. 517, s. 39.

Article 11A.

Medical Care Data.

§ 131E-214. Title and purpose.

(a)   This Article is the Medical Care Data Act.

(b)   The General Assembly finds that, as a result of rising medical care costs and the concern expressed by medical care providers, medical care consumers, third-party payors, and health care planners involved with planning for the provision of medical care, there is an urgent and continuing need to understand patterns and trends in the use and cost of medical care services in this State. The purposes of this Article are as follows:

(1)   To ensure that there is an information base containing medical care data from throughout the State that can be used to improve the appropriate and efficient use of medical care services and maintain an acceptable quality of health care services in this State.

(2)   To ensure that the necessary medical care data is available to university researchers, State public policymakers, and all other interested persons to improve the decision-making process regarding access, identified needs, patterns of medical care, charges, and use of appropriate medical care services.

(3)   To ensure that a data processor receiving data under this Article protects patient confidentiality.

These purposes are to be accomplished by requiring that all hospitals and freestanding ambulatory surgical facilities submit information necessary for a review and comparison of charges, utilization patterns, and quality of medical services to a data processor that maintains a statewide database of medical care data and that makes medical care data available to interested persons, including medical care providers, third-party payors, medical care consumers, and health care planners. (1995, c. 517, s. 39(b).)

§ 131E-214.1. Definitions.

As used in this Article:

(1)   "Division" means the Division of Health Service Regulation of the Department of Health and Human Services.

(2)   "Freestanding ambulatory surgical facility" means a facility licensed under Part D of Article 6 of this Chapter.

149

(3)   "Hospital" means a facility licensed under Article 5 of this Chapter or Article 2 of Chapter 122C of the General Statutes, but does not include the following:

a.   A facility with all of its beds designated for medical type "LTC" (long-term care).

b.   A facility with the majority of its beds designated for medical type "PSY-3" (mental retardation).

c.   A facility operated by the Division of Adult Correction of the Department of Public Safety.

(4)   "Patient data" means data that includes a patient's age, sex, race, ethnicity, zip code, third-party coverage, principal and other diagnosis, date of admission, procedure and discharge date, principal and other procedures, total charges and components of the total charges, attending physician identification number, and hospital or freestanding ambulatory surgical facility identification number.

(5)   "Patient identifying information" means the name, address, social security number, or similar information by which the identity of a patient can be determined with reasonable accuracy and speed either directly or by reference to other publicly available information. The term does not include a number assigned to a patient by a health care provider if that number does not consist of or contain numbers, including social security or drivers license numbers, that could be used to identify a patient with reasonable accuracy and speed from sources external to the health care provider.

(6)   "Statewide data processor" means a data processor certified by the Division as capable of complying with the requirements of G.S. 131E-214.4. The Division may deny, suspend, or revoke a certificate, in accordance with Chapter 150B of the General Statutes, if the statewide data processor does not comply with or is not capable of complying with the requirements of G.S. 131E-214.4. The Division is authorized to promulgate rules concerning the receipt, consideration, and limitation of a certificate applied for or issued under this Article. (1995, c. 517, s. 39(b); 1997-443, s. 11A.118(a); 2007-182, s. 1; 2008-119, s. 2; 2011-145, s. 19.1(h); 2012-83, s. 44.)

§ 131E-214.2. Data submission required.

Except as prohibited by federal law or regulation, each hospital and freestanding ambulatory surgical facility shall submit patient data to a statewide data processor within 60 calendar days after the close of each calendar quarter for patients that were discharged or died during that quarter. (1995, c. 517, s. 39(b).)

§ 131E-214.3. Patient data not public records.

(a)   The following are not public records under Chapter 132 of the General Statutes:

(1)   Patient data furnished to and maintained by a statewide data processor pursuant to this Article.

(2)   Compilations of patient data prepared for release or dissemination by a statewide data processor pursuant to this Article.

(3)   Patient data furnished by a statewide data processor to the State.

(b)   Compilations of data under subdivision (a)(3) of this section, prepared for release or dissemination by the State, are public records.

(c)   The State shall not allow proprietary information, including patient data, that it receives from a statewide data processor to be used by a person for commercial purposes. The State shall require the person requesting this information to certify that it will not use the information for commercial purposes.

(d)   A person is immune from liability for actions arising from the required submission of data under this Article. (1995, c. 517, s. 39(b).)

§ 131E-214.4. Statewide data processor.

(a)   A statewide data processor shall perform the following duties:

(1)   Make available annually to the Division, at no charge, a report that includes a comparison of the 35 most frequently reported charges of hospitals and freestanding ambulatory surgical facilities. The report is a public record and shall be made available to the public in accordance with Chapter 132 of the General Statutes. Publication or broadcast by the news media shall not constitute a resale or use of the data for commercial purposes.

(2)   Receive patient data from hospitals and freestanding ambulatory surgical facilities throughout this State.

(3)   Compile and maintain a uniform set of data from the patient data submitted.

(4)   Analyze the patient data.

(5)   Compile reports from the patient data and make the reports available upon request to interested persons at a reasonable charge determined by the data processor.

(6)   Ensure that adequate measures are taken to provide system security for all data and information received from hospitals and freestanding ambulatory surgical facilities pursuant to this Article.

(7)   Protect the confidentiality of patient records and comply with applicable laws and regulations concerning patient confidentiality, including the confidentiality of patient-identifying information. The data processor shall not disclose patient-identifying information unless (i) the information was originally submitted by the party requesting disclosure or (ii) the State Health Director requests specific individual records for the purpose of protecting and promoting the public health under Chapter 130A of the General Statutes, and the disclosure is not otherwise prohibited by federal law or regulation. Such records shall be made available to the State Health Director at a reasonable charge. Such records made available to the State Health Director are not public records; the State Health Director shall maintain their confidentiality and shall not make the records available notwithstanding G.S. 130A-374(a)(2).

(b)   The Department of Health and Human Services may take adverse action against a hospital under G.S. 131E-78 or G.S. 122C-24 or against a freestanding ambulatory surgical center under G.S. 131E-148 for a violation of this Article. (1995, c. 517, s. 39(b); 1997-443, s. 11A.118(a).)

§§ 131E-214.5 through 131E-214.10. Reserved for future codification purposes.

Article 11B.

Transparency in Health Care Costs.

§ 131E-214.11. Title.

This article shall be known as the Health Care Cost Reduction and Transparency Act of 2013. (2013-382, s. 10.1.)

§ 131E-214.12. Purpose; Department to publish price information.

(a)   It is the intent of this Article to improve transparency in health care costs by providing information to the public on the costs of the most frequently reported diagnostic related groups (DRGs) for hospital inpatient care and the most common surgical procedures and imaging procedures provided in hospital outpatient settings and ambulatory surgical facilities.

(b)   The Department of Health and Human Services shall make available to the public on its internet Web site the most current price information it receives from hospitals and ambulatory surgical facilities pursuant to G.S. 131E-214.13. The Department shall provide this information in a manner that is easily understood by the public and meets the following minimum requirements:

(1)   Information for each hospital shall be listed separately and hospitals shall be listed in groups by category as determined by the North Carolina Medical Care Commission in rules adopted pursuant to G.S. 131E-214.13.

(2)   Information for each hospital outpatient department and each ambulatory surgical facility shall be listed separately.

(c)   Any data disclosed to the Department by a hospital or ambulatory surgical facility pursuant to the Health Care Cost Reduction and Transparency Act of 2013 shall be and will remain the sole property of the facility that submitted the data. Any data or product derived from the data disclosed pursuant to this act, including a consolidation or analysis of the data, shall be and will remain the sole property of the State. The Department shall not allow

153

proprietary information it receives pursuant to this act to be used by any person or entity for commercial purposes. (2013-382, s. 10.1.)

§ 131E-214.13. Disclosure of prices for most frequently reported DRGs, CPTs, and HCPCSs.

(a)   The following definitions apply in this Article:

(1)   Ambulatory surgical facility. - A facility licensed under Part 4 of Article 6 of this Chapter.

(2)   Commission. - The North Carolina Medical Care Commission.

(3)   Health insurer. - As defined in G.S. 108A-55.4, provided that "health insurer" shall not include self-insured plans and group health plans as defined in section 607(1) of the Employee Retirement Income Security Act of 1974.

(4)   Hospital. - A medical care facility licensed under Article 5 of this Chapter or under Article 2 of Chapter 122C of the General Statutes.

(5)   Public or private third party. - Includes the State, the federal government, employers, health insurers, third-party administrators, and managed care organizations.

(b)   Beginning with the quarter ending June 30, 2014, and quarterly thereafter, each hospital shall provide to the Department of Health and Human Services, utilizing electronic health records software, the following information about the 100 most frequently reported admissions by DRG for inpatients as established by the Commission:

(1)   The amount that will be charged to a patient for each DRG if all charges are paid in full without a public or private third party paying for any portion of the charges.

(2)   The average negotiated settlement on the amount that will be charged to a patient required to be provided in subdivision (1) of this subsection.

(3)   The amount of Medicaid reimbursement for each DRG, including claims and pro rata supplemental payments.

(4)   The amount of Medicare reimbursement for each DRG.

(5)   For the five largest health insurers providing payment to the hospital on behalf of insureds and teachers and State employees, the range and the average of the amount of payment made for each DRG. Prior to providing this information to the Department, each hospital shall redact the names of the health insurers and any other information that would otherwise identify the health insurers.

A hospital shall not be required to report the information required by this subsection for any of the 100 most frequently reported admissions where the reporting of that information reasonably could lead to the identification of the person or persons admitted to the hospital in violation of the federal Health Insurance Portability and Accountability Act of 1996 (HIPAA) or other federal law.

(c)   The Commission shall adopt rules on or before March 1, 2014, to ensure that subsection (b) of this section is properly implemented and that hospitals report this information to the Department in a uniform manner. The rules shall include all of the following:

(1)   The 100 most frequently reported DRGs for inpatients for which hospitals must provide the data set out in subsection (b) of this section.

(2)   Specific categories by which hospitals shall be grouped for the purpose of disclosing this information to the public on the Department's Internet Web site.

(d)   Beginning with the quarter ending September 30, 2014, and quarterly thereafter, each hospital and ambulatory surgical facility shall provide to the Department, utilizing electronic health records software, information on the total costs for the 20 most common surgical procedures and the 20 most common imaging procedures, by volume, performed in hospital outpatient settings or in ambulatory surgical facilities, along with the related CPT and HCPCS codes. Hospitals and ambulatory surgical facilities shall report this information in the same manner as required by subdivisions (b)(1) through (5) of this section, provided that hospitals and ambulatory surgical facilities shall not be required to report the information required by this subsection where the reporting of that information reasonably could lead to the identification of the person or persons admitted to the hospital in violation of the federal Health Insurance Portability and Accountability Act of 1996 (HIPAA) or other federal law.

(e)   The Commission shall adopt rules on or before June 1, 2014, to ensure that subsection (d) of this section is properly implemented and that hospitals and ambulatory surgical facilities report this information to the Department in a uniform manner. The rules shall include the list of the 20 most common surgical procedures and the 20 most common imaging procedures, by volume, performed in a hospital outpatient setting and those performed in an ambulatory surgical facility, along with the related CPT and HCPCS codes.

(f)   Upon request of a patient for a particular DRG, imaging procedure, or surgery procedure reported in this section, a hospital or ambulatory surgical facility shall provide the information required by subsection (b) or subsection (d) of this section to the patient in writing, either electronically or by mail, within three business days after receiving the request. (2013-382, s. 10.1.)

§ 131E-214.14. Disclosure of charity care policy and costs.

(a)   Requirements. - A hospital or ambulatory surgical facility required to file Schedule H, federal form 990, under the Code must provide the public access to its financial assistance policy and its annual financial assistance costs reported on its Schedule H, federal form 990. The information must be submitted annually to the Department in the time, manner, and format required by the Department. The Department must post the information on its internet Web site. The information must also be displayed in a conspicuous place in the organization's place of business.

(b)   Definitions. - The following definitions apply in this section:

(1)   Code. - Defined in G.S. 105-228.90.

(2)   Financial assistance costs. - The information reported on Schedule H, federal form 990, related to the organization's financial assistance at cost and the amounts reported on that schedule related to the organization's bad debt expense and the estimated amount of the organization's bad debt expense attributable to patients eligible under the organization's financial assistance policy.

(3)   Financial assistance policy. - A policy that meets the requirements of section 501(r) of the Code. (2013-382, s. 10.1.)

Article 12.

Disclosure and Contract Requirements for Continuing Care Facilities.

§§ 131E-215 through 131E-224: Repealed by Session Laws 1989, c. 758, s. 2.

§§ 131E-225 through 131E-229. Reserved for future codification purposes.

Article 13.

Temporary Management of Long-Term Care Facilities.

§ 131E-230. Legislative findings.

The General Assembly finds that:

(1)   A substantial number of citizens of this State now reside, or in the future may reside, in long-term care facilities within this State;

(2)   Improper operation of long-term care facilities may tend to create a substantial risk of serious physical injury to residents;

(3)   The closure of a long-term care facility can have adverse effects on the residents thereof, especially if the closure and transfer of residents is done hastily;

(4)   The general health and welfare of the people of this State, particularly those persons residing in long-term care facilities within this State, would be enhanced by development of a procedure for the court appointment of a temporary manager to assure the proper operation of a long-term care facility in certain instances until a manager chosen by the facility is prepared to properly operate the facility, or until the residents can be safely transferred to a proper alternative setting; and

(5)   The use of a temporary manager is intended as a temporary measure and the ongoing or long-term operation of a nursing facility by a temporary manager is neither beneficial nor appropriate. (1993, c. 390, s. 1.)

157

§ 131E-231. Definitions.

As used in this Article, unless otherwise specified:

(1)   "Long-term care facility" means a nursing home as defined in G.S. 131E-101(6) and an adult care home as defined in G.S. 131D-2.1(3) or G.S. 131E-101(4).

(2)   "Resident" means a person who has been admitted to a long-term care facility.

(3)   "Respondent" means the person or entity holding a license pursuant to G.S. 131E-102 or G.S. 131D-2.4 or a person or entity operating a long-term care facility subject to licensure without a license. (1993, c. 390, s. 1; 1995, c. 535, s. 26; 2008-187, s. 38(b); 2009-462, s. 4(l).)

§ 131E-232. Who may petition; contents of petition.

The Department may petition a court of competent jurisdiction to appoint a temporary manager to operate a long-term care facility. The petition shall set forth material facts showing that one or more of the grounds for appointment of a temporary manager set forth in G.S. 131E-234 exist, that the facts set forth in the petition have been brought to the attention of the respondent, and that the conditions described in the petition have not been remedied within a reasonable period of time. The petition shall also set forth a brief description of the action or actions necessary to remedy the alleged conditions. (1993, c. 390, s. 1.)

§ 131E-233. Procedures for appointment; evidence in defense.

(a)   The procedure for petitioning the superior court for the appointment of a temporary manager, including service of process shall be in accordance with the North Carolina Rules of Civil Procedure. If personal service of a copy of the petition cannot be made with due diligence upon the respondent, service may be made upon the respondent by sending a copy of the summons and petition to the respondent by registered mail at the respondent's last known address and by hand-delivering or mailing a copy to the administrative or staff person in charge of the facility.

(b)   A hearing shall be held on the petition within 20 days of service of the petition upon the respondent. Both the Department and the respondent may present evidence and written and oral argument at the hearing regarding the allegations of the petition. It shall be relevant evidence in defense to a petition that the conditions alleged in the petition do not in fact exist, that such conditions do not exist to the extent alleged, or that such conditions have been remedied or removed.

(c)   (1)   Upon petition by the Department for emergency intervention, a court may order the appointment of an emergency temporary manager after finding that there is reasonable cause to believe that:

a.   Conditions or a pattern of conditions exist in the long-term care facility that create an immediate substantial risk of death or serious physical harm to residents; or

b.   The long-term care facility is closing or intends to close before the time in which a hearing would ordinarily be scheduled, and:

1.   Adequate arrangements for relocating residents have not been made, or

2.   Quick relocation would not be in the best interest of residents.

(2)   The court shall appoint an emergency temporary manager to serve until a hearing is conducted in accordance with ordinary procedures and shall direct the temporary manager to make only such changes in administration as necessary to protect the health or safety of residents until the emergency condition is resolved.

(3)   The court shall schedule a hearing on the appointment of an emergency temporary manager within three days after service of notice of the filing of the petition. Notice of the filing of the petition and other relevant information, including the factual basis of the belief that an emergency temporary manager is needed shall be served upon the facility as provided in this Article. The notice shall be given at least 24 hours prior to the hearing of the petition for emergency intervention, except that the court may issue an immediate emergency order ex parte upon a finding as fact that:

a.   The conditions specified above exist, and

159

b.	There is likelihood that a resident may suffer irreparable injury or death if the order is delayed.

The order shall contain a show-cause notice to each person upon whom the notice is served directing the person to appear immediately or at any time up to and including the time for the hearing of the petition for emergency services and show cause, if any exists, for the dissolution or modification of the order. Unless dissolved by the court for good cause shown, the emergency order ex parte shall be in effect until the hearing is held on the petition for emergency services. At the hearing, if the court determines that the emergency continues to exist, the court may order the provision of emergency services in accordance with subsections (a) and (b) of this section. (1993, c. 390, s. 1; 1999-334, s. 1.11.)

§ 131E-234. Grounds for appointment of temporary manager.

Upon a showing by the Department that one or more of the following grounds exist, the court may appoint a temporary manager for an initial period of 30 days or the first review by a superior court judge pursuant to G.S. 131E-243, whichever is longer:

(1)	Conditions or a pattern of conditions exist in the long-term care facility that create a substantial risk of death or serious physical harm to residents or that death or serious physical harm has occurred, and it is probable that the facility will not or cannot immediately remedy those conditions or pattern of conditions, or the facility has shown a pattern of failure to comply with applicable laws and rules and continues to fail to comply;

(2)	The long-term care facility is operating without a license;

(3)	The license of the long-term care facility has been revoked or the long-term care facility is closing or intends to close and: (i) adequate arrangements for relocating residents have not been made, or (ii) quick relocation would not be in the best interest of the residents; or

(4)	A previous court order has been issued requiring the respondent to act or refrain from acting in a manner directly affecting the care of the residents and the respondent has failed to comply with the court order. (1993, c. 390, s. 1; 1999-334, s. 1.12.)

§ 131E-235. Alternative to appointment of temporary manager.

(a)   After the hearing described in G.S. 131E-233(b), if the court finds that the evidence warrants the granting of the relief sought and the respondent applies to the court for permission to promptly remove or remedy the conditions or pattern specified in the petition and demonstrates the ability to promptly undertake and complete the removal or remedying of such conditions or pattern, the court, in lieu of appointing a temporary manager, may issue an order permitting the respondent to remove or remedy the conditions in accordance with a time schedule and subject to conditions determined by the court, including the posting of security for the performance of the work as may be fixed by the court.

(b)   If, after entry of an order pursuant to subsection (a) of this section, it appears that the respondent is not proceeding in accordance with the court's order in removing or remedying the conditions found by the court to exist, the Department, upon notice to the respondent, may move the court for an order appointing a temporary manager pursuant to the court's findings at the original hearing. If upon hearing the matter, the court finds that the respondent is not proceeding in accordance with the court's order, the court may appoint a temporary manager as authorized by G.S. 131E-234. If the respondent has posted security to ensure removal or remedying of the conditions found by the court, the security or any part of the security as is necessary may be used by the temporary manager to remedy the conditions. (1993, c. 390, s. 1.)

§ 131E-236. Compensation of temporary manager.

The court shall set the compensation of the temporary manager. (1993, c. 390, s. 1.)

§ 131E-237. Candidates for temporary managers.

In the petition the Department shall nominate at least one candidate for temporary manager and shall include the name, address, and qualifications of each nominee. The Department shall maintain a list of persons qualified to act as temporary managers. The person or persons nominated by the Department to serve as temporary manager shall either be employed by the Department or

161

be one of the persons on the list of qualified persons maintained by the Department. This nominee shall be approved by the court reviewing the Department's petition for appointment of a temporary manager. (1993, c. 390, s. 1.)

§ 131E-238. Temporary manager; powers and duties.

A temporary manager appointed under this section:

(1)   May exercise those powers and shall perform those duties ordered by the court;

(2)   Shall operate the long-term care facility in compliance with State and federal laws and assure the safety of the residents and the delivery of services to them;

(3)   May operate the facility under a temporary license issued by the Department in the event that the license of the original operator has been revoked or suspended or was never issued;

(4)   Shall have the same rights as the respondent to possession of the building in which the long-term care facility is located and of all goods and fixtures located in the building at the time the temporary manager is appointed. If the court finds that between the time the petition is filed and the temporary manager is appointed, the respondent has transferred assets for the purpose of frustrating the intent of this section, the court may require the respondent to repay to the temporary manager the value of such transferred assets. The temporary manager shall take all actions necessary to protect and conserve the assets and property of which the temporary manager takes possession, and the proceeds of any transfer, and may use them only in the performance of the powers and duties set forth in this section and as may be ordered by the court;

(5)   May use the building, fixtures, furnishings, and any accompanying consumable goods in providing care and services to residents and to any other persons receiving services from the long-term care facility at the time the petition for temporary management was filed. The temporary manager shall collect payment for all goods and services provided to residents or others at the same rate and method of payment as was charged by the respondent at the time the petition for temporary management was filed, unless a different rate is

set by the State or other third-party payors. The temporary manager shall owe a duty to the owner of the long-term care facility to protect and preserve, and to avoid the waste or diminution of, the building, fixtures, furnishings, consumable goods, receipts, and other assets of the facility and to prevent the use of those assets for any purpose other than the reasonable operation of the facility;

(6)   May correct or eliminate any deficiency in the structure or furnishings of the long-term care facility that endangers the safety or health of residents, provided the total cost of correction of all such deficiencies does not exceed one thousand dollars ($1,000);

(7)   Shall submit to the court a plan in accordance with G.S. 131E-239 for correction or elimination of any deficiency or deficiencies in the structure or furnishings of the long-term care facility that endanger the safety or health of residents and that are estimated to exceed one thousand dollars ($1,000), and shall carry out the plan with any modification approved by the court;

(8)   May enter into contracts and hire agents and employees to carry out the powers and duties created under this section, provided that the temporary manager must notify the court and the respondent prior to entering into any substantially new contract obligating the respondent to pay more than one thousand dollars ($1,000);

(9)   Except as specified in G.S. 131E-241, shall honor all leases, mortgages, and secured transactions governing the building in which the long-term care facility is located and all goods and fixtures in the building of which the temporary manager has taken possession, but, in the case of a rental agreement, only to the extent of payments that are for the use of the property during the period of the temporary management, or, in the case of a purchase agreement, come due during the period of the temporary management;

(10)   Shall have full power to direct, manage, and discharge employees of the long-term care facility, consistent with applicable State and federal laws governing the employment of these employees;

(11)   If transfer of the residents is necessary, shall cooperate with the Department or local departments of social services or both in carrying out the transfer of residents to an alternative placement;

(12)   Shall be entitled to and shall take possession of all property or assets of residents in the possession of the respondents. The temporary manager shall

preserve all property, assets, and records of residents of which the temporary manager takes possession and shall provide for the prompt transfer of the property, assets, and records to the alternative placement of any transferred resident. No owner, licensee, or administrator of a facility under temporary management shall be liable for the waste, mismanagement, or other negligent or intentional wrongful act of a temporary manager with respect to the property or assets of residents; and

(13)   May be held liable in his personal capacity only for his own gross negligence or intentional acts. (1993, c. 390, s. 1.)

§ 131E-239. Plan for correction of deficiencies in excess of one thousand dollars ($1,000).

(a)   If the temporary manager determines that it is necessary to correct a deficiency or deficiencies in the structure or furnishings reasonably estimated by the temporary manager to cost in excess of one thousand dollars ($1,000), the temporary manager shall submit to the court a written plan that contains the following:

(1)   A description of the deficiency or deficiencies that require correction;

(2)   A description of the method proposed by the temporary manager for correction of the deficiency or deficiencies; and

(3)   An estimate of the cost of the correction or corrections.

(b)   A copy of the plan shall be served upon the Department and the respondent on the same day that it is submitted to the court.

(c)   If the Department or respondent makes a written request for a hearing within seven days after the submission of the plan to the court, a hearing on the proposed plan of correction shall be held. If a hearing is requested by a party, the hearing shall be held within 14 days of the written request. The Department, respondent, and temporary manager shall have the opportunity to present evidence at the hearing regarding the proposed plan. Upon hearing the evidence, the court may approve the plan, modify the plan, or, if the court determines as a result of the evidence that the alleged deficiency does not require correction, it may reject the plan. If no party requests a hearing on the plan in accordance with this subsection, the court may order the temporary manager to proceed to implement the plan.

(d)   In the event of an emergency situation involving the structure or furnishings of the facility the correction of which will cost in excess of one thousand dollars ($1,000) and where failure to correct the situation immediately will likely result in serious physical harm or death to residents, the temporary manager may proceed to correct the situation in the most economical and efficient manner under the circumstances without prior court approval of a plan. If the court later determines pursuant to G.S. 131E-244(b) that the expenditure was not necessary or reasonable under the circumstances, payment for the expenditure or any part determined to be unreasonable or unnecessary by the court, must be paid from the contingency fund described in G.S. 131E-242. If the payment was initially made by the temporary manager from the contingency fund, the respondent shall have no obligation to repay those funds to the contingency fund upon a finding that the expenditure was unreasonable or unnecessary. If the payment was initially made by the temporary manager from operating revenues of the facility, the respondent shall be entitled to repayment of those amounts from the contingency fund. (1993, c. 390, s. 1.)

§ 131E-240. Payment to temporary manager.

(a)   A person served with notice of an order of the court appointing a temporary manager and of the temporary manager's name and address shall be liable to pay the temporary manager for any goods or services provided by the temporary manager after the date of the order if the person would have been liable for the goods or services supplied by the respondent or an agent of the respondent. The temporary manager shall give a receipt for each payment and shall keep a copy of each receipt on file. The temporary manager shall deposit amounts received in a special account and shall use this account for all disbursements.

(b)   The temporary manager may bring an action to enforce the liability created by subsection (a) of this section. Proof of payment to the temporary manager is as effective in favor of the person making the payment as payment of the amount to the person who, but for this subsection, would have been entitled to receive the sum paid.

165

(c)   A resident may not be discharged, nor may any contract or rights be forfeited or impaired, nor may forfeiture or liability be increased, by reason of an omission to pay a respondent, licensee, or other person a sum paid to the temporary manager. (1993, c. 390, s. 1.)

§ 131E-241. Avoidance of preexisting leases, mortgages, and contracts.

(a)   A temporary manager shall not be required to honor any lease, mortgage, secured transaction, or other wholly or partially executory contract entered into by the respondent, licensee, or administrator of the long-term care facility if the temporary manager demonstrates to the court that the rental price, rate of interest, or other compensation to be paid under the contract or agreement is unreasonable in light of conditions existing at the time the agreement was entered into by the parties or in light of the relationship of the parties.

(b)   If the temporary manager is in possession of real estate or goods subject to a lease, mortgage, security interest, or other contract that the temporary manager is permitted to avoid under subsection (a) of this section, and if the real estate or goods are necessary for the continued operation of the long-term care facility, the temporary manager may apply to the court to set a reasonable rental price, rate of interest, or other compensation to be paid by the temporary manager during the duration of the temporary management. The court shall hold a hearing on the application within 15 days after receipt of the application. At least 10 days prior to the hearing, the temporary manager shall send notice of the application to any known person with any beneficial interest in the property involved.

(c)   Payment by the temporary manager of the amount determined by the court to be reasonable is a defense to any action against the temporary manager for payment or for possession of the goods or real estate subject to the lease, mortgage, security interest, or other contract involved by any person who received such notice, but the payment does not relieve the obligee of liability for the difference between the amount paid by the temporary manager and the amount due under the original lease, mortgage, or security interest involved. (1993, c. 390, s. 1.)

§ 131E-242. Contingency fund.

(a)   The Department may maintain a temporary management contingency fund.

(b)   Upon a showing that proper expenses of the temporary management under this Article exceed the operating funds of the long-term care facility, the court, in its discretion, may order that the Department provide funds from the contingency fund to the temporary manager to operate the facility and compensate the temporary manager.

(c)   When the total funds available in the contingency fund exceed five hundred thousand dollars ($500,000), the Department may reallocate any or all of the amount in excess of five hundred thousand dollars ($500,000) for other activities intended to protect the health and property of residents. (1993, c. 390, s. 1; 1995, c. 535, s. 27; 1998-215, s. 78(d); 1999-334, s. 1.13.)

§ 131E-243. Review and termination of temporary management.

(a)   The operations and continuing need for a temporary manager shall be reviewed by the court every 30 days following the appointment of the temporary manager.

(b)   The court may order the replacement of a temporary manager upon a showing that the temporary manager has mismanaged the long-term care facility.

(c)   The court shall order the termination of the temporary management upon the recommendation of the Department or upon a showing that the conditions leading to imposition of the temporary management have been resolved.

(d)   When a long-term care facility is returned to its owner, the court may impose conditions to assure compliance with applicable laws and regulations. (1993, c. 390, s. 1.)

§ 131E-244. Accounting lien for expenses.

(a)   Within 30 days after termination of the temporary management, the temporary manager shall give the court a complete accounting of:

(1)   All property of which the temporary manager took possession;

(2)   All funds collected under this Article;

(3)   Expenses of the temporary management; and

(4)   All disbursements or transfers of facility funds or other assets made during the period of temporary management. On the same day the accounting is filed with the court, the temporary manager shall serve on the respondent by registered mail a copy of this accounting.

(b)   If the operating funds collected during the temporary management exceed the reasonable expenses of the temporary management, the court shall order payment of the excess to the respondent, after reimbursement to the contingency fund. If the operating funds are insufficient to cover the reasonable expenses of the temporary management, the respondent shall be liable for the deficiency, except as described in this section. If the respondent demonstrates to the court that repayment of amounts spent from the contingency fund would significantly impair the provision of appropriate care or services to residents, the court may order repayment over a period of time with or without interest or may order that the respondent be required to repay only part or none of the amount spent from the contingency fund. In reaching this decision, the court may consider all assets, revenues, debts and other obligations of the long-term care facility, the likelihood of the sale of the long-term care facility where repayment forgiveness would result in unjust enrichment of the respondent, and shall consider the impact of its determination on the provision of care to residents. The respondent may petition the court to determine the reasonableness of any expenses of the temporary management. The respondent shall not be responsible for expenses in excess of amounts the court finds to be reasonable. Payment recovered from the respondent shall be used to reimburse the contingency fund for amounts used by the temporary manager.

(c)   The court may order that the Department have a lien for any reasonable costs of the temporary management that are not covered by the operating funds collected by the temporary manager and for any funds paid out of the contingency fund during the temporary management upon any beneficial interest, direct or indirect, of any respondent in the following property:

168

(1)   The building in which the long-term care facility is located;

(2)   The land on which the long-term care facility is located;

(3)   Any fixtures, equipment, or goods used in the operation of the long-term care facility; or

(4)   The proceeds from any conveyance of property described in subdivisions (1), (2), and (3) of this subsection made by the respondent within one year prior to the filing of the petition for temporary management unless such transfers were made in good faith, in the ordinary course of business, and without intent to frustrate the intent of subsection (b) of this section. Transfers made coincidental with serious deficiencies in resident care may be considered evidence of intent to frustrate the intent of subsection (b) of this section.

(d)   To the extent permitted by other provisions of applicable State or federal law, the lien provided for in this section is superior to any lien or other interest that arises subsequent to the filing of the petition for temporary management under this section, except for a construction or mechanic's lien arising out of work performed with the express consent of the temporary manager.

(e)   The clerk of court in the county in which the long-term care facility is located shall record the filing of the petition for temporary management in the lien docket opposite the names of the respondents and licensees named in the petition.

(f)   Within 60 days after termination of the temporary management, the temporary manager shall file a notice of any lien created under this section. If the lien is on real property, the notice shall be filed with the clerk of court in the county where the long-term care facility is located and entered on the lien docket. If the lien is on personal property, the lien shall be filed with the person against whom the lien is claimed, and shall state the name of the temporary manager, the date of the petition for temporary management, the date of the termination of temporary management, a description of the property involved, and the amount claimed. No lien shall exist under this section against any person, on any property, or for any amount not specified in the notice filed under this section. (1993, c. 390, s. 1.)

§ 131E-245. Obligations of licensee.

169

Nothing in this Article shall relieve any respondent, licensee, or administrator of a long-term care facility placed in temporary management of any civil or criminal liability, or any duty imposed by law, by reason of acts or omissions of the respondent, licensee, or administrator prior to the appointment of the temporary manager. Nothing in this Article shall suspend during the temporary management any obligation of the respondent, licensee, or administrator for payment of taxes, other operating and maintenance expenses of the long-term care facility, nor the respondent, licensee, or administrator or any other person for the payment of mortgages or liens. No owner, licensee, or administrator shall be held personally liable for acts or omissions of the temporary manager or the temporary manager's employees during the term of the temporary management. No licensee or administrator may be held responsible or liable for licensure fines, sanctions or penalties, or other administrative sanctions, arising or imposed as a result of acts or omissions occurring during the period of temporary management unless those sanctions result from acts or omissions by the licensee or administrator. (1993, c. 390, s. 1.)

§ 131E-246. Conflict of laws.

In the event of a conflict between federal laws or regulations and State law or rules, the federal laws or regulations shall control. (1993, c. 390, s. 1.)

§ 131E-247. Reserved for future codification purposes.

§ 131E-248. Reserved for future codification purposes.

§ 131E-249. Reserved for future codification purposes.

Article 14.

Disposal of Surplus Property to Aid Other Countries.

§ 131E-250. Disposition of surplus property by public and State hospitals.

(a)   As used in this section, "public hospital" has the same meaning as in G.S. 159-39. A State hospital is any hospital operated by the State.

(b)   A public hospital or a State hospital may donate medical equipment it determines is no longer needed by the hospital to any of the following if the property so donated is to be used by a hospital or medical facility in another country:

(1)   A corporation that is exempt from taxation under section 501(c) of the Internal Revenue Code of 1986.

(2)   The United States or any agency of it.

(3)   The government of a foreign country or any political subdivision of that country.

(4)   The United Nations or an agency of it.

(5)   Other eleemosynary institutions and groups. (1993, c. 529, s. 7.6; 1995, c. 509, s. 73.)

§§ 131E-251 through 131E-254. Reserved for future codification purposes.

Article 15.

Health Care Personnel Registry.

§ 131E-255. Nurse Aide Registry.

(a)   Pursuant to 42 U.S.C. § 1395i-3(e) and 42 U.S.C. § 1396r(e), the Department shall establish and maintain a registry containing the names of all nurse aides working in nursing facilities in North Carolina. The Department shall include in the nurse aide registry any findings by the Department of neglect of a resident in a nursing facility or abuse of a resident in a nursing facility or misappropriation of the property of a resident in a nursing facility by a nurse aide.

(b)   A nurse aide who wishes to contest a finding of resident neglect, resident abuse, or misappropriation of resident property made against the aide, is entitled to an administrative hearing as provided by the Administrative

171

Procedure Act, Chapter 150B of the General Statutes. A petition for a contested case shall be filed within 30 days of the mailing of the written notice by certified mail of the Department's intent to place findings against the aide in the nurse aide registry.

(c)   "Nursing facility", as used in this section, means a "combination home" as defined in G.S. 131E-101(1) and a "nursing home" as defined in G.S. 131E-101(6) and also means "facility" as that term is defined in G.S. 131E-116(2).

(d)   The Commission shall adopt, amend, and repeal all rules necessary for the implementation of this section.

(e)   No person shall be liable for providing any information for the nurse aide registry if the information is provided in good faith. Neither an employer, potential employer, nor the Department shall be liable for using any information from the nurse aide registry if the information is used in good faith for the purpose of screening prospective applicants for employment or reviewing the employment status of an employee. (1991, c. 185, s. 1; c. 761, s. 26; 1995 (Reg. Sess., 1996), c. 713, ss. 3(a), (b).)

§ 131E-256. Health Care Personnel Registry.

(a)   The Department shall establish and maintain a health care personnel registry containing the names of all health care personnel working in health care facilities in North Carolina who have:

(1)   Been subject to findings by the Department of:

a.   Neglect or abuse of a resident in a health care facility or a person to whom home care services as defined by G.S. 131E-136 or hospice services as defined by G.S. 131E-201 are being provided.

b.   Misappropriation of the property of a resident in a health care facility, as defined in subsection (b) of this section including places where home care services as defined by G.S. 131E-136 or hospice services as defined by G.S. 131E-201 are being provided.

c.   Misappropriation of the property of a health care facility.

d.   Diversion of drugs belonging to a health care facility.

d1.   Diversion of drugs belonging to a patient or client of the health care facility.

e.   Fraud against a health care facility.

e1.   Fraud against a patient or client for whom the employee is providing services.

(2)   Been accused of any of the acts listed in subdivision (1) of this subsection, but only after the Department has screened the allegation and determined that an investigation is required.

The Health Care Personnel Registry shall also contain all findings by the Department of neglect of a resident in a nursing facility or abuse of a resident in a nursing facility or misappropriation of the property of a resident in a nursing facility by a nurse aide that are contained in the nurse aide registry under G.S. 131E-255.

(a1)   The Department shall include in the registry a brief statement of any individual disputing the finding entered against the individual in the health care personnel registry pursuant to subdivision (1) of subsection (a) of this section.

(b)   For the purpose of this section, the following are considered to be "health care facilities":

(1)   Adult Care Homes as defined in G.S. 131D-2.1.

(2)   Hospitals as defined in G.S. 131E-76.

(3)   Home Care Agencies as defined in G.S. 131E-136.

(4)   Nursing Pools as defined by G.S. 131E-154.2.

(5)   Hospices as defined by G.S. 131E-201.

(6)   Nursing Facilities as defined by G.S. 131E-255.

(7)   State-Operated Facilities as defined in G.S. 122C-3(14)f.

(8)   Residential Facilities as defined in G.S. 122C-3(14)e.

(9)   24-Hour Facilities as defined in G.S. 122C-3(14)g.

(10)   Licensable Facilities as defined in G.S. 122C-3(14)b.

(11)   Multiunit Assisted Housing with Services as defined in G.S. 131D-2.1.

(12)   Community-Based Providers of Services for the Mentally Ill, the Developmentally Disabled, and Substance Abusers that are not required to be licensed under Article 2 of Chapter 122C of the General Statutes.

(13)   Agencies providing in-home aide services funded through the Home and Community Care Block Grant Program in accordance with G.S. 143B-181.1(a)11.

(c)   For the purpose of this section, the term "health care personnel" means any unlicensed staff of a health care facility that has direct access to residents, clients, or their property. Direct access includes any health care facility unlicensed staff that during the course of employment has the opportunity for direct contact with an individual or an individual's property, when that individual is a resident or person to whom services are provided.

(d)   Health care personnel who wish to contest findings under subdivision (a)(1) of this section are entitled to an administrative hearing as provided by the Administrative Procedure Act, Chapter 150B of the General Statutes. A petition for a contested case shall be filed within 30 days of the mailing of the written notice of the Department's intent to place its findings about the person in the Health Care Personnel Registry.

(d1)   Health care personnel who wish to contest the placement of information under subdivision (a)(2) of this section are entitled to an administrative hearing as provided by the Administrative Procedure Act, Chapter 150B of the General Statutes. A petition for a contested case hearing shall be filed within 30 days of the mailing of the written notice of the Department's intent to place information about the person in the Health Care Personnel Registry under subdivision (a)(2) of this section. Health care personnel who have filed a petition contesting the placement of information in the health care personnel registry under subdivision (a)(2) of this section are deemed to have challenged any findings made by the Department at the conclusion of its investigation.

174

(d2)   Before hiring health care personnel into a health care facility or service, every employer at a health care facility shall access the Health Care Personnel Registry and shall note each incident of access in the appropriate business files.

(e)   The Department shall provide an employer at a health care facility or potential employer at a health care facility of any person listed on the Health Care Personnel Registry information concerning the nature of the finding or allegation and the status of the investigation.

(f)   No person shall be liable for providing any information for the health care personnel registry if the information is provided in good faith. Neither an employer, potential employer, nor the Department shall be liable for using any information from the health care personnel registry if the information is used in good faith for the purpose of screening prospective applicants for employment or reviewing the employment status of an employee.

(g)   Health care facilities shall ensure that the Department is notified of all allegations against health care personnel, including injuries of unknown source, which appear to be related to any act listed in subdivision (a)(1) of this section. Facilities must have evidence that all alleged acts are investigated and must make every effort to protect residents from harm while the investigation is in progress. The results of all investigations must be reported to the Department within five working days of the initial notification to the Department.

(g1)   Health care facilities defined in subsection (b) of this section are permitted to provide confidential or other identifying information to the Health Care Personnel Registry, including social security numbers, taxpayer identification numbers, parent's legal surname prior to marriage, and dates of birth, for verifying the identity of accused health care personnel. Confidential or other identifying information received by the Health Care Personnel Registry is not a public record under Chapter 132 of the General Statutes.

(h)   The North Carolina Medical Care Commission shall adopt, amend, and repeal all rules necessary for the implementation of this section.

(i)   In the case of a finding of neglect under subdivision (1) of subsection (a) of this section, the Department shall establish a procedure to permit health care personnel to petition the Department to have his or her name removed from the registry upon a determination that:

175

(1)	The employment and personal history of the health care personnel does not reflect a pattern of abusive behavior or neglect;

(1a)	The health care personnel's name was added to the registry for a single finding of neglect;

(2)	The neglect involved in the original finding was a singular occurrence; and

(3)	The petition for removal is submitted after the expiration of the one-year period which began on the date the petitioner's name was added to the registry under subdivision (1) of subsection (a) of this section.

(i1)	Health care personnel who wish to contest a decision by the Department to deny a removal of a single finding of neglect from the Health Care Personnel Registry under subdivision (1a) of subsection (i) of this section are entitled to an administrative hearing under Chapter 150B of the General Statutes. A petition for a contested case hearing shall be filed within 30 days of the mailing of the written notice of the Department's denial of a removal of a finding of neglect.

(j)	Removal of a finding of neglect from the registry under this section may occur only once with respect to any person. (1995 (Reg. Sess., 1996), c. 713, s. 3(b); 1998-212, s. 12.16E; 1999-159, s. 1; 2000-55, s. 1; 2004-203, ss. 52(a), (b), (c); 2007-544, s. 2; 2009-316, ss. 1(a), (b), 2; 2009-462, s. 4(m).)

§ 131E-256.1. Adverse action on a license; appeal procedures.

(a)	The Department may suspend, cancel, or amend a license when a facility subject to this Article has substantially failed to comply with this Article or rules adopted under this Article.

(b)	Administrative action taken by the Department under this section shall be in accordance with Chapter 150B of the General Statutes. (2000-55, s. 2.)

Article 15A.

Public Hospital Personnel Act.

§ 131E-257. Title; purpose; applicability of other laws; "public hospital" defined.

(a)   This Article shall be known and may be cited as the "Public Hospital Personnel Act".

(b)   The purpose of this Article is to protect the privacy of the personnel records of public hospital employees and to authorize public hospitals to determine employee compensation and personnel policies and to establish employee benefit plans.

(c)   Unless otherwise provided, none of the provisions of Part 4, Article 5, Chapter 153A and Part 4, Article 7, Chapter 160A shall apply to public hospitals.

(d)   If any provision of this Article is inconsistent with any provision of any other law, the provision of this Article shall be controlling.

(e)   As used in this Article, unless the context clearly indicates otherwise, the term "public hospital" has the same meaning as in G.S. 159-39. (1997-517, s. 2.)

§ 131E-257.1. Compensation; personnel policies; employee benefits plans.

(a)   A public hospital shall determine the pay, expense allowances, and other compensation of its officers and employees, and may establish position classification and pay plans and incentive compensation plans.

(b)   A public hospital may:

(1)   Adopt personnel policies and procedures regarding, without limitation, vacations, personal leave, service award programs, other personnel policies and procedures, and any other measures that enhance the ability of a public hospital to hire and retain employees.

(2)   Determine the work hours, workdays, and holidays applicable to its employees.

(3)   Establish and pay all or part of the cost of benefit plans for its employees and former employees, including without limitation, life, health and

177

disability plans, pension, profit sharing, deferred compensation and other retirement plans, and other fringe benefit plans.

(4)   Pay severance payments and provide other employee severance benefits to its employees and former employees pursuant to a severance plan established in connection with a reduction in the size of the workforce of a public hospital or, with respect to an individual employee, pursuant to an employment agreement entered into prior to the date the employee receives notice of termination of employment.

(c)   The provisions of G.S. 159-30 and G.S. 159-31 are not applicable to public hospitals with respect to the investment of escrowed or trusteed retirement and deferred compensation funds. Public hospitals may invest such escrowed and trusteed funds in property or securities in which trustees, guardians, personal representatives, and others acting in a fiduciary capacity may legally invest funds under their control. (1997-517, s. 2.)

§ 131E-257.2. Privacy of employee personnel records.

(a)   Notwithstanding the provisions of G.S. 132-6 or any other general law or local act concerning access to public records, personnel files of employees and applicants for employment maintained by a public hospital are subject to inspection and may be disclosed only as provided by this section. For purposes of this section, an employee's personnel file consists of any information in any form gathered by the public hospital with respect to an employee and, by way of illustration but not limitation, relating to the employee's application, selection or nonselection, performance, promotions, demotions, transfers, suspensions and other disciplinary actions, evaluation forms, employment contracts, leave, salary, and termination of employment. As used in this section, "employee" includes both current and former employees of a public hospital.

(b)   The following information with respect to each public hospital employee is a matter of public record:

(1)   Name.

(2)   Age.

(3)   Date of original employment.

(4)   Current position title.

(5)   Date of the most recent promotion, demotion, transfer, suspension, separation or other change in position classification.

(6)   The office to which the employee is currently assigned.

In addition, the following information with respect to each licensed medical provider employed by or having privileges to practice in a public hospital shall be a matter of public record: educational history and qualifications, date and jurisdiction or original and current licensure; and information relating to medical board certifications or other qualifications of medical specialists.

(b1)   In addition, the following information for the last completed fiscal year, beginning with the fiscal year ending in 2008, of a public hospital with respect to each Covered Officer and the five key employees (who are not Covered Officers) with the highest annual compensation of a public hospital is a matter of public record:

(1)   Base salary.

(2)   Bonus compensation.

(3)   Plan-based incentive compensation.

(4)   Dollar value of all other compensation, which includes any perquisites and other personal benefits.

(b2)   As used in this section:

(1)   "Covered Officer" means each of the following:

a.   All individuals serving as the public hospital's chief executive officer or acting in a similar capacity at any time during the last completed fiscal year, regardless of compensation level.

b.   The public hospital's four most highly compensated executive officers, determined by the aggregate amount reportable under subdivisions (1) through (4) of subsection (b1) of this section, other than the chief executive officer, who were serving as executive officers at the end of the last completed fiscal year.

179

c.   Any individual for whom disclosure would have been provided pursuant to sub-subdivision b. of this subsection but for the fact that the individual's service as an executive officer of the public hospital terminated during the last completed fiscal year.

(2)   "Executive officer" means each employee of the public hospital specifically appointed by the governing board of the public hospital to serve as an officer.

(3)   "Key employee" means any person having responsibilities, powers, or influence similar to those of an officer. The term includes the chief management and administrative officials of a public hospital.

(b3)   The governing board of a public hospital shall determine in what form and by whom this information will be maintained. Any person may have access to this information for the purpose of inspection, examination, and copying, during regular business hours, subject only to such rules and regulations for the safekeeping of public records as the governing board of the public hospital may have adopted. Any person denied access to this information may apply to the appropriate division of the General Court of Justice for an order compelling disclosure, and the court shall have jurisdiction to issue such orders.

(c)   All information contained in a public hospital employee's personnel file, other than the information made public by subsection (b) of this section, is confidential and shall be open to inspection only in the following instances:

(1)   The employee or the employee's duly authorized agent may examine all portions of the employee's personnel file, except letters of reference solicited prior to employment.

(2)   A licensed physician designated in writing by the employee may examine the employee's medical record.

(3)   A public hospital employee having supervisory authority over the employee may examine all material in the employee's personnel file.

(4)   By order of a court of competent jurisdiction, any person may examine such portion of an employee's personnel file as may be ordered by the court.

(5)   An official of an agency of the State or federal government, or any political subdivision of the State, may inspect any portion of a personnel file

when the inspection is deemed by the person having custody of the file to be inspected to be necessary and essential to the pursuance of a proper function of the inspecting agency, but no information shall be divulged for the purpose of assisting in criminal prosecution of the employee, or for the purpose of assisting in an investigation of the employee's tax liability. However, the official having custody of the records may release the name, address, and telephone number from a personnel file for the purpose of assisting in a criminal investigation.

(6)   An employee may sign a written release, to be placed with the employee's personnel file, that permits the person with custody of the file to provide, either in person, by telephone, or by mail, information specified in the release to prospective employers, educational institutions, or other persons specified in the release.

(d)   Even if considered part of an employee's personnel file, the following information need not be disclosed to an employee nor to any other person:

(1)   Testing or examination material used solely to determine individual qualifications for appointment, employment, or promotion in the public hospital's service, when disclosure would compromise the objectivity or the fairness of the testing or examination process.

(2)   Investigative reports or memoranda and other information concerning the investigation of possible criminal actions of an employee, until the investigation is completed and no criminal action taken, or until the criminal action is concluded.

(3)   Information that might identify an undercover law enforcement officer or a law enforcement informer.

(4)   Notes, preliminary drafts, and internal communications concerning an employee. In the event such materials are used for any official personnel decision, then the employee or his duly authorized agent shall have a right to inspect such materials.

(e)   The governing board of a public hospital may permit access, subject to limitations they may impose, to selected personnel files by a professional representative of a training, research, or academic institution if that representative certifies that he or she will not release information identifying the employees whose files are opened and that the information will be used solely

181

for statistical, research, or teaching purposes. This certification shall be retained by the public hospital as long as each personnel file so examined is retained.

(f) The governing board of a public hospital that maintains personnel files containing information other than the information mentioned in subsection (b) of this section shall establish procedures whereby an employee who objects to material in his or her file on grounds that it is inaccurate or misleading may seek to have the material removed from the file or may place in the file a statement relating to the material.

(g) A public hospital director, trustee, officer, or employee who knowingly, willfully, and with malice permits any person to have access to information contained in a personnel file, except as is permitted by this section, is guilty of a Class 3 misdemeanor; however, conviction under this subsection shall be punishable only by a fine not to exceed five hundred dollars ($500.00).

(h) Any person not specifically authorized by this section to have access to a personnel file designated as confidential, who shall knowingly and willfully examine in its official filing place, or remove, or copy any portion of a confidential personnel file shall be guilty of a Class 3 misdemeanor; however, conviction under this subsection shall be punishable, in the discretion of the court, by a fine not to exceed five hundred dollars ($500.00). (1997-517, s. 2; 2007-508, s. 5.5.)

§§ 131E-258 through 131E-264. Reserved for future codification purposes.

Article 16.

Miscellaneous Provisions.

§ 131E-265. Criminal history record checks required for certain applicants for employment.

(a) Requirement; Nursing Home or Home Care Agency. - An offer of employment by a nursing home licensed under this Chapter to an applicant to fill a position that does not require the applicant to have an occupational license is conditioned on consent to a criminal history record check of the applicant. If the applicant has been a resident of this State for less than five years, then the offer of employment is conditioned on consent to a State and national criminal history record check of the applicant. The national criminal history record check shall include a check of the applicant's fingerprints. If the applicant has been a resident of this State for five years or more, then the offer is conditioned on consent to a State criminal history record check of the applicant. An offer of employment by a home care agency licensed under this Chapter to an applicant to fill a position that requires entering the patient's home is conditioned on consent to a criminal history record check of the applicant. In addition, employment status change of a current employee of a home care agency licensed under this Chapter from a position that does not require entering the patient's home to a position that requires entering the patient's home shall be conditioned on consent to a criminal history record check of that current employee. If the applicant for employment or if the current employee who is changing employment status has been a resident of this State for less than five years, then the offer of employment or change in employment status is conditioned on consent to a State and national criminal history record check. The national criminal history record check shall include a check of the applicant's or current employee's fingerprints. If the applicant or current employee has been a resident of this State for five years or more, then the offer is conditioned on consent to a State criminal history record check of the applicant or current employee applying for a change in employment status. A nursing home or a home care agency shall not employ an applicant who refuses to consent to a criminal history record check required by this section. In addition, a home care agency shall not change a current employee's employment status from a position that does not require entering the patient's home to a position that requires entering the patient's home who refuses to consent to a criminal history record check required by this section. Within five business days of making the conditional offer of employment, a nursing home or home care agency shall submit a request to the Department of Justice under G.S. 114.19.10 to conduct a State or national criminal history record check required by this section, or shall submit a request to a private entity to conduct a State criminal history record check required by this section. Notwithstanding G.S. 114-19.10, the Department of Justice shall return the results of national criminal history record checks for employment positions not covered by Public Law 105-277 to the Department of Health and Human Services, Criminal Records Check Unit. Within five business days of receipt of the national criminal history of the person, the Department of Health and Human Services, Criminal Records Check Unit, shall notify the nursing home or home care agency as to whether the information received may affect the employability of the applicant. In no case shall the results of the national criminal history record check be shared with the nursing home or home care agency. Nursing homes and home care agencies shall make available upon request verification that a criminal history check has

183

been completed on any staff covered by this section. All criminal history information received by the home or agency is confidential and may not be disclosed, except to the applicant as provided in subsection (b) of this section.

(a1)   Requirement; Contract Agency of Nursing Home or Home Care Agency. - An offer of employment by a contract agency of a nursing home or home care agency licensed under this Chapter to an applicant to fill a position that does not require the applicant to have an occupational license is conditioned upon consent to a criminal history record check of the applicant. If the applicant has been a resident of this State for less than five years, then the offer of employment is conditioned on consent to a State and national criminal history record check of the applicant. The national criminal history record check shall include a check of the applicant's fingerprints. If the applicant has been a resident of this State for five years or more, then the offer is conditioned on consent to a State criminal history record check of the applicant. A contract agency of a nursing home or home care agency shall not employ an applicant who refuses to consent to a criminal history record check required by this section. Within five business days of making the conditional offer of employment, a contract agency of a nursing home or home care agency shall submit a request to the Department of Justice under G.S. 114-19.10 to conduct a State or national criminal history record check required by this section, or shall submit a request to a private entity to conduct a State criminal history record check required by this section. Notwithstanding G.S. 114-19.10, the Department of Justice shall return the results of national criminal history record checks for employment positions not covered by Public Law 105-277 to the Department of Health and Human Services, Criminal Records Check Unit. Within five business days of receipt of the national criminal history of the person, the Department of Health and Human Services, Criminal Records Check Unit, shall notify the contract agency of the nursing home or home care agency as to whether the information received may affect the employability of the applicant. In no case shall the results of the national criminal history record check be shared with the contract agency of the nursing home or home care agency. Contract agencies of nursing homes and home care agencies shall make available upon request verification that a criminal history check has been completed on any staff covered by this section. All criminal history information received by the contract agency is confidential and may not be disclosed, except to the applicant as provided by subsection (b) of this section.

(b)   Action. - If an applicant's criminal history record check reveals one or more convictions of a relevant offense, the nursing home or home care agency,

184

or the contract agency of a nursing home or home care agency, shall consider all of the following factors in determining whether to hire the applicant:

(1)   The level and seriousness of the crime.

(2)   The date of the crime.

(3)   The age of the person at the time of the conviction.

(4)   The circumstances surrounding the commission of the crime, if known.

(5)   The nexus between the criminal conduct of the person and the job duties of the position to be filled.

(6)   The prison, jail, probation, parole, rehabilitation, and employment records of the person since the date the crime was committed.

(7)   The subsequent commission by the person of a relevant offense.

The fact of conviction of a relevant offense alone shall not be a bar to employment; however, the listed factors shall be considered by the nursing home or home care agency, or the contract agency of the nursing home or home care agency. If a nursing home, home care agency, or contract agency of a nursing home or home care agency disqualifies an applicant after consideration of the relevant factors, then the nursing home, home care agency, or contract agency may disclose information contained in the criminal history record check that is relevant to the disqualification, but may not provide a copy of the criminal history record check to the applicant.

(c)   Limited Immunity. - An entity and an officer or employee of an entity that, in good faith, complies with this section is not liable for the failure of the entity to employ an individual on the basis of information provided in the criminal history record check of the individual.

(d)   Relevant Offense. - As used in this section, the term "relevant offense" has the same meaning as in G.S. 131D-40.

(e)   Penalty for Furnishing False Information. - Any applicant for employment who willfully furnishes, supplies, or otherwise gives false information on an employment application that is the basis for a criminal history record check under this section shall be guilty of a Class A1 misdemeanor.

185

(f)   Conditional Employment. - A nursing home or home care agency may employ an applicant conditionally prior to obtaining the results of a criminal history record check regarding the applicant if both of the following requirements are met:

(1)   The nursing home or home care agency shall not employ an applicant prior to obtaining the applicant's consent for a criminal history record check as required in subsection (a) of this section or the completed fingerprint cards as required in G.S. 114-19.10.

(2)   The nursing home or home care agency shall submit the request for a criminal history record check not later than five business days after the individual begins conditional employment.

(g)   Immunity From Liability. - An entity and officers and employees of an entity shall be immune from civil liability for failure to check an employee's history of criminal offenses if the employee's criminal history record check is requested and received in compliance with this section.

(h)   For purposes of this section, the term "private entity" means a business regularly engaged in conducting criminal history record checks utilizing public records obtained from a State agency. (1995 (Reg. Sess., 1996), c. 606, s. 3; 1997-125, s. 2; 1997-140, s. 4; 2000-154, ss. 3(a),(b); 2004-124, s. 10.19D(a); 2005-4, ss. 8, 9; 2007-444, s. 3.2.)

§ 131E-266. Compliance history provider file.

The Department of Health and Human Services shall establish and maintain a provider file to record and monitor compliance histories of facilities, owners, operators, and affiliates of nursing homes and adult care homes. (1999-334, s. 3.8.)

§ 131E-267. Fees for departmental review of licensed health care facility or Medical Care Commission bond-financed construction projects.

(a)   The Department of Health and Human Services shall charge a fee for the review of each health care facility construction project to ensure that project plans and construction are in compliance with State law. The fee shall be charged on a one-time, per-project basis as provided in this section. In no event may a fee imposed under this section exceed two hundred thousand dollars ($200,000) for any single project. The first seven hundred twelve thousand six hundred twenty-six dollars ($712,626) in fees collected under this section shall remain in the Division of Health Service Regulation. Additional fees collected shall be credited to the General Fund as nontax revenue and are intended to offset rather than replace appropriations made for this purpose.

(b)   The fee imposed for the review of a hospital construction project varies depending upon the square footage of the project:

Over	Up To	Project Fee
0 square foot	5,000	$1,500 plus $0.25 per
5,000 square foot	10,000	$3,000 plus $0.25 per
10,000 square foot	20,000	$4,500 plus $0.45 per
20,000 square foot	NA	$6,000 plus $0.45 per

(c)   The fee imposed for the review of a nursing home construction project varies depending upon the square footage of the project:

Over	Up To	Project Fee
0 square foot	2,000	$250.00 plus $0.15 per
2,000 square foot	NA	$500.00 plus $0.25 per

(d)   The fee imposed for the review of an ambulatory surgical facility construction project varies depending upon the square footage of the project:

Over	Up To	Project Fee

187

0 square foot	2,000	$200.00 plus $0.15 per
2,000 square foot	NA	$400.00 plus $0.25 per

(e)   The fee imposed for the review of a psychiatric hospital construction project varies depending upon the square footage of the project:

Over	Up To	Project Fee
0 square foot	5,000	$750.00 plus $0.25 per
5,000 square foot	10,000	$1,500.00 plus $0.25 per
10,000 square foot	20,000	$2,250.00 plus $0.45 per
20,000 square foot	NA	$3,000.00 plus $0.45 per

(f)   The fee imposed for the review of an adult care home construction project varies depending upon the square footage of the project:

Over	Up To	Project Fee
0 square foot	2,000	$175.00 plus $0.10 per
2,000 square foot	NA	$350.00 plus $0.20 per

(g)   The fee imposed for the review of the following residential construction projects is:

Residential Project	Project Fee
Family Care Homes	$225.00 flat fee

188

ICF/MR Group Homes	$350.00 flat fee
Group Homes: 1-3 beds	$125.00 flat fee
Group Homes: 4-6 beds	$225.00 flat fee
Group Homes: 7-9 beds	$275.00 flat fee

Other residential:

More than 9 beds square foot of project space.	$275.00 plus $0.15 per

(2003-284, s. 34.11(a); 2005-276, s. 41.2(j); 2006-66, s. 10.22; 2007-323, s. 30.5(a); 2008-107, s. 29.5(a).)

§ 131E-268. Reserved for future codification purposes.

§ 131E-269. Authorization to charge fee for certification of facilities suitable to perform abortions.

The Department of Health and Human Services shall charge each hospital or clinic certified by the Department as a facility suitable for the performance of abortions, as authorized under G.S. 14-45.1, a nonrefundable annual certification fee in the amount of seven hundred dollars ($700.00). (2003-284, s. 34.7(a); 2005-276, s. 41.2(g).)

§ 131E-270. Medication Aide Registry.

(a)   The Department shall establish and maintain a Medication Aide Registry containing the names of all health care personnel in North Carolina who have successfully completed a medication aide training program that has been approved by the North Carolina Board of Nursing, passed a State-administered medication aide competency exam, and met any other requirements set by the Medical Care Commission.

189

(b)   Before allowing an individual to serve as a medication aide, an employer shall access the Medication Aide Registry to verify that the individual is listed on the Registry and shall note each incidence of access in the appropriate business file. Employers may not use an individual as a medication aide unless the individual is listed on the Medication Aide Registry.

(c)   Employers shall access the Health Care Personnel Registry prior to employing a medication aide. Any substantiated action as defined in G.S. 131E-256(a)(1) listed against the medication aide shall disqualify the medication aide from employment in any facility or agency covered by Part 1 of Article 6 of this Chapter. (2005-276, s. 10.40C(c); 2007-444, s. 4(b).)

§ 131E-271: Reserved for future codification purposes.

§ 131E-272. Initial licensure fees for new facilities.

The following fees are initial licensure fees for new facilities and are applicable as follows:

Facility Type	Number of Beds	Initial License Fee	Initial Bed Fee
Adult Care Licensure $19.00	More than 6	$400.00	
	6 or Fewer	$350.00	$ -
Acute and Home Care			
General Acute Hospitals $19.00	1-49	$550.00	
$19.00	50-99	$750.00	
$19.00	100-199	$950.00	

190

	200-399	$1150.00	
$19.00			
	400-699	$1550.00	
$19.00			
	700+	$1950.00	
$19.00			
Other Hospitals		$1050.00	
$19.00			
Home Care	-	$560.00	$ -
Ambulatory Surgical Ctrs.	-	$900.00	
$85.00			
Hospice (Free Standing)	-	$450.00	$ -
Abortion Clinics	-	$750.00	$ -
Cardiac Rehab. Centers	-	$425.00	$ -
Nursing Home & L&C			
Nursing Homes		$470.00	
$19.00			
All Others		$ -	
$19.00			
Mental Health Facilities			
Nonresidential		$265.00	$ -

191

Non ICF-MR	6 or fewer	$350.00	$ -
ICF-MR only	6 or fewer	$900.00	$ -
Non ICF-MR $19.00	More than 6	$525.00	
ICF-MR only $19.00."	More than 6	$850.00	

(2009-451, s. 10.77.)

§ 131E-273. Certain charges/payments prohibited.

It shall be unlawful for any provider of health care services to charge or accept payment for any health care procedure or component of any health care procedure that was not performed or supplied. If a procedure requires the informed consent of a patient, the charge for any component of the procedure performed prior to consent being given shall not exceed the actual cost to the provider if the patient elects not to consent to the procedure. (2013-382, s. 11.1; 2013-393, s. 1.)

§ 131E-274: Reserved for future codification purposes.

Article 17.

Provider Sponsored Organization Licensing.

§ 131E-275. General provisions.

(a)   The General Assembly acknowledges that section 1855, et seq., of the federal Social Security Act permits provider sponsored organizations that are organized and licensed under State law as risk-bearing entities, or that are otherwise certified as such by the federal government, to be eligible to offer Medicare health insurance or health benefits coverage in each state in which the provider sponsored organization offers a Medicare+Choice plan. The General Assembly declares that provider sponsored organizations are beneficial to North Carolina citizens who are Medicare beneficiaries and should be encouraged, subject to appropriate regulation by the Division of Medical Assistance of the Department of Health and Human Services. The General Assembly further declares that, because provider sponsored organizations provide health care directly and assume responsibility for the provision of health care services to Medicare beneficiaries under the requirements of the federal Medicare program, they require different regulatory oversight to protect the public than health maintenance organizations and insurance companies. The General Assembly further declares that the organizers and operators of provider sponsored organizations which are licensed under the terms of this Article as risk-bearing entities authorized to contract directly with the federal Medicare+Choice program shall not be subject to Chapter 58 of the General Statutes or the insurance laws of this State, unless otherwise specified in this Article.

It is the intent of the General Assembly to encourage innovative methods by which sponsoring providers can directly or indirectly share substantial financial risk in the PSO in any lawful manner.

(b)   As set forth in this Article, the Division of Medical Assistance of the Department of Health and Human Services shall be the agency of the State authorized to license provider sponsored organizations to contract with Medicare to provide health care services to Medicare beneficiaries and to engage in the other related activities described in this Article.

(c)   Each provider sponsored organization shall obtain a license from the Division or shall otherwise be certified by the federal government prior to establishing, maintaining, and operating a health care plan in this State for Medicare+Choice beneficiaries. Nothing in this Article shall be construed to authorize a provider sponsored organization to establish, maintain, or operate a health care plan other than exclusively for Medicare+Choice beneficiaries. (1998-227, s. 1.)

§ 131E-276. Definitions.

As used in this Article, unless the context clearly implies otherwise, the following definitions apply:

(1)   "Affiliated provider" means a health care provider that is affiliated with another provider if, through contract, ownership, or otherwise: (i) one provider directly controls, is controlled by, or is under common control with the other provider; (ii) each provider participates in a lawful combination under which they share substantial financial risk for the organization's operation; (iii) both providers are part of a controlled group of corporations as defined under section 1563 of the Internal Revenue Code of 1986; or (iv) both providers are part of an affiliated service group under section 414 of this Code. Control is presumed if one party directly or indirectly owns, controls, or holds the power to vote, or proxies for, at least fifty-one percent (51%) of the voting or governance rights of another.

(2)   "Beneficiary" or "beneficiaries" means a beneficiary or beneficiaries of the Medicare+Choice program who are enrolled with the provider sponsored organization (PSO) under the terms of a contract between the PSO and the Medicare program.

(3)   "Current assets" means cash, marketable securities, accounts receivable, and other current items that will be converted into cash within 12 months.

(4)   "Current liabilities" means accounts payable and other accrued liabilities, including payroll, claims, and taxes that will need to be paid within 12 months.

(5)   "Current ratio" means the ratio of current assets divided by current liabilities calculated at the end of any accounting period.

(6)   "Division" means the Division of Medical Assistance of the Department of Health and Human Services.

(7)   "Emergency services" has the same meaning as defined in G.S. 58-50-61(a)(5).

(8)   "Health care delivery assets" means any tangible asset that is part of a PSO operation, including hospitals, medical facilities, and their ancillary equipment, and any property that may reasonably be required for the PSO's principal office or for any purposes that may be necessary in the transaction of the business of the PSO.

(9)   "Health plan contract" or "Medicare contract" means a PSO's direct contract with the United States Department of Health and Human Services under section 1857 of the federal Social Security Act.

(10)   "Out-of-network services" means health care items or services that are covered services under a PSO's Medicare contract and that are provided to beneficiaries by health care providers that are not participating providers in the PSO's network of health care providers.

(11)   "Parent of a sponsoring provider" means the public or private entity that owns or controls a controlling interest in the sponsoring provider or that has the power to appoint a controlling number of the governing board of a sponsoring provider or that has the power to direct the management policy and decisions of the sponsoring provider.

(12)   "Provider" or "health care provider" means: (i) any individual that is engaged in the delivery of health care services and that is required by North Carolina law or regulation to be licensed to engage in the delivery of these health care services and is so licensed; (ii) any entity that is engaged in the delivery of health care services and that is required by North Carolina law or regulation to be licensed to engage in the delivery of these health care services and is so licensed; or (iii) any entity that is owned or controlled entirely by individuals or entities described in subparts (i) or (ii) of this definition.

(13)   "Provider sponsored organization" or "PSO" means a public or private entity domiciled in this State, including a business corporation, a nonprofit corporation, a partnership, a limited liability company, a professional limited liability company, a professional corporation, a sole proprietorship, a public hospital, a hospital authority, a hospital district, or a body politic: (i) that is established, organized, and operated by sponsoring providers; (ii) in which physicians licensed pursuant to Article 1 of Chapter 90 of the General Statutes or to the laws of any state of the United States comprise no less than fifty percent (50%) of the governing board or body, unless otherwise prohibited by law; and (iii) that provides a substantial proportion of the services under each Medicare contract directly through the sponsoring provider. The requirement in subpart (ii) of this definition shall not preclude a PSO that includes a tax-exempt hospital from adopting a bylaw provision that provides a veto for the tax-exempt hospital over actions of the PSO necessary to maintain the hospital's tax-exempt status. A PSO shall not be out of compliance with the requirement in subpart (ii) due to temporary vacancies on its governing board or body. Subpart (ii) of this subdivision applies only if a hospital licensed under this Chapter or

195

Chapter 122C of the General Statutes is the sponsoring provider or a member of the group of affiliated health care providers that comprises the sponsoring provider.

(14)   "Sponsoring providers" of a PSO means the health care provider domiciled in this State that assumes, or group of affiliated health care providers that directly or indirectly shares, substantial financial risk in the PSO and that has at least a majority financial interest in the PSO.

(15)   "Substantial proportion of the services" means at least seventy percent (70%), or sixty percent (60%) for PSOs whose beneficiaries reside primarily in rural areas, of the annual health care expenditures. (1998-227, s. 1.)

§ 131E-277. Direct or indirect sharing of substantial financial risk.

In order for sponsoring providers to directly or indirectly share substantial financial risk in the PSO, the PSO shall do one or more of the following:

(1)   Provide services under its Medicare contract at a capitated rate;

(2)   Provide designated services or classes of services under its Medicare contract for a predetermined percentage of premium or revenue from the Medicare program;

(3)   Use significant financial incentives for its sponsoring providers, as a group to achieve specified cost-containment and utilization management goals either by:

a.   Withholding from all sponsoring providers a substantial amount of the compensation due to them, with distribution of that amount to the sponsoring providers based on performance of all sponsoring providers in meeting the cost-containment goals of the network as a whole; or

b.   Establishing overall cost or utilization targets for the PSO, with the sponsoring providers subject to subsequent substantial financial rewards or penalties based on group performance in meeting the targets; or

(4)   Agree to provide a complex or extended course of treatment that requires the substantial coordination of care by sponsoring providers in different

specialties offering a complementary mix of services, for a fixed, predetermined payment, when the costs of that course of treatment for any individual patient can vary greatly due to the individual patient's treatment or other factors; or

(5)   Agree to any other arrangement that the Division determines to provide for the sharing of substantial financial risk by the sponsoring providers. (1998-227, s. 1.)

§ 131E-278. Applicability of other laws.

Unless otherwise required by federal law, provider sponsored organizations licensed pursuant to the terms of this Article are exempt from all regulation under Chapter 58 of the General Statutes. Plan contracts, provider contracts, and other arrangements related to the provision of covered services by these licensed networks or by health care providers of these PSOs when operating through these PSOs shall likewise be exempt from regulation under Chapter 58 of the General Statutes. (1998-227, s. 1.)

§ 131E-279. Approval.

(a)   Unless otherwise required by federal law, the Division shall be the agency of the State that shall license provider sponsored organizations that seek to contract with the federal government to provide health care services directly to Medicare beneficiaries under the Medicare+Choice program.

(b)   Provider sponsored organizations which have been granted a waiver pursuant to 42 U.S.C. § 1395w-25(a)(2) and which otherwise meet the requirements of the PSO's Medicare contract shall be deemed by the State to be licensed under this Article for so long as the waiver or Medicare contract remains in effect. The foregoing shall not limit the Division's authority to regulate such PSOs and their respective sponsoring providers and affiliated providers as may be permitted in 42 U.S.C. § 1395w-25(a)(2)(G) or the PSO's Medicare contract.

(c)   The Division shall license a PSO as a risk-bearing entity eligible to offer health benefits coverage in this State to Medicare beneficiaries if the PSO complies with the requirements of this Article. This license shall be granted or

197

denied by the Division not longer than 90 days after the receipt of a substantially complete application for licensing. Within 45 days after the Division receives an application for licensing, the Division shall either notify the applicant that the application is substantially complete, or clearly and accurately specify in writing to the applicant all additional specific information required by the applicant to make the application a substantially completed application. This agency response shall set forth a date and time for a meeting within 30 days after it is sent to the applicant, at which a representative of the Division will explain with particularity the additional information required by the Division in the response to make the application substantially complete. The Division shall be bound by the response unless the Division determines that it must be modified in order to meet the purposes of this Article. The Division shall not delegate the authority to modify the response. If an applicant provides the additional information set forth in the response, the application shall be considered substantially complete. If the Division has not acted on an application within 90 days after it is deemed substantially complete, the Division shall immediately issue a license to the applicant, and the applicant shall be considered to have been licensed by the Division. Any reapplication which corrects the deficiencies which were specified by the Division in the response shall be approved by the Division.

(d)   For purposes of determining, under 42 U.S.C. § 1395w-25(a)(2)(B), or any successor thereof, the date of receipt by the State of a substantially complete application, the date the Division receives the applicant's written response to the agency response or an earlier date considered by the Division shall be considered to be that date. The foregoing shall not limit the Division's authority to consider an application not substantially complete under subsection (c) of this section if the applicant's response to the response does not provide substantially the information specified in the response.

(e)   A license shall be denied only after the Division complies with the requirements of G.S. 131E-305. (1998-227, s. 1.)

§ 131E-280. Applicants for license.

Each application for licensing as a provider sponsored organization authorized to do business in North Carolina shall be certified by an officer or authorized representative of the applicant, shall be in a form prescribed by the Division, and shall be set forth or be accompanied by the following:

(1)   A copy of the basic organizational document, if any, of the applicant and each sponsoring organization that holds greater than a five percent (5%) interest in the PSO, such as the articles of incorporation, articles of organization, partnership agreement, trust agreement, or other applicable documents, and all amendments thereto;

(2)   A copy of the respective bylaws, rules and regulations, or similar documents, if any, regulating the conduct of the internal affairs of the applicant and each sponsoring provider which holds greater than a five percent (5%) interest in the PSO;

(3)   Copies of the document evidencing the arrangements between the applicant and each sponsoring provider that create the relationships and obligations described in G.S. 131E-276(1);

(4)   A list of the names, addresses, and official positions of persons who are to be responsible for the conduct of the affairs of the applicant and of each sponsoring provider that holds greater than a five percent (5%) interest in the PSO, respectively, including all members of the respective boards of directors, boards of trustees, executive committees, or other governing boards or committees, the principal officers in the case of a corporation, and the partners or members in the case of a partnership or association;

(5)   A copy of any contract form made or to be made between any class of providers and the PSO and a copy of any contract form made or to be made between third-party administrators, marketing consultants, or persons listed in subdivision (3) of this subsection and the PSO;

(6)   A statement generally describing the provider sponsored organization, its sponsoring providers, its health care plan or plans, facilities, and personnel and certifying that its medical director or other person charged with determining and overseeing the PSO's medical policies is a medical doctor holding an unrestricted license to practice medicine under Article 1 of Chapter 90 of the General Statutes;

(7)   A copy of the hospital license of each sponsoring provider that is a hospital, a copy of the license to practice medicine of each sponsoring provider or owner of a sponsoring provider that is a licensed physician, and a copy of the health care service or facility license held by any other licensed sponsoring provider;

199

(8)   Financial statements showing the applicant's assets, liabilities, sources of financial support, and the financial statements of each sponsoring provider that holds greater than a five percent (5%) interest in the PSO showing the sponsoring provider's assets, liabilities, and sources of support. If the applicant's or any such sponsoring provider's financial affairs are audited by independent certified public accountants, a copy of the applicant's or sponsoring provider's most recent regular certified financial statement shall be considered to satisfy this requirement unless the Division directs that additional or more recent financial information is required for the proper administration of this Article;

(9)   If the applicant's obligations under G.S. 131E-282, 131E-283, 131E-297, 131E-298, and 131E-299 are guaranteed by one or more guarantors:

a.   Documentation that each guarantor meets the following requirements:

1.   The guarantor is a legal entity authorized to conduct business in North Carolina.

2.   The guarantor is not under federal bankruptcy or State receivership or rehabilitation proceedings.

3.   The guarantor has a net worth, not including other guarantees, intangibles, and restricted reserves, equal to three times the amount of the PSO's guarantee.

b.   Financial statements showing each guarantor's assets, liabilities, and source of financial support.

c.   If a guarantor's financial affairs are audited by independent certified public accountants, a copy of the guarantor's most recent regular audited financial statement shall be considered to satisfy this requirement unless the Division directs that additional or more recent financial information is required for the proper administration of this Article.

d.   The guarantee document, including a statement of the financial obligation covered by the guarantee, an agreement to unconditionally fulfill the financial obligations covered by the guarantee, an agreement not to subordinate the guarantee to any other claim on the resources of the guarantor and a declaration that the guarantor must act on a timely basis to satisfy the financial obligations covered by the guarantee.

(10)	A financial plan, satisfactory to the Division, covering the first 12 months of operation under the PSO's Medicare contract and which meets the requirements of G.S. 131E-283. If the financial plan projects losses, the financial plan must cover the period through 12 months beyond the projected breakeven;

(11)	A statement reasonably describing the geographic area or areas to be served;

(12)	A description of the procedures to be implemented to meet the protection against insolvency requirements of G.S. 131E-298; and

(13)	Any other information the Division may require to make the determinations required in G.S. 131E-282. (1998-227, s. 1.)

§ 131E-281.	Additional information.

(a)	In addition to the information filed under G.S. 131E-280, each application shall include a description of the following:

(1)	The program to be used to evaluate whether the applicant's network of sponsoring providers and contracted providers is sufficient, in numbers and types of providers, to assure that all health care services will be accessible without unreasonable delay;

(2)	The program used to evaluate whether the sponsoring providers provide a substantial portion of services under each Medicare contract of the PSO;

(3)	The program to be used for verifying provider credentials;

(4)	The utilization review program for the review and control of health care services provided or paid for by the applicant;

(5)	The quality management program to assure quality of care and health care services managed and provided through the health care plan; and

(6)	The applicant's network of sponsoring providers and contracted providers and evidence of the ability of that network to provide all health care services other than out-of-network services and emergency services to the applicant's prospective beneficiaries.

201

(b)   The Division may promulgate rules and regulations exempting from the filing requirements of subsection (a) of this section those items it deems unnecessary. (1998-227, s. 1.)

§ 131E-282. Issuance of license.

(a)   Before issuing a PSO license, the Division may make an examination or investigation as it deems expedient. The Division shall issue a license after receipt of a substantially complete application and upon satisfaction of the following requirements:

(1)   The applicant is duly organized as a provider sponsored organization as defined by this Article.

(2)   The PSO has initially a minimum net worth of one million five hundred thousand dollars ($1,500,000). In the event the PSO submits a financial plan that demonstrates that the PSO does not have to create but has or has available to it an administrative infrastructure that shall reduce the PSO's start-up costs, the Division may lower the initial minimum net worth required to one million dollars ($1,000,000) or to any lower amount as determined by the Division if the PSO operates primarily in rural areas.

(3)   The PSO shall have at least seven hundred fifty thousand dollars ($750,000) in cash or equivalents on its balance sheet, except that the Division may permit a PSO operating primarily in rural areas to have a lesser amount held in cash or equivalents on its balance sheets.

(4)   The applicant submits a financial plan satisfactory to the Division which covers the first 12 months of operation of the PSO's Medicare contract and which meets the requirements of G.S. 131E-283. If the plan projects losses, the financial plan shall cover the period through 12 months beyond projected breakeven.

(5)   The Division determines that the applicant has sufficient cash flow to meet its obligations as they become due. In making that determination, the Division shall consider the following:

a.   The timeliness of payment;

b.   The extent to which the current ratio is maintained at one-to-one, or whether there is a change in the current ratio over a period of time; and

c.   The availability of outside financial resources.

(b)   In calculating the net worth of a PSO, the Division shall admit the following:

(1)   One hundred percent (100%) of the book value of health care delivery assets on the balance sheet of the applicant.

(2)   One hundred percent (100%) of the value of cash and cash equivalents on the balance sheet of the applicant.

(3)   If at least one million dollars ($1,000,000) of the initial minimum net worth requirement is met by cash or cash equivalents, then one hundred percent (100%) of the book value of the PSO's intangible assets up to twenty percent (20%) of the minimum net worth amount required. If less than one million dollars ($1,000,000) of the initial minimum net worth requirement is met by cash or cash equivalents or if the Division has used its discretion to reduce the initial net worth requirement below one million five hundred thousand dollars ($1,500,000), then the Division shall admit one hundred percent (100%) of the book value of intangible assets of the PSO up to ten percent (10%) of the minimum net worth amount required.

(4)   Standard accounting principles treatment shall be given to other assets of the PSO not used in the delivery of health care for the purposes of meeting the minimum net worth requirement.

(5)   Deferred acquisition costs shall not be admitted. (1998-227, s. 1.)

§ 131E-283. Financial plan.

(a)   The financial plan shall include the following:

(1)   A detailed marketing plan;

(2)   Statements of revenue and expense on an accrual basis;

(3)   Cash flow statements;

(4)   Balance sheets; and

(5)   The assumptions and justifications in support of the financial plan.

(b)   In the financial plan, the PSO shall demonstrate that it has the resources available to meet the projected losses for the entire period to break even. Except for the use of guaranties as provided in subsection (c) of this section, letters of credit as provided in subsection (e) of this section, and other means as provided in subsection (f) of this section, the resources must be assets on the balance sheet of the PSO in a form that is either cash or convertible to cash in a timely manner, pursuant to the financial plan.

(c)   Guaranties shall be acceptable as a resource to meet projected losses, under the following conditions:

(1)   For the first year of the PSO's operation of the PSO's Medicare contract, the guarantor must provide the PSO with cash or cash equivalents to fund the projected losses, as follows:

a.   Prior to the beginning of the first quarter, in the amount of the projected losses for the first two quarters;

b.   Prior to the beginning of the second quarter, in the amount of the projected losses through the end of the third quarter; and

c.   Prior to the beginning of the third quarter, in the amount of the projected losses through the end of the fourth quarter.

(2)   If the guarantor provides the cash or cash equivalents to the PSO in a timely manner on the above schedule, this funding shall be considered in compliance with the guarantor's commitment to the PSO. In the third quarter, the PSO shall notify the Division if the PSO intends to reduce the period of funding of projected losses. The Division shall notify the PSO within 60 days of receiving the PSO's notice if the reduction is not acceptable.

(3)   If the above guaranty requirements are not met, the Division may take appropriate action, such as requiring funding of projected losses through means other than a guaranty. The Division retains discretion which shall be reasonably exercised to require other methods or timing of funding, considering factors

such as the financial condition of the guarantor and the accuracy of the financial plan.

(d)   The Division may modify the conditions in subsection (c) of this section in order to clarify the acceptability of guaranty arrangements.

(e)   An irrevocable, clean, unconditional letter of credit may be used as an acceptable resource to fund projected losses in place of cash or cash equivalents if satisfactory to the Division.

(f)   If approved by the Division, based on appropriate standards promulgated by the Division, PSOs may use the following to fund projected losses for periods after the first year: lines of credit from regulated financial institutions, legally binding agreements for capital contributions, or other legally binding contracts of a similar level of reliability.

(g)   The exceptions in subsections (c), (e), and (f) of this section may be used in an appropriate combination or sequence. (1998-227, s. 1.)

§ 131E-284. Modifications.

(a)   A provider sponsored organization shall file a notice describing any significant change in the information required by the Division under G.S. 131E-280. Such notice shall be filed with the Division prior to the change. If the Division does not disapprove within 90 days after the filing, this modification shall be considered approved. Changes subject to the terms of this section include expansion of service area, addition or deletion of sponsoring providers, changes in provider contract forms, and group contract forms when the distribution of risk is significantly changed, and any other changes that the Division describes in properly adopted rules. Every PSO shall report to the Division for the Division's information material changes in the network of sponsoring providers and affiliated providers of services to beneficiaries enrolled with the PSO, the addition or deletion of any Medicare contracts of the PSO or any other information the Division may require. This information shall be filed with the Division within 15 days after implementation of the reported changes. Every PSO shall file with the Division all subsequent changes in the information or forms that are required by this Article to be filed with the Division.

205

(b)   The Division may adopt rules exempting from the filing requirements of subsection (a) of this section those items it considers unnecessary. (1998-227, s. 1.)

§ 131E-285. Deposits.

(a)   At the time of application, the Division shall require a deposit of one hundred thousand dollars ($100,000) in cash or securities or a combination thereof for all provider sponsored organizations. The deposits shall be included in the calculations of a PSO's or applicant's net worth.

(b)   All deposits required by this section shall be restricted to use in the event of insolvency to help assume continuation of services or pay costs associated with receivership or liquidation. (1998-227, s. 1.)

§ 131E-286. Ongoing financial standards - Net worth.

(a)   Beginning the first day of operation of the PSO and except as otherwise provided in subsection (d) of this section, every PSO shall maintain a minimum net worth equal to the greatest of the following amounts:

(1)   One million dollars ($1,000,000);

(2)   Two percent (2%) of annual premium revenues as reported on the most recent annual financial statement filed with the Division on the first one hundred fifty million dollars ($150,000,000) of premium and one percent (1%) of annual premium on the premium in excess of one hundred fifty million dollars ($150,000,000);

(3)   An amount equal to the sum of three months uncovered health care expenditures as reported on the most recent financial statement filed with the Division;

(4)   An amount equal to the sum of:

a.   Eight percent (8%) of annual health care expenditures paid on a noncapitated basis to nonaffiliated providers as reported on the most recent financial statement filed with the Division; and

b.   Four percent (4%) of annual health care expenditures paid on a capitated basis to nonaffiliated providers plus annual health care expenditures paid on a noncapitated basis to affiliated providers; and

c.   Zero percent (0%) of annual health care expenditures paid on a capitated basis to affiliated providers regardless of downstream arrangements from the affiliated provider.

(b)   In calculating net worth, liabilities shall not include fully subordinated debt or subordinated liabilities. For purposes of this provision, subordinated liabilities are claims liabilities otherwise due to providers that are retained by the PSO to meet net worth requirements and are fully subordinated to all creditors.

(c)   In calculating net worth for purposes of this section, the items described in G.S. 131E-282(b) shall be admitted, except as follows:

(1)   For intangible assets, if at least the greater of one million dollars ($1,000,000) or sixty-seven percent (67%) of the ongoing minimum net worth requirement is met by cash or cash equivalents, then the Division shall admit the book value of intangible assets up to twenty percent (20%) of the minimum net worth amount required. If less than the greater of one million dollars ($1,000,000) or sixty-seven percent (67%) of the ongoing minimum net worth requirement is met by cash or cash equivalents, then the Division shall admit the book value of intangible assets up to ten percent (10%) of the minimum net worth amount required; and

(2)   Deferred acquisition costs shall not be admitted.

(d)   The Division may lower the minimum ongoing net worth threshold, and the amount held in cash or cash equivalents for PSOs that operate primarily in rural areas.

(e)   During the start-up phase of the PSO, the pre-break-even financial plan requirements shall apply. After the point of breakeven, the financial plan requirement shall address cash needs and the financing required for the next three years.

207

(f)   If a PSO, or the legal entity of which the PSO is a component, did not earn a net operating surplus during the most recent fiscal year, the PSO shall submit a financial plan, satisfactory to the Division, meeting all of the requirements established for the initial financial plan. (1998-227, s. 1.)

§ 131E-287. PSO Reporting.

(a)   The PSO shall file with the Division financial information relating to PSO solvency standards described in this Article, according to the following schedule:

(1)   On a quarterly basis until breakeven; and

(2)   On an annual basis after breakeven, if the PSO has a net operating surplus; or

(3)   On a quarterly or monthly basis, as specified by the Division, after breakeven, if the PSO does not have a net operating surplus.

(b)   To the extent not preempted by federal law or otherwise mandated by the Medicare program, the PSO shall annually, on or before the first day of March of each year, file with the Division the following information for the previous calendar year:

(1)   The number of and reasons for grievances and complaints received from Medicare beneficiaries enrolled with the PSO under the PSO's Medicare contract regarding medical treatment. The report shall include the number of covered lives, total number of grievances categorized by reason for the grievance, the number of grievances referred to the second level grievance review, the number of grievances resolved at each level and their resolution, and a description of the actions that are being taken to correct the problems that have been identified through grievances received. Every PSO shall file with the Division, as part of its annual grievance report, a certificate of compliance stating that the PSO has established and follows, for its Medicare contract, grievance procedures that comply with this Article.

(2)   The number of Medicare beneficiaries enrolled with the PSO under the PSO's Medicare contract who terminated their enrollment with the PSO for any reason.

(3)   The number of provider contracts between the PSO and network providers for the provision of covered services to Medicare beneficiaries that were terminated and reasons for termination. This information shall include the number of providers leaving the PSO network and the number of new providers in the network. The report shall show voluntary and involuntary terminations separately.

(4)   Data relating to the utilization, quality, availability, and accessibility of service. The report shall include the following:

a.   Information on the PSO's program to determine the level of network availability, as measured by the numbers and types of network providers, required to provide covered services to covered persons. This information shall include the PSO's methodology under its Medicare+Choice program for:

1.   Establishing performance targets for the numbers and types of providers by specialty, area of practice, or facility type, for each of the following categories: primary care physicians, specialty care physicians, nonphysician health care providers, hospitals, and nonhospital health care facilities.

2.   Determining when changes in PSO Medicare+Choice program enrollees will necessitate changes in the provider network.

The report shall also include: the availability performance targets for the previous and current years; the numbers and types of providers currently participating in the PSO's provider network; and an evaluation of actual plan performance against performance targets.

b.   The PSO's method for arranging or providing health care services from nonnetwork providers, both within and outside of its service area, when network providers are not available to provide covered services.

c.   Information on the PSO's program under its Medicare+Choice program to determine the level of provider network accessibility necessary to serve its Medicare enrollees. This information shall include the PSO's methodology for establishing performance targets for member access to covered services from primary care physicians, specialty care physicians, nonphysician health care providers, hospitals, and nonhospital health care facilities. The methodology shall establish targets for:

1.   The proximity of network providers to members, as measured by member driving distance, to access primary care, specialty care, hospital-based services, and services of nonhospital facilities.

2.   Expected waiting time for appointments for urgent care, acute care, specialty care, and routine services for prevention and wellness.

The report shall also include: the accessibility performance targets for the previous and current years; data on actual overall accessibility as measured by driving distance and average appointment waiting time; and an evaluation of actual Medicare+Choice plan performance against performance targets. Measures of actual accessibility may be developed using scientifically valid random sample techniques.

d.   A statement of the PSO's methods and standards for determining whether in-network services are reasonably available and accessible to a Medicare enrollee for the purpose of determining whether such enrollee should receive the in-network level of coverage for services received from a nonnetwork provider.

e.   A description of the PSO's program to monitor the adequacy of its network availability and accessibility methodologies and performance targets, Medicare+Choice plan performance, and network provider performance.

f.   A summary of the PSO's utilization review program activities for the previous calendar year under its Medicare+Choice program. The report shall include the number of: each type of utilization review performed, noncertifications for each type of review, each type of review appealed, and appeals settled in favor of Medicare enrollees. The report shall be accompanied by a certification from the carrier that it has established and follows procedures that comply with this Article.

(5)   Aggregate financial compensation data, including the percentage of providers paid under a capitation arrangement, discounted fee-for-service or salary, the services included in the capitation payment, and the range of compensation paid by withhold or incentive payments. This information shall be submitted on a form prescribed by the Division.

The name, or group or institutional name, of an individual provider may not be disclosed pursuant to this subsection. No civil liability shall arise from compliance with the provisions of this subsection, provided that the acts or omissions are made in good faith and do not constitute gross negligence, willful or wanton misconduct, or intentional wrongdoing.

(c)   Disclosure Requirements. - To the extent not otherwise prohibited by federal law or under the terms of the PSO's Medicare contract, each PSO shall provide the following applicable information to Medicare beneficiaries enrolled with the PSO under the PSO's Medicare contract and bona fide prospective enrollees upon request:

(1)   The evidence of coverage under the Medicare+Choice plan provided by the PSO to Medicare beneficiaries under the terms of the PSO's Medicare contract;

(2)   An explanation of the utilization review criteria and treatment protocol under which treatments are provided for conditions specified by the prospective enrollee. This explanation shall be in writing if so requested;

(3)   If denied a recommended treatment, written reasons for the denial and an explanation of the utilization review criteria or treatment protocol upon which the denial was based;

(4)   The plan's restrictive formularies or prior approval requirements for obtaining prescription drugs, whether a particular drug or therapeutic class of drugs is excluded from its formulary, and the circumstances under which a nonformulary drug may be covered; and

(5)   The procedures and medically based criteria under the PSO's Medicare contract for determining whether a specified procedure, test, or treatment is experimental.

(d)   Effective January 1, 1999, PSOs shall make the reports that are required under subsection (b) of this section and that have been filed with the Division available on their business premises and shall provide any Medicare beneficiary enrolled with the PSO access to them upon request, unless otherwise prohibited by federal law or under the terms of the PSO's Medicare contract.

(e)   Every PSO licensed under this Article shall annually on or before the first day of March of each year, file with the Division a sworn statement verified by at least two of the principal officers of the PSO showing its condition on the thirty-first day of December, then next preceding; which shall be in such form as the Division shall prescribe. In case the PSO fails to file the annual statement as

211

herein required, the Division is authorized to suspend the license issued to the PSO until the statement shall be properly filed.

(f)   A PSO shall report to the Division the efforts it has undertaken to foster measurable improvements in the health status of the community's Medicare population, increase access to health care for noncovered benefits, and address critical health care needs of the community's Medicare population. (1998-227, s. 1.)

§ 131E-288. Liquidity.

(a)   Each PSO shall have sufficient cash flow to meet its obligations as they become due. In determining the ability of a PSO to meet this requirement, the Division shall consider the following:

(1)   The timeliness of payment;

(2)   The extent to which the current ratio is maintained at one-to-one or whether there is a change in the current ratio over a period of time; and

(3)   The availability of outside financial resources.

(b)   The following corresponding remedies apply:

(1)   If the PSO fails to pay obligations as they become due, the Division shall require the PSO to initiate corrective action to pay all overdue obligations.

(2)   The Division may require the PSO to initiate corrective action if either of the following is evident: (i) the current ratio declines significantly; or (ii) there is a continued downward trend in the current ratio. The corrective action may include a change in the distribution of assets, a reduction of liabilities, or alternative arrangements to secure additional funding requirements to restore the current ratio to one-to-one.

(3)   If there is a change in the availability of the outside resources, the Division shall require the PSO to obtain funding from alternative financial resources.

(c)   Nothing in the foregoing liquidity requirements shall be interpreted to require the PSO to maintain a current ratio of one-to-one if the PSO can demonstrate to the Division that it is able to pay its obligations as they become due and the current ratio maintained by the PSO has neither declined significantly nor is on a continued downward trend. (1998-227, s. 1.)

§ 131E-289. Minimum of net worth that must be in cash or cash equivalents.

(a)   Except as otherwise provided in subsection (b) of this section, each PSO shall, on an ongoing basis, maintain a minimum net worth in cash or cash equivalents of the greater of:

(1)   Seven hundred fifty thousand dollars ($750,000) cash or cash equivalents; or

(2)   Forty percent (40%) of the minimum net worth required.

(b)   The Division may lower the threshold for minimum net worth held in cash or cash equivalents by PSOs that operate primarily in rural areas.

(c)   Cash or cash equivalents held to meet the net worth requirement shall be current assets of the PSO. (1998-227, s. 1.)

§ 131E-290. Prohibited practice.

(a)   No provider sponsored organization or sponsoring provider, unless licensed as an insurer under Chapter 58 of the General Statutes may use in its name, contracts, or literature any of the words "insurance", "casualty", "surety", "mutual", or any other words descriptive of the insurance, casualty, or surety business or deceptively similar to the name or description of any insurance or surety corporation doing business in this State.

(b)   No provider sponsored organization or sponsoring provider shall engage in any activity or conduct which is prohibited by the terms of the PSO's Medicare contract.

(c)   Unless otherwise preempted by federal law or mandated by the Medicare program, a PSO shall not discriminate with respect to participation, reimbursement, or indemnification as to any provider who is acting within the scope of the provider's license or certification under applicable State law, solely on the basis of that license or certification. This subsection does not preclude a PSO from including providers only to the extent necessary to meet the needs of the organization's enrollees or from establishing any measure designed to maintain quality and control costs consistent with the responsibilities of the organization. (1998-227, s. 1.)

§ 131E-291. Collaboration with local health departments.

A provider sponsored organization and a local health department shall collaborate and cooperate within available resources regarding health promotion and disease prevention efforts that are necessary to protect the public health. (1998-227, s. 1.)

§ 131E-292. Coverage.

(a)   Provider sponsored organizations subject to this Article shall provide coverage for the medically appropriate and necessary services specified under the PSO's Medicare contract.

(b)   In the event a PSO's Medicare contract or federal law, regulations, or rules governing coverage by the PSO of items or services to Medicare beneficiaries permits a PSO, sponsoring provider, or participating provider to object on moral or religious grounds to providing an item or service to Medicare beneficiaries, it is the policy of this State to permit this objection and allow the participating provider to refuse to provide the item or service. (1998-227, s. 1.)

§ 131E-293. Rates.

Rates charged by provider sponsored organizations to the Medicare program and charges by PSOs and sponsoring providers for items or services to beneficiaries shall be governed by the terms of the PSO's Medicare contract. (1998-227, s. 1.)

§ 131E-294. Additional consumer protection and quality standards.

Unless otherwise preempted by federal law or mandated by the Medicare program, the Division shall apply to provider sponsored organizations the same standards and requirements that the Department of Insurance applies to health maintenance organizations under Chapter 58 of the General Statutes with respect to the following consumer protection and quality matters:

(1)   Quality management programs (11 NCAC 20.0500, et seq.);

(2)   Utilization review procedures (G.S. 58-67-61 and G.S. 58-67-62);

(3)   Unfair or deceptive trade practices (Article 63 of Chapter 58 of the General Statutes);

(4)   Antidiscrimination (G.S. 58-3-25(b) and (c), 58-3-120, 58-63-15(7), and 58-67-75);

(5)   Provider accessibility and availability (11 NCAC 20.0300, et seq.);

(6)   Network provider credentialing (11 NCAC 20.0400, et seq.); and

(7)   Data reporting requirements under G.S. 58-67-50(e). (1998-227, s. 1.)

§ 131E-295. Powers of insurers and medical service corporations.

Notwithstanding any provision of the insurance and hospital or medical service corporation laws contained in Articles 1 through 67 of Chapter 58 of the General Statutes, an insurer or a hospital or medical service corporation may contract with a provider sponsored organization to provide insurance or similar protection against the cost of care provided through provider sponsored organizations and their sponsoring providers to beneficiaries and to provide coverage in the event of the failure of the provider sponsored organization or its sponsoring providers to meet its obligations under the PSO's Medicare contract. The beneficiaries of a provider sponsored organization constitute a permissible group under these laws. Among other things, under these contracts, the insurer or hospital or medical service corporation may make benefit payments to provider sponsored organizations for health care services rendered by providers pursuant to the health care plan. (1998-227, s. 1.)

§ 131E-296. Examinations.

The Division may make an examination of the affairs of any provider sponsored organization and the contracts, agreements, or other arrangements pursuant to its health care plan as often as the Division considers necessary for the protection of the interests of the people of this State but not less frequently than once every three years. (1998-227, s. 1.)

§ 131E-297. Hazardous financial condition.

(a)   Whenever the financial condition of any provider sponsored organization indicates a condition such that the continued operation of the provider sponsored organization might be hazardous to its beneficiaries, creditors, or the general public, then the Division may order the provider sponsored organization to take any action that may be reasonably necessary to rectify the existing condition, including one or more of the following steps:

(1)   To reduce the total amount of present and potential liability for benefits by reinsurance;

(2)   To reduce the volume of new business being accepted;

(3)   To reduce the expenses by specified methods;

(4)   To suspend or limit the writing of new business for a period of time;

(5)   To require an increase to the provider sponsored organization's net worth by contribution;

(6)   To add or delete sponsoring providers;

(7)   To increase the amount of payments from the PSO which sponsoring providers agree to forego; or

(8)   To require additional guaranties from sponsoring providers or from parents of sponsoring providers.

(b)   If the Division determines that the standards in G.S. 131E-286, 131E-288, and 131E-289 do not provide sufficient early warning that the continued operation of any provider sponsored organization might be hazardous to its beneficiaries, creditors, or the general public, the Division may adopt rules to set uniform standards and criteria for such an early warning and to set standards for evaluating the financial condition of any provider sponsored organization, which standards shall be consistent with the purposes expressed in subsection (a) of this section. (1998-227, s. 1.)

§ 131E-298. Protection against insolvency.

(a)   The Division shall require deposits in accordance with the provisions of G.S. 131E-285.

(b)   If a provider sponsored organization fails to comply with the net worth requirements of G.S. 131E-286, the Division may take appropriate action to assure that the continued operation of the provider sponsored organization will not be hazardous to the beneficiaries enrolled with the PSO.

(c)   Every provider sponsored organization shall have and maintain at all times an adequate plan for protection against insolvency acceptable to the Division. In determining the adequacy of such a plan, the Division shall consider:

(1)   A reinsurance agreement preapproved by the Division covering excess loss, stop-loss, or catastrophies. The agreement shall provide that the Division will be notified no less than 60 days prior to cancellation or reduction of coverage;

(2)   A conversion policy or policies that will be offered by an insurer to the beneficiaries in the event of the provider sponsored organization's insolvency;

(3)   Legally binding unconditional guaranties by adequately capitalized sponsoring provider or adequately capitalized sponsoring corporations of sponsoring providers;

(4)   Legally binding obligations of sponsoring providers to forego payment for items or services provided by the sponsoring provider in order to avoid the financial insolvency of the PSO;

(5)   Legally binding obligations of sponsoring providers or parents of sponsoring providers to make capital infusions to the PSO; and

(6)   Any other arrangements offering protection against insolvency that the Division may require. (1998-227, s. 1.)

§ 131E-299. Hold harmless agreements or special deposit.

(a)   Unless the PSO maintains a special deposit in accordance with subsection (b) of this section, each contract between every PSO and a participating provider of health care services shall be in writing and shall set forth that in the event the PSO fails to pay for health care services as set forth in the contract, the Medicare subscriber or beneficiary shall not be liable to the provider for any sums owed by the PSO. No other provisions of these contracts shall, under any circumstances, change the effect of this provision. No participating provider or agent, trustee, or assignee thereof may maintain any action at law against a subscriber or beneficiary to collect sums owed by the PSO.

(b)   In the event that the participating provider contract has not been reduced to writing or that the contract fails to contain the required prohibition, the PSO shall maintain a special deposit in cash or cash equivalent as follows:

(1)   If at any time uncovered expenditures exceed ten percent (10%) of total health care expenditures the PSO shall either:

a.   Place an uncovered expenditures insolvency deposit with the Division, or with any organization or trustee acceptable to the Division through which a custodial or controlled account is maintained, cash or securities that are acceptable to the Division. This deposit shall at all times have a fair market value in an amount of one hundred twenty percent (120%) of the PSO's

218

outstanding liability for uncovered expenditures for enrollees, including incurred but not reported claims, and shall be calculated as of the first day of the month and maintained for the remainder of the month. If a PSO is not otherwise required to file a quarterly report, it shall file a report within 45 days of the end of the calendar quarter with information sufficient to demonstrate compliance with this section; or

b.   Maintain adequate insurance or a guaranty arrangement approved in writing by the Division, to pay for any loss to beneficiaries claiming reimbursement due to the insolvency of the PSO. The Division shall approve a guaranty arrangement if the guarantying organization is a sponsoring provider, has been operating for at least 10 years, and has a net worth, including organization-related land, buildings, and equipment of at least fifty million dollars ($50,000,000), unless the Division finds that the approval of this guaranty may be financially hazardous to beneficiaries.

(2)   The deposit required under sub-subdivision a. of subdivision (1) of this subsection is an admitted asset of the PSO in the determination of net worth. All income from these deposits or trust accounts shall be assets of the PSO and may be withdrawn from the deposit or account quarterly with the approval of the Division;

(3)   A PSO that has made a deposit may withdraw that deposit or any part of the deposit if (i) a substitute deposit of cash or securities of equal amount and value is made, (ii) the fair market value exceeds the amount of the required deposit, or (iii) the required deposit under this subsection is reduced or eliminated. Deposits, substitutions, or withdrawals may be made only with the prior written approval of the Division;

(4)   The deposit required under sub-subdivision a. of subdivision (1) of this section is in trust and may be used only as provided under this section. The Division may use the deposit of an insolvent PSO for administrative costs associated with administering the deposit and payment of claims of enrollees of the PSO.

(c)   Whenever the reimbursements described in this section exceed ten percent (10%) of the PSO's total costs for health care services over the immediately preceding six months, the PSO shall file a written report with the Division containing the information necessary to determine compliance with sub-subdivision a. of subdivision (1) of subsection (b) of this section no later than 30 business days from the first day of the month. Upon an adequate showing by

219

the PSO that the requirements of this section should be waived or reduced, the Division may waive or reduce these requirements to an amount it deems sufficient to protect beneficiaries of the PSO consistent with the intent and purpose of this Article. (1998-227, s. 1.)

§ 131E-300. Continuation of benefits.

The Division shall require that each PSO have a plan for handling insolvency, which plan allows for continuation of benefits for the duration of the contract period for which premiums have been paid and continuation of benefits to beneficiaries who are confined in an inpatient facility until their discharge or expiration of benefits. In considering such a plan, the Division may require:

(1)   Insurance to cover the expenses to be paid for benefits after an insolvency;

(2)   Provisions in provider contracts that obligate the provider to provide services for the duration of the period after the PSO's insolvency for which premium payment has been made and until the beneficiaries' discharge from inpatient facilities;

(3)   Insolvency reserves as the Division may require;

(4)   Letters of credit acceptable to the Division;

(5)   Additional guaranties from a sponsoring provider of the PSO or from the parent of a sponsoring provider;

(6)   Legally binding obligations of sponsoring providers to forego payment from the PSO for services provided to beneficiaries in order to avoid the insolvency of the PSO; and

(7)   Any other arrangements to assure that benefits are continued as specified. (1998-227, s. 1.)

§ 131E-301. Insolvency.

(a)   In the event of an insolvency of a PSO upon order of the Division, all providers that were sponsoring providers of the PSO within the previous 12 months from the order of the Division shall, for 30 days after the order, offer all beneficiaries enrolled with the insolvent PSO, covered services without charge other than for any applicable co-payments, deductibles, or coinsurance permitted to be charged to beneficiaries under the PSO's Medicare contract.

(b)   If the Division determines that the sponsoring providers lack sufficient health care delivery resources to assure that health care services will be available and accessible to all of the beneficiaries of the insolvent PSO, then, in the event the Health Care Financing Administration of the United States Department of Health and Human Services fails to make such allocations in a timely manner, the Division shall allocate the insolvent PSO's contracts for these groups among all other PSOs that operate within a portion of the insolvent PSO's service area, taking into consideration the health care delivery resources of each PSO. Each PSO to which beneficiaries are so allocated by the Division shall offer such group or groups that PSO's existing coverage that is most similar to each beneficiary's coverage with the insolvent PSO at rates determined in accordance with the successor PSO's existing rating methodology.

(c)   Taking into consideration the health care delivery resources of each such PSO, then in the event the Health Care Financing Administration of the United States Department of Health and Human Services fails to make such allocations in a timely manner, the Division shall also allocate among all PSOs that operate within a portion of the insolvent PSO's service area the insolvent PSO's beneficiaries who are unable to obtain other coverage. Each PSO to which beneficiaries are so allocated by the Division shall offer such beneficiaries that PSO's existing coverage for individual or conversion coverage as determined by the beneficiary's type of coverage in the insolvent PSO at rates determined in accordance with the successor PSO's Medicare contract. (1998-227, s. 1.)

§ 131E-302. Replacement coverage.

(a)   Any carrier providing replacement coverage with respect to hospital, medical, or surgical expense or service benefits, within a period of 60 days from the date of discontinuance of a prior PSO contract or policy providing these hospital, medical, or surgical expense or service benefits, shall immediately cover all beneficiaries who were validly covered under the previous PSO contract or policy at the date of discontinuance and who would otherwise be eligible for coverage under the succeeding carrier's contract, regardless of any provisions of the contract relating to hospital confinement or pregnancy.

(b)   Except to the extent benefits for the condition would have been reduced or excluded under the prior carrier's contract or policy, no provision in a succeeding carrier's contract of replacement coverage that would operate to reduce or exclude benefits on the basis that the condition giving rise to benefits preceded the effective date of the succeeding carrier's contract shall be applied with respect to those beneficiaries validly covered under the prior carrier's contract on the date of discontinuance. (1998-227, s. 1.)

§ 131E-303. Incurred but not reported claims.

(a)   Every PSO shall, when determining liability, include an amount estimated in the aggregate to provide for any unearned premium and for the payment of all claims for health care expenditures that have been incurred, whether reported or unreported, that are unpaid and for which such PSO is or may be liable, and to provide for the expense of adjustment or settlement of such claims.

(b)   These liabilities shall be computed in accordance with rules adopted by the Division upon reasonable consideration of the ascertained experience and character of the PSO. (1998-227, s. 1.)

§ 131E-304. Suspension or revocation of license.

(a)   The Division may suspend, revoke, or refuse to renew a PSO license if the Division finds that the PSO:

(1)   Is operating significantly in contravention of its basic organizational document, or in a manner contrary to that described in and reasonably inferred from any other information submitted under G.S. 131E-280, unless amendments to these submissions have been filed with and approved by the Division;

(2)   Issues evidences of coverage or uses a schedule of premiums for health care services that do not comply with Medicare or Medicaid program requirements as applicable;

(3)   No longer maintains the financial reserve specified in G.S. 131E-286 or is no longer financially responsible and may reasonably be expected to be unable to meet its obligations to beneficiaries or prospective beneficiaries;

(4)   Knowingly or repeatedly fails or refuses to comply with any law or rule applicable to the PSO or with any order issued by the Division after notice and opportunity for a hearing;

(5)   Has knowingly made to the Division any false statement or report;

(6)   Has sponsoring providers that fail to provide a substantial proportion of the services under any health plan during any 12-month period;

(7)   Has itself or through any person on its behalf advertised or merchandised its items or services in an untrue, misrepresentative, misleading, or unfair manner;

(8)   If continuing to operate would be hazardous to beneficiaries; or

(9)   Has otherwise substantially failed to comply with this Article.

(b)   A license shall be suspended or revoked only after compliance with G.S. 131E-305.

(c)   When a PSO license is suspended, the PSO shall not, during the suspension, enroll any additional beneficiaries and shall not engage in any advertising or solicitation.

(d)   When a PSO license is revoked, the PSO shall proceed, immediately following the effective date of the order of revocation, to wind up its affairs and shall conduct no further business except as may be essential to the orderly conclusion of the affairs of the PSO. The PSO shall engage in no advertising or solicitation. The Division may, by written order, permit any further operation of the PSO that the Division may find to be in the best interest of beneficiaries, to the end that beneficiaries will be afforded the greatest practical opportunity to obtain continuing health care coverage. (1998-227, s. 1.)

§ 131E-305. Administrative procedures.

(a)   When the Division has cause to believe that grounds for the denial of an application for a license exist, or that grounds for the suspension or revocation of a license exist, it shall notify the provider sponsored organization in writing specifically stating the grounds for denial, suspension, or revocation and fixing a time of at least 30 days thereafter for a hearing on the matter.

(b)   After this hearing, or upon the failure of the provider sponsored organization to appear at this hearing, the Division shall take the action it considers advisable or make written findings that shall be mailed to the provider sponsored organization. The action of the Division shall be subject to review by the Superior Court of Wake County. The court may, in disposing of the issue before it, modify, affirm, or reverse the order of the Division in whole or in part.

(c)   The provisions of Chapter 150B of the General Statutes apply to proceedings under this section to the extent that they are not in conflict with subsections (a) and (b) of this section. (1998-227, s. 1.)

§ 131E-306. Expired.

§ 131E-307. Penalties and enforcement.

(a)   The provisions of G.S. 58-2-70, modified to replace the word "Commissioner" by the word "Division", applies to this Article. The Division may, in addition to or in lieu of suspending or revoking a license under G.S. 131E-304, proceed under G.S. 58-2-70, as so modified, provided that the provider sponsored organization has a reasonable time within which to remedy the defect in its operations that gave rise to the procedure under G.S. 58-2-70.

(b)   Any person who violates this Article shall be guilty of a Class 1 misdemeanor.

(c)   If the Division shall for any reason have cause to believe that any violation of this Article has occurred or is threatened, the Division may give notice to the provider sponsored organization and to the representatives or other persons who appear to be involved in such suspected violation to arrange a conference with the alleged violators or their authorized representatives for the purpose of attempting to ascertain the facts relating to such suspected violation, and, in the event it appears that any violation has occurred or is threatened, to arrive at an adequate and effective means of correcting or preventing such violation.

Proceedings under this subsection shall not be governed by any formal procedural requirements and may be conducted in such manner as the Division may deem appropriate under the circumstances.

(d)   The Division may issue an order directing a provider sponsored organization or a representative of a provider sponsored organization to cease and desist from engaging in any act or practice in violation of the provisions of this Article.

Within 30 days after service of the order of cease and desist, the respondent may request a hearing on the question of whether acts or practices in violation of this Article have occurred. These hearings shall be conducted pursuant to Chapter 150B of the General Statutes, and judicial review shall be available as provided by this Chapter.

(e)   In the case of any violation of the provisions of this Article, if the Division elects not to issue a cease and desist order, or in the event of noncompliance with a cease and desist order issued pursuant to subsection (d) of this section, the Division may institute a proceeding to obtain injunctive relief, or seeking other appropriate relief, in the Superior Court of Wake County. (1998-227, s. 1.)

§ 131E-308. Statutory construction and relationship to other laws.

(a)   Except as otherwise provided in this Article, provisions of the insurance laws and provisions of hospital or medical service corporation laws shall not be applicable to any provider sponsored organization granted a license under this Article or to its sponsoring providers when operating under such a license. This provision shall not apply to an insurer or hospital or medical service corporation licensed and regulated pursuant to the insurance laws or the hospital or medical service corporation laws of this State except with respect to its provider sponsored organization activities authorized and regulated pursuant to this Article.

225

(b)   Solicitation of beneficiaries by a provider sponsored organization granted a license, or its representatives, shall not be construed to violate any provision of law relating to solicitation or advertising by health professionals or health care providers.

(c)   Any provider sponsored organization licensed under this Article shall not be considered to be a provider of medicine and shall be exempt from the provisions of Chapter 90 of the General Statutes relating to the practice of medicine: provided, however, that this exemption does not apply to individual providers under contract with or employed by the provider sponsored organization or sponsoring providers or to the sponsoring providers.

(d)   Except as otherwise limited by this Article, a PSO may organize in the same manner and may exercise the same prerogatives, powers, and privileges as other entities that are organized and existing under the same laws as the PSO. (1998-227, s. 1.)

§ 131E-309. Filings and reports as public documents.

Except for information that constitutes a bona fide trade secret, proprietary information or competitively sensitive information of a sponsoring provider or parent of a sponsoring provider, all applications, filings, and reports required under this Article shall be treated as public documents. (1998-227, s. 1.)

§ 131E-310. Confidentiality of medical information.

Any data or information pertaining to the diagnosis, treatment, or health of any beneficiary or applicant obtained from the person or from any provider by any provider sponsored organization or by any provider acting pursuant to its provider contract with a provider sponsored organization shall be held in confidence and shall not be disclosed to any person except to the extent that it may be necessary to carry out the purposes of this Article; or upon the express consent of the beneficiary or applicant; or pursuant to statute; or pursuant to court order for the production of evidence or the discovery thereof; or in the event of claim or litigation between such person and the provider sponsored organization wherein such data or information is pertinent. A provider sponsored organization shall be entitled to claim any statutory privileges against such disclosure which the provider who furnished such information to the provider sponsored organization is entitled to claim. (1998-227, s. 1; 1999-272, s. 2.)

§ 131E-311. Conflicts; severability.

To the extent that the provisions of this Article may be in conflict with any other provision of this Chapter, the provisions of this Article shall prevail and apply with respect to provider sponsored organizations. Notwithstanding the absence of adopted rules, the Division shall continue to process applications for provider sponsored organization licenses as described in this Article. If any section, term, or provision of this Article shall be adjudged invalid for any reason, these judgments shall not affect, impair, or invalidate any other section, term, or provision of this Article, but the remaining sections, terms, and provisions shall be and remain in full force and effect. (1998-227, s. 1.)

§ 131E-312. Regulations.

This Article shall be self-implementing. No later than six months after the date of enactment of this Article, the Division may adopt rules consistent with this Article to authorize and regulate provider sponsored organizations to contract directly with the federal Medicare program to provide health care services to the beneficiaries of such programs. The Division shall issue permanent rules and, may issue temporary rules, to the extent these rules may be necessary. The Division shall limit its regulation of provider sponsored organizations to the licensing and regulating of these organizations as risk-bearing entities contracting directly with the Medicare program and to the consumer protection and quality standards as provided in G.S. 131E-294 and shall not regulate any matters described in 42 U.S.C. § 1395W-26(b)(3), or any successor thereof. (1998-227, s. 1.)

§ 131E-313. Utilization review and grievances.

Unless otherwise preempted by federal law or mandated by the Medicare program, the provisions of G.S. 58-50-61 and G.S. 58-50-62 apply to a PSO licensed under this Article as if the PSO was an "insurer" under those sections, except that the Division rather than the Commissioner of Insurance shall regulate a PSO's compliance with those sections. (1998-227, s. 1.)

§ 131E-314. Division Reporting.

The Division of Medical Assistance of the Department of Health and Human Services shall report quarterly to the Joint Legislative Oversight Committee on Health and Human Services on its regulatory activities in the enforcement of this Article and shall provide the Committee with a summary of nonconfidential information on the financial plans and operations of PSOs. The report to the Committee shall include a description and explanation of any regulations or regulatory interpretations that differ from Department of Insurance regulations applicable to HMOs. The report shall also include PSO efforts to improve community health status. The Division shall develop processes or methods to measure improvements in health outcomes for Medicare beneficiaries served by managed care organizations and shall report quarterly to the Joint Legislative Oversight Committee on Health and Human Services on the development of these standards. (1998-227, ss. 4, 5; 2011-291, s. 2.49.)

Chapter 131F.

Solicitation of Contributions.

Article 1.

General Provisions.

§ 131F-1. Purpose.

The General Assembly recognizes the right of persons or organizations to conduct solicitation activities. It is the intent of the General Assembly to protect the public by requiring full disclosure by persons who solicit contributions from the public of the purposes for which the contributions are solicited and how the contributions are actually used. It is the intent of the General Assembly to prohibit deception, fraud, and misrepresentation in the solicitation and reporting of contributions. (1981, c. 886, s. 1; 1993 (Reg. Sess., 1994), c. 759, s. 2.)

§ 131F-2. Definitions.

The following definitions apply in this Chapter:

(1) "Association" means any voluntary statewide organization of persons for common ends especially as in an organized group working together or periodically meeting because of common interests, beliefs, or professions. These associations may serve charitable organizations including environmental, health, educational, humane, patriotic, scientific, artistic, social welfare, and civic.

(2) "Charitable" means for a benevolent purpose, including environmental, health, educational, humane, patriotic, scientific, artistic, social welfare, and civic.

(3) "Charitable organization" means any person who has or holds out as having a section 501(c)(3) tax exempt determination by the Internal Revenue Service and operates for a charitable purpose, or a person who is or holds himself out to be established for a charitable or civic purpose; or a person who employs a charitable or civic appeal as the basis of a solicitation, or employs an appeal that suggests there is a charitable or civic purpose for the appeal. "Charitable organization" includes a chapter, branch, area office, or similar affiliate soliciting contributions within the State for a charitable organization which has its principal place of business outside the State.

(4) "Charitable sales promotion" means an advertising or sales campaign that represents that the purchase or use of goods or services offered by a coventurer is to benefit a charitable organization. The provision of advertising services alone to a charitable organization does not constitute a charitable sales promotion.

(4a) "Collection Receptacle" means an unattended box, bin, canister, or other similar container used for the solicitation and collection of clothing and household goods and other miscellaneous items.

(5) "Contribution" means a promise, pledge, grant of any money or property, financial assistance, or any other thing of value in response to a solicitation. "Contribution" includes, in the case of a charitable organization or sponsor offering a good or service to the public, the excess of the price at which the charitable organization or sponsor or any person acting on behalf of the charitable organization or sponsor sells the good or service to the public over

229

the fair market value of the good or service. "Contribution" does not include bona fide fees, dues, or assessments paid by members if the membership is not conferred solely as consideration for making a contribution in response to a solicitation. "Contribution" does not include funds obtained by a charitable organization or sponsor under government grants or contracts.

(6)   "Coventurer" means any person who, for compensation, conducts a charitable sales promotion or a sponsor sales promotion, other than in connection with the solicitation of contributions.

(7)   "Department" means the Department of the Secretary of State.

(8)   "Emergency service employees" means employees who are firefighters, ambulance drivers, emergency medical technicians, or paramedics.

(9)   "Federated fund-raising organization" means a federation of independent charitable organizations which have voluntarily joined together, including a united way, united arts fund, or community chest, for the purpose of raising and distributing contributions and where membership does not confer operating authority and control of the individual organization upon the federated group organization.

(10)   "Fund-raising consultant" means any person who meets all of the following:

a.   Is retained by a charitable organization or sponsor for a fixed fee or rate under a written agreement to plan, manage, conduct, consult, or prepare material for the solicitation of contributions in this State.

b.   Does not solicit contributions or employ, procure, or engage any person to solicit contributions.

c.   Does not at any time have custody or control of contributions.

(11)   "Fund-raising costs" means those costs incurred in inducing others to make contributions to a charitable organization or sponsor for which the contributors will receive no direct economic benefit. Fund-raising costs include salaries, rent, acquiring and obtaining mailing lists, printing, mailing, all direct and indirect costs of soliciting, and the cost of unsolicited merchandise sent to encourage contributions.

(12)   "Law enforcement officers" means persons who are elected, appointed, or employed by the State or any political subdivision of the State and who meet either of the following:

a.   Are vested with the authority to bear arms and make arrests and have primary responsibility to prevent and detect crime or enforce the criminal, traffic, or highway laws of the State.

b.   Have responsibility for supervision, protection, care, custody, or control of inmates within a correctional institution.

(12a)   "Maintenance" means to keep in working order in order to ensure that something continues to work properly and includes regular checks and the completion of any required repairs and adjustments.

(13)   "Membership" means the relationship of a person to an organization that entitles that person to the privileges, professional standing, honors, or other direct benefits of the organization in addition to the right to vote, elect officers, and hold office in the organization.

(14)   "Owner" means any person who has a direct or indirect interest in any fund-raising consultant or solicitor.

(15)   "Parent organization" means that part of a charitable organization or sponsor which coordinates, supervises, or exercises control over policy, fund-raising, and expenditures, or assists or advises one or more chapters, branches, or affiliates of a charitable organization or sponsor.

(16)   "Person" means any individual, organization, trust, foundation, association, group, entity, partnership, corporation, society, or any combination of these acting as a unit.

(17)   "Religious institution" means any church, ecclesiastical, or denominational organization, or any established physical place for worship in this State at which nonprofit religious services and activities are regularly conducted, and any bona fide religious groups that do not maintain specific places of worship. "Religious institution" includes any separate group or corporation that forms an integral part of a religious institution that is exempt from federal income tax under the provisions of section 501(c)(3) of the Internal Revenue Code, and that is primarily supported by funds solicited inside its own membership or congregation.

231

(18)   "Solicitation" means a request, directly or indirectly, for money, property, financial assistance, or any other thing of value on the plea or representation that it will be used for a charitable or sponsor purpose or will benefit a charitable organization or sponsor. "Solicitation" may occur by any of the following methods:

a.   Any oral or written request.

b.   Any announcement to the press, radio, or television, by telephone or telegraph, or by any other communication device.

c.   Distributing, posting, or publishing any handbill, written advertisement, or other publication that directly or by implication seeks to obtain any contribution.

d.   Selling or offering or attempting to sell any good, service, chance, right, or any thing of value to benefit a charitable organization or sponsor.

The selling or offering or attempting to sell is a "solicitation" whether or not the person making the solicitation receives any contribution. It is not a "solicitation" when a person applies for a grant or an award to the government or to an organization that is exempt from federal income taxation under section 501(a) of the Internal Revenue Code and described in section 501(c) of the Internal Revenue Code.

e.   Placing or maintaining a collection receptacle in public view for the purpose of collecting donated clothing, household items, and other items for resale.

(19)   "Solicitor" means any person who, for compensation, does not qualify as a fund-raising consultant and does either of the following:

a.   Performs any service, including the employment or engagement of other persons or services, to solicit contributions for a charitable organization or sponsor.

b.   Plans, conducts, manages, consults, whether directly or indirectly, in connection with the solicitation of contributions for a charitable organization or sponsor.

(20)   "Sponsor" means a person who is or holds out to others as soliciting contributions by the use of any name that implies affiliation with emergency

service employees or law enforcement officers and who is not a charitable organization. "Sponsor" includes a chapter, branch, or affiliate that has its principal place of business outside the State, if this chapter, branch, or affiliate solicits or holds out to be soliciting contributions in this State.

(21)   "Sponsor purpose" means any program or endeavor performed to benefit emergency service employees or law enforcement officers.

(22)   "Sponsor sales promotion" means an advertising or sales campaign conducted by a coventurer who represents that the purchase or use of goods or services offered by the coventurer will be used for a sponsor purpose or donated to a sponsor. The provision of advertising services alone to a sponsor does not constitute a sponsor sales promotion. (1981, c. 886, s. 1; 1985, c. 497, s. 2; 1993 (Reg. Sess., 1994), c. 759, s. 2; 1997-443, s. 11A.118(a); 1998-212, s. 12.14(b); 2011-319, ss. 1, 2.)

§ 131F-3. Exemptions.

The following are exempt from the provisions of this Chapter:

(1)   Any person who solicits charitable contributions for a religious institution.

(2)   Solicitation of charitable contributions by the federal, State, or local government, or any of their agencies.

(3)   Any person who receives less than twenty-five thousand dollars ($25,000) in contributions in any calendar year and does not provide compensation to any officer, trustee, organizer, incorporator, fund-raiser, or solicitor.

(4)   Any educational institution, the curriculum of which, in whole or in part, is registered, approved, or accredited by the Southern Association of Colleges and Schools or an equivalent regional accrediting body, any educational institution in compliance with Article 39 of Chapter 115C of the General Statutes, any foundation or department having an established identity with any of these educational institutions, and any organization with a membership that is composed solely of 20 or more educational institutions as defined under this Chapter.

233

(5)   Any hospital licensed pursuant to Article 5 of Chapter 131E or Article 2 of Chapter 122C of the General Statutes and any foundation or department having an established identity with that hospital if the governing board of the hospital, authorizes the solicitation and receives an accounting of the funds collected and expended.

(6)   Any noncommercial radio or television station.

(7)   A qualified community trust as provided in 26 C.F.R. § 1.170A-9(e)(10) through (e)(14).

(8)   A bona fide volunteer or bona fide employee or salaried officer of a charitable organization or sponsor.

(9)   An attorney, investment counselor, or banker who advises a person to make a charitable contribution.

(10)   A volunteer fire department, REACT (Radio Emergency Associated Communications Teams), rescue squad, or emergency medical service.

(11)   A Young Men's Christian Association or a Young Women's Christian Association.

(12)   A nonprofit continuing care facility licensed under Article 64 of Chapter 58 of the General Statutes.

(13)   Any tax exempt nonprofit fire or emergency medical service organization involved in the sale of goods or services that does not ask for a donation. (1981, c. 886, s. 1; 1983, c. 320, ss. 1, 2; 1991, c. 45, s. 24; 1993 (Reg. Sess., 1994), c. 759, s. 2; 1995 (Reg. Sess., 1996), c. 650, s. 1; 1997-329, s. 1; 2003-373, s. 3; 2005-230, s. 1; 2011-27, s. 1.)

§ 131F-4. Reserved for future codification purposes.

Article 2.

Charitable Organizations and Sponsors.

§ 131F-5. Licensure of charitable organizations and sponsors required.

(a)   License Required. - Unless exempted under G.S. 131F-3, a charitable organization, sponsor, or person that intends to solicit contributions in this State, to have funds solicited on its behalf, or to participate in a charitable sales promotion or sponsor sales promotion shall obtain a license by filing an application with the Department, obtaining approval of that application by the Department, and paying the applicable fee.

(b)   Departmental Review. - The Department shall examine each application filed by a charitable organization or sponsor and shall determine whether the licensing requirements are satisfied. If the Department determines that the requirements are not satisfied, the Department shall notify the charitable organization or sponsor within 10 days after its receipt of the application. If the Department does not notify the charitable organization or sponsor within 10 days, the application is deemed to be approved and the license shall be granted. Within seven days after receipt of a notification that the requirements are not satisfied, the charitable organization or sponsor may file a petition for a contested case. The State has the burden of proof in the contested case. The contested case hearing must be held within seven days after the petition is filed. A final decision must be made within five days of the hearing. The contested case hearing proceedings shall be conducted in accordance with Chapter 150B of the General Statutes except that the time limits and provisions set forth in this section shall prevail to the extent of any conflict. The applicant shall be permitted to continue to operate or continue operations pending judicial review of the Department's denial of the application. The Department shall make rules regarding the custody and control of any funds collected during the review period and disposal of such funds in the event the denial of the application is affirmed on appeal.

(c)   License Renewal. - The license shall be renewed on an annual basis. Any change in information from the original application for a license shall be filed annually on or before the fifteenth day of the fifth calendar month after the close of each fiscal year in which the charitable organization or sponsor solicited in this State, or by the date of any applicable extension of the federal filing date, whichever is later, provided that extensions given under this section shall not exceed three months after the initial renewal date or eight months after the conclusion of the year for which financial information is due at the time of renewal. A charitable organization or sponsor whose federal filing date has been extended shall, within seven days after receipt, forward a copy of the document granting the extension to the Department.

(d)   Extension of Time. - For good cause shown, the Department may extend the time for the license renewal and the annual filing of updated information for a period not to exceed 60 days, during which time the previous license shall remain in effect. (1981, c. 886, s. 1; 1985, c. 497, s. 3; 1987, c. 827, ss. 1, 239; 1989, c. 566, s. 1; 1993 (Reg. Sess., 1994), c. 759, s. 2; 2011-398, s. 47.)

§ 131F-6. Information required for licensure.

(a)   Initial Information Required. - The initial application for a license for a charitable organization or sponsor shall be submitted on a form provided by the Department, signed under oath by the treasurer or chief fiscal officer of the charitable organization or sponsor, and shall include the following:

(1)   The name of the charitable organization or sponsor, the purpose for which it is organized, the name under which it intends to solicit contributions, and the purpose for which the contributions to be solicited will be used.

(2)   The principal street address and telephone number of the charitable organization or sponsor and the street address and telephone numbers of any offices in this State or, if the charitable organization or sponsor does not maintain an office in this State, the name, street address, and telephone number of the person who has custody of its financial records. The parent organization that files a consolidated registration statement under G.S. 131F-7 on behalf of its chapters, branches, or affiliates shall additionally provide the street addresses and telephone numbers of all of its locations in this State.

(3)   The names and street addresses of the officers, directors, trustees, and the salaried executive personnel.

(4)   The date when the charitable organization's or sponsor's fiscal year ends.

(5)   A list or description of the major program activities.

(6)   The names, street addresses, and telephone numbers of the individuals or officers who have final responsibility for the custody of the contributions and who will be responsible for the final distribution of the contributions.

236

(7)   The name of the individuals or officers who are in charge of any solicitation activities.

(8)   A financial report for the immediately preceding fiscal year upon a form provided by the Department. The report shall include the following:

a.   The balance sheet.

b.   A statement of support, revenue, and expenses, and any change in the fund balance.

c.   Repealed by Session Laws 1995 (Regular Session, 1996), c. 748, s. 1.3.

d.   A statement of expenses in the following categories:

1.   Program.

2.   Management and general.

3.   Fund-raising.

(9)   In substitution for the information described in subdivisions (3), (4), (5), (6), and (8) of this subsection, a charitable organization or sponsor may submit, at the time the application is filed, a copy of its Internal Revenue Service Form 990 and Schedule A filed for the preceding fiscal year, or a copy of its Form 990-EZ filed for the preceding fiscal year.

(10)   A charitable organization or sponsor may include a financial report which has been audited by an independent certified public accountant or an audit with opinion by an independent certified public accountant. In the event that a charitable organization or sponsor elects to file this, this optional filing shall be noted in the Department's annual report submitted under G.S. 131F-30.

(11)   A newly organized charitable organization or sponsor with no financial history shall file a budget for the current fiscal year.

(12)   A statement indicating all of the following:

a.   Whether or not the charitable organization or sponsor is authorized by any other state to solicit contributions.

b.   Whether or not the charitable organization or sponsor or any of its officers, directors, trustees, or salaried executive personnel have been enjoined in any jurisdiction from soliciting contributions or have been found to have engaged in unlawful practices in the solicitation of contributions or administration of charitable assets.

c.   Whether or not the charitable organization or sponsor has had its authority denied, suspended, or revoked by any governmental agency, together with the reasons for the denial, suspension, or revocation.

d.   Whether or not the charitable organization or sponsor has voluntarily entered into an assurance of voluntary compliance or agreement similar to that set forth in G.S. 131F-24(c), together with a copy of that agreement.

(13)   The names, street addresses, and telephone numbers of any solicitor, fund-raising consultant, or coventurer who is acting or has agreed to act on behalf of the charitable organization or sponsor, together with a statement setting forth the specific terms of the arrangements for salaries, bonuses, commissions, expenses, or other compensation to be paid the fund-raising consultant, solicitor, or coventurer, and the amounts received from each of them, if any.

(14)   With initial licensing only, when and where the organization was established, the tax-exempt status of the organization, and a copy of any federal tax exemption determination letter. If the charitable organization or sponsor has not received a federal tax exemption determination letter at the time of initial licensing, a copy of the determination shall be filed with the Department within 30 days after receipt of the determination by the charitable organization or sponsor. If the organization is subsequently notified by the Internal Revenue Service of any challenge to its continued entitlement to federal tax exemption, the charitable organization or sponsor shall notify the Department of this fact within 30 days after receipt.

(b)   Renewal Information Required. - A license shall be renewed on an annual basis. The charitable organization or sponsor shall submit any changes in the information submitted from the initial application. (1981, c. 886, s. 1; 1993 (Reg. Sess., 1994), c. 759, s. 2; 1995 (Reg. Sess., 1996), c. 748, s. 1.3.)

§ 131F-7. Consolidated application and renewal.

238

(a)   Election to File Consolidated Application. - Each chapter, branch, member, or affiliate of a parent organization or association that is required to obtain a license under G.S. 131F-5 shall either file a separate application or shall report the required information to its parent organization or association. The parent organization or association may then file, on a form provided by the Department, a consolidated application for the parent organization or association and its chapters, branches, members, and affiliates located in this State.

(b)   Consolidated Financial Information. - If all contributions received by chapters, branches, or affiliates are remitted directly into the parent organization's centralized accounting system from which all disbursements are made, the parent organization may submit one consolidated financial report as part of the application on a form provided by the Department.

(c)   Renewal Information. - The parent organization or association may file the information required for a renewal of a license in a consolidated form provided by the Department. (1993 (Reg. Sess., 1994), c. 759, s. 2.)

§ 131F-8. License fees.

(a)   Required Fees. - Except as provided in subsections (b) and (c) of this section, every charitable organization or sponsor shall pay the following fees with each license application:

(1)   Fifty dollars ($50.00), if the contributions received for the last fiscal year were less than one hundred thousand dollars ($100,000).

(2)   One hundred dollars ($100.00), if the contributions received for the last fiscal year were one hundred thousand dollars ($100,000) or more, but less than two hundred thousand dollars ($200,000).

(3)   Two hundred dollars ($200.00), if the contributions received for the last fiscal year were two hundred thousand dollars ($200,000) or more.

(b)   Exemption. - A licensed charitable organization or sponsor that received less than five thousand dollars ($5,000) in the last calendar or fiscal year shall not pay a fee.

(c)   Parent Organization. - A parent organization or association filing on behalf of one or more chapters, branches, members, or affiliates shall pay a single license fee for itself and its other chapters, branches, members, or affiliates. These license fees shall be imposed as follows:

(1)   One hundred dollars ($100.00) for a parent organization or association and one to five chapters, branches, members, or affiliates.

(2)   Two hundred dollars ($200.00) for a parent organization or association and 6 to 10 chapters, branches, members, or affiliates.

(3)   Two hundred fifty dollars ($250.00) for a parent organization or association and 11 to 15 chapters, branches, members, or affiliates.

(4)   Four hundred dollars ($400.00) for a parent organization or association and 16 or more chapters, branches, members, or affiliates.

(d)   Late Filing. - A charitable organization or sponsor which fails to file the renewal information by the due date may be assessed an additional fee for the late filing. The late filing fee shall be established by rule of the Department and shall not exceed twenty-five dollars ($25.00) for each month or part of a month after the date on which the information was due to be filed or after the period of extension granted for the filing. (1981, c. 886, s. 1; 1993 (Reg. Sess., 1994), c. 759, s. 2.)

§ 131F-9. Disclosure requirements of charitable organizations and sponsors.

(a)   Contributions for Expressed Purpose. - A charitable organization or sponsor shall solicit contributions only for the purpose expressed in its application and may apply contributions only in a manner substantially consistent with that purpose.

(b)   Disclosures. - A charitable organization or sponsor soliciting in this State shall include all of the following disclosures at the point of solicitation:

(1)   The name of the charitable organization and state of the principal place of business of the charitable organization or sponsor.

(2)   A description of the purpose for which the solicitation is being made.

(3)   Upon request, the name and either the address or telephone number of a representative to whom inquiries could be addressed.

(4)   Upon request, the amount of the contribution which may be deducted as a charitable contribution under federal income tax laws.

(5)   Upon request, the source from which a written financial statement may be obtained. The financial statement shall be for the immediate past fiscal year and shall be consistent with G.S. 131F-6. The written financial statement shall be provided within 14 days after the request and shall state the purpose for which funds are raised, the total amount of all contributions raised, the total costs and expenses incurred in raising contributions, the total amount of contributions dedicated to the stated purpose or disbursed for the stated purpose, and whether the services of another person or organization have been contracted to conduct solicitation activities.

(c)   Printed Disclosure. - Every charitable organization or sponsor that is required to obtain a license under G.S. 131F-5 shall conspicuously display in type of a minimum size nine points, the following statement on every printed solicitation, written confirmation, receipt, or reminder of a contribution:

"Financial information about this organization and a copy of its license are available from the State Solicitation Licensing Branch at [telephone number]. The license is not an endorsement by the State."

The statement shall be made conspicuous by use of one or more of the following: underlining, a border, or bold type. When the solicitation consists of more than one piece, the statement shall be displayed prominently in the solicitation materials, but not necessarily on every page.

(d)   Collection Receptacle Disclosure. - Any person who is required to obtain a license under any provision of this Chapter and who is soliciting donated clothing, household items, and other items for resale through the use of a collection receptacle shall display on all sides of each collection receptacle a permanent sign or label with the name of the charitable organization or sponsor for whom the solicitation is made and the phone number or electronic mail address of a contact at the charitable organization or sponsor. The sign or label shall be placed on all sides of the collection receptacle with the required information printed in letters that are no less than three inches in height and no less than one-half inch in width and in a color that contrasts with the color of the collection receptacle so that the sign or label is clearly visible. Upon request, the

241

charitable organization or sponsor must provide the donor with documentation of its tax exempt status and license issued under this Chapter. (1985, c. 497, s. 8; 1989, c. 566, s. 3; 1993 (Reg. Sess., 1994), c. 759, s. 2; 1995 (Reg. Sess., 1996), c. 748, s. 1.1; 2011-319, s. 3.)

§ 131F-10. Disclosure requirements for other organizations.

Any person who is not a charitable organization or sponsor and who places or maintains a collection receptacle in public view for the purpose of collecting donated clothing, household items, and other items for resale shall display on all sides of each collection receptacle a permanent sign or label with the phone number or electronic mail address of a contact for the person and the following statement: "This is not a charity. Donations made here support a for-profit business and are not tax deductible." The sign or label shall be placed on all sides of the collection receptacle with the required information printed in letters that are no less than three inches in height and no less than one-half inch in width and in a color that contrasts with the color of the collection receptacle so that the sign or label is clearly visible. Upon request, the person must provide the donor with documentation of its license issued under this Chapter. (2011-319, s. 4.)

§ 131F-11. Reserved for future codification purposes.

§ 131F-12. Reserved for future codification purposes.

§ 131F-13. Reserved for future codification purposes.

§ 131F-14. Reserved for future codification purposes.

Article 3.

Fund-Raising Consultants, Solicitors, and Coventurers.

§ 131F-15. License required for fund-raising consultant.

(a)   License Required. - Unless exempted under G.S. 131F-3, a person shall not act as a fund-raising consultant in this State unless that person has obtained a license from the Department.

(b)   License Application. - Applications for a license or renewal of a license shall be submitted on a form provided by the Department, shall be signed under oath, and shall include the following:

(1)   The street address and telephone number of the principal place of business of the applicant and any street addresses of business locations in this State if the principal place of business is located outside this State.

(2)   The form of the applicant's business.

(3)   The names and residence addresses of all officers, directors, and owners.

(4)   Whether any of the owners, directors, officers, or employees of the applicant are related as parent, child, spouse, or sibling to any of the following individuals:

a.   Other directors, officers, owners, or employees of the applicant.

b.   Any officer, director, trustee, or employee of any charitable organization or sponsor under contract to the applicant.

c.   Any supplier or vendor providing goods or services to any charitable organization or sponsor under contract to the applicant.

(5)   Whether the applicant or any of the applicant's officers, directors, employees, or owners have, within the last five years, been convicted of any felony, or of any misdemeanor arising from the conduct of a solicitation for a charitable organization or sponsor or charitable or sponsor purpose, or been enjoined from violating a charitable solicitation law in this or any other state.

(c)   Fees. - The application for an initial or renewal license shall be accompanied by a license fee of two hundred dollars ($200.00). A fund-raising consultant that is a partnership or corporation may obtain a license for and pay a single fee on behalf of all of its partners, members, officers, directors, agents, and employees. In that case, the names and street addresses of all of the officers, employees, and agents of the fund-raising consultant and all other

243

persons with whom the fund-raising consultant has contracted to work under its direction shall be listed in the license application. Each license is valid for one year or a part of one year and expires on March 31 of each year. The license may be renewed on or before March 31 of each year for additional one-year periods upon application to the Department and payment of the license fee.

(d)   Contracts. - Every contract or agreement between a fund/y-raising consultant and a charitable organization or sponsor shall be in writing, signed by two authorized officials of the charitable organization or sponsor, and filed by the fund-raising consultant with the Department at least five days prior to the performance of any service by the fund-raising consultant. Solicitation under the contract or agreement shall not begin before the filing of the contract or agreement. The contract shall contain all of the following provisions:

(1)   A statement of the charitable purpose or sponsor purpose for which the solicitation campaign is being conducted.

(2)   A statement of the respective obligations of the fund-raising consultant and the charitable organization or sponsor.

(3)   A clear statement of the fee that will be paid to the fund-raising consultant.

(4)   The effective and termination dates.

(5)   A statement that the fund-raising consultant shall not, at any time, have control or custody of contributions.

(e)   Departmental Review. - The Department shall examine each application or renewal filed by a fund-raising consultant and determine whether the requirements are satisfied. If the Department determines that the requirements are not satisfied, the Department shall notify the fund-raising consultant within 10 days after its receipt of the application or renewal. If the Department does not respond within 10 days, the license is deemed approved. Within seven days after receipt of a notification that the license requirements are not satisfied, the applicant may file a petition for a contested case. The State has the burden of proof in the contested case. The contested case hearing must be held within seven days after the petition is filed. A final decision must be made within five days of the hearing. The contested case hearing proceedings shall be conducted in accordance with Chapter 150B of the General Statutes, except that the time limits and provisions set forth in this section shall prevail to the

244

extent of any conflict. The applicant shall be permitted to continue to operate or continue operations pending judicial review of the Department's denial of the application. The Department shall make rules regarding the custody and control of any funds collected during the review period and disposal of such funds in the event the denial of the application is affirmed on appeal.

(f)   Fund. - All license fees shall be paid to the Department and deposited into the Solicitation of Contributions Fund to be used to pay the costs incurred in administering and enforcing this Chapter.

(g)   Change in Information. - Unless otherwise provided, any material change in information filed with the Department pursuant to this section shall be reported in writing to the Department within seven working days after the change occurred. (1981, c. 886, s. 1; 1985, c. 497, s. 1; 1989, c. 566, s. 2; 1993 (Reg. Sess., 1994), c. 759, s. 2; 2011-398, s. 48.)

§ 131F-16. License required for solicitors.

(a)   Licensure Required. - Unless exempted under G.S. 131F-3, a person shall not act as a solicitor in this State unless that person has obtained a license from the Department and paid the applicable fees.

(b)   Applications. - Applications for a license or renewal of a license shall be submitted on a form provided by the Department, shall be signed under oath, and shall include the following information:

(1)   The street address and telephone number of the principal place of business of the applicant and any North Carolina street addresses if the principal place of business is located outside this State.

(2)   The form of the applicant's business.

(3)   The place and date when the applicant, if other than an individual, was legally established.

(4)   The names and residence addresses of all officers, directors, and owners.

245

(5)   A statement as to whether any of the owners, directors, officers, or employees of the applicant are related as parent, spouse, child, or sibling to:

a.   Any other directors, officers, owners, or employees of the applicant.

b.   Any officer, director, trustee, or employee of any charitable organization or sponsor under contract to the applicant.

c.   Any supplier or vendor providing goods or services to any charitable organization or sponsor under contract to the applicant.

(6)   A statement as to whether the applicant or any of the directors, officers, persons with a controlling interest in the applicant, or employees or agents involved in solicitation have been convicted, within the last five years, of any felony, or of a misdemeanor arising from the conduct of a solicitation for any charitable organization or sponsor or charitable or sponsor purpose, or been enjoined from violating a charitable solicitation law in this or any other state.

(7)   The names of all persons in charge of any solicitation activity.

(c)   Fees. - The application for an initial or renewal license shall be accompanied by a fee of two hundred dollars ($200.00). A solicitor that is a partnership or corporation may register for and pay a single fee on behalf of all of the partners, members, officers, directors, agents, and employees. In that case, the names and street addresses of all the officers, employees, and agents of the solicitor and all other persons with whom the solicitor has contracted to work under that solicitor's direction, including solicitors, shall be listed in the license application or furnished to the Department within five days after the date of employment or contractual arrangement. Each license is valid for one year or a part of one year and expires on March 31 of each year. The license may be renewed on or before March 31 of each year for an additional one-year period upon application to the Department and payment of the license fee.

(d)   Bond. - A solicitor shall, at the time of application or renewal of the license, file with and have approved by the Department a bond with a surety authorized to do business in this State and to which the solicitor is the principal obligor. The amount of the bond shall be determined as follows:

(1)   Twenty thousand dollars ($20,000), if the contributions received for the last fiscal year were less than one hundred thousand dollars ($100,000).

246

(2)   Thirty thousand dollars ($30,000), if the contributions received for the last fiscal year were at least one hundred thousand dollars ($100,000) but less than two hundred thousand dollars ($200,000).

(3)   Fifty thousand dollars ($50,000), if the contributions received for the last fiscal year were at least two hundred thousand dollars ($200,000).

The solicitor shall maintain the bond in effect as long as the license is in effect. The liability of the surety under the bond shall not exceed an all-time aggregate liability of fifty thousand dollars ($50,000). The bond, which may be in the form of a rider to a larger blanket liability bond, shall be payable to the State and to any person who may have a cause of action against the principal obligor of the bond for any liability arising out of a violation by the obligor of any provision of this Chapter or any rule adopted under this Chapter.

(d1)   In lieu of the bond required under subsection (d) of this section, a solicitor may submit a certificate of deposit in the amount as for a bond pursuant to subsection (d) of this section. The certificate of deposit shall be payable to the State and unrestrictively endorsed to the Department; or, in the case of a negotiable certificate of deposit, unrestrictively endorsed to the Department; or, in the case of a nonnegotiable certificate of deposit, assigned to the Department in a form satisfactory to the Department. Access to the certificate of deposit in favor of the State is subject to the same conditions as for a bond under subsection (d) of this section and shall extend for a period not less than four years after the solicitor ceases activities that are subject to this Chapter. The Department shall deliver to the State Treasurer certificates of deposit submitted under this section.

(e)   Departmental Review. - The Department shall examine each application filed by a solicitor. If the Department determines that the requirements are not satisfied, the Department shall notify the solicitor within 10 days after its receipt of the application. If the Department does not respond within 10 days, the license is deemed approved. Within seven days after receipt of a notification that the requirements are not satisfied, the applicant may request a hearing. The state shall bear the burden of proof at such hearing. The hearing shall be held within seven days after receipt of the request. Any recommended order, if one is issued, shall be rendered within three days after the hearing. The final order shall then be issued within two days after the recommended order. If there is no recommended order, the final order shall be issued within five days after the hearing. The proceedings shall be conducted in accordance with Chapter 150B of the General Statutes, except that the time limits and provision set forth in this

247

subsection prevail to the extent of any conflict. The applicant shall be permitted to continue to operate or continue operations pending judicial review of the Department's denial of the application. The Department shall make rules regarding the custody and control of any funds collected during the review period and disposal of such funds in the event the denial of the application is affirmed on appeal.

(f)　　Solicitation Notice. - No less than five days before commencing any solicitation campaign or event, the solicitor shall file with the Department a solicitation notice on a form provided by the Department. The notice shall be signed and sworn to by the contracting officer of the solicitor and shall include:

(1)　　A description of the solicitation event or campaign.

(2)　　Each location and telephone number from which the solicitation is to be conducted.

(3)　　The legal name and residence address of each person responsible for directing and supervising the conduct of the campaign.

(4)　　A statement as to whether the solicitor will, at any time, have custody of contributions.

(5)　　The account number and location of each bank account where receipts from the campaign are to be deposited.

(6)　　A full and fair description of the charitable or sponsor program for which the solicitation campaign is being carried out as provided in the contract between the solicitor and the charitable organization or sponsor.

(7)　　The fund-raising methods to be used.

(8)　　A copy of the contract executed in accordance with subsection (g) of this section.

(g)　　Contracts. - Each contract or agreement between a solicitor and a charitable organization or sponsor for each solicitation campaign shall be in writing, shall be signed by two authorized officials of the charitable organization or sponsor, one of whom shall be a member of the organization's governing body and one of whom shall be the authorized contracting officer for the solicitor. Each contract or agreement shall contain all of the following provisions:

248

(1)   A statement of the charitable or sponsor purpose and program for which the solicitation campaign is being conducted.

(2)   A statement of the respective obligations of the solicitor and the charitable organization or sponsor.

(3)   A statement of the guaranteed minimum percentage of the gross receipts from contributions which will be remitted to the charitable organization or sponsor. If the solicitation involves the sale of goods, services, or tickets to a fund-raising event, the percentage of the purchase price which will be remitted to the charitable organization or sponsor. Any stated percentage shall exclude any amount which the charitable organization or sponsor shall pay as fund-raising costs.

(4)   A statement of the percentage of the gross revenue for which the solicitor shall be compensated. If the compensation of the professional solicitor is not contingent upon the number of contributions or the amount of revenue received, the compensation shall be expressed as a reasonable estimate of the percentage of the gross revenue, and the contract shall clearly disclose the assumptions upon which the estimate is based. The stated assumptions shall be based upon all of the relevant facts known to the solicitor regarding the solicitation to be conducted by the solicitor.

(5)   The effective and termination dates of the contract.

(h)   Financial Report. - Within 90 days after a solicitation campaign has been completed and on the anniversary of the commencement of a solicitation campaign lasting more than one year, the solicitor shall provide to the charitable organization or sponsor and file with the Department a financial report of the campaign, including the gross revenue received, an itemization of all expenses incurred, and the fixed percentage of the gross revenue that the charitable organization or sponsor received as a benefit from the solicitation campaign. The report shall be completed on a form provided by the Department and shall be signed by an authorized official of the solicitor who shall certify under oath that the report is true and correct.

(i)   Handling of Contributions. - Each contribution collected by or in the custody of the solicitor shall be solely in the name of the charitable organization or sponsor on whose behalf the contribution was solicited. Not later than two days after receipt of each contribution, the solicitor shall deposit the entire amount of the contribution in an account at a bank or other federally insured

249

financial institution, which account shall be in the name of that charitable organization or sponsor. The charitable organization or sponsor shall have sole control of all withdrawals from the account and the solicitor shall not be given the authority to withdraw any deposited funds from the account.

(j)   Records of Solicitors. - During each solicitation campaign, and for not less than three years after its completion, the solicitor shall maintain the following records:

(1)   The date and amount of each contribution received and the name, address, and telephone number of each contributor.

(2)   The name and residence street address of each employee, agent, and any other person, however designated, who is involved in the solicitation, the amount of compensation paid to each, and the dates on which the payments were made.

(3)   A record of all contributions that at any time are in the custody of the solicitor.

(4)   A record of all expenses incurred by the solicitor for the payment of which the solicitor is liable.

(5)   A record of all expenses incurred by the solicitor for the payment of which the charitable organization or sponsor is liable.

(6)   The location of each bank or financial institution in which the solicitor has deposited revenue from the solicitation campaign and the account number of each account in which the deposits were made.

(7)   A copy of each pitch sheet or solicitation script used during the completed solicitation campaign.

(8)   If a refund of a contribution has been requested, the name and address of each person requesting the refund. If a refund was made, the amount and the date it was made.

(k)   Records of Tickets. - If the solicitor sells tickets to any event and represents that the tickets will be donated for use by another person, the solicitor shall maintain for at least three years the following records:

(1)   The name and address of each contributor who purchases or donates tickets and the number of tickets purchased or donated by the contributor.

(2)   The name and address of each organization that receives the donated tickets for the use of others, and the number of tickets received by the organization.

(l)   Review of Records. - Any of the records described in this section shall be made available to the Department upon request and shall be furnished within 10 days after the request.

(m)   Change in Information. - Unless otherwise provided in this Chapter, any change in any information filed with the Department under this section shall be reported in writing to the Department within seven days after the change occurs.

(n)   License Rescinded. - Any person licensed as a solicitor shall permanently lose that person's license if it is determined that that person, any officer or director thereof, any person with a ten percent (10%) or greater interest therein, or any person the solicitor employs, engages, or procures to solicit for compensation, has been convicted in the last five years of a crime arising from the conduct of a solicitation for a charitable organization or sponsor or a charitable purpose or sponsor purpose. (1981, c. 886, s. 1; 1985, c. 497, s. 1; 1989, c. 566, s. 2; 1993 (Reg. Sess., 1994), c. 759, s. 2; 1997-124, s. 1; 2003-373, s. 2.)

§ 131F-17. Disclosure requirements of solicitors.

(a)   General Disclosures. - A solicitor shall comply with the following disclosures:

(1)   Prior to orally requesting a contribution or along with a written request for a contribution, a solicitor shall clearly disclose:

a.   The name of the solicitor as on file with the Department.

b.   If the individual acting on behalf of the solicitor identifies himself by name, the individual's legal name.

c.   That the caller is a paid solicitor.

251

(2)   In the case of a solicitation campaign conducted orally, whether by telephone or otherwise, any written confirmation, receipt, or reminder sent to any person who has contributed or has pledged to contribute, shall include a clear disclosure of the information required under subdivision (1) of this subsection.

(3)   In addition to the information required by subdivision (1) of this subsection, any written confirmation, receipt, or reminder of contribution made pursuant to an oral solicitation and any written solicitation shall conspicuously state in type of a minimum of nine points:

"Financial information about the solicitor and a copy of its license are available from the State Solicitation Licensing Branch at [telephone number]. The license is not an endorsement by the State."

The statement shall be made conspicuous by use of one or more of the following: underlining, a border, or bold type. When the solicitation materials consist of more than one piece, the statement shall be displayed prominently in the solicitation materials, but not necessarily on every page.

(4)   If requested by the person being solicited, the solicitor shall inform that person, in writing, within 14 days of the request, of the fixed percentage of the gross revenue or the reasonable estimate of the percentage of the gross revenue that the charitable organization or sponsor will receive as a benefit from the solicitation campaign.

(5)   If requested by the person being solicited, the solicitor shall inform that person, in writing, within 14 days of the request, of the percentage of the contribution which may be deducted as a charitable contribution under federal income tax laws.

(b)   Tickets. - A solicitor shall not represent that tickets to any event will be donated for use by another person, unless:

(1)   The solicitor has the written commitments from persons stating that they will accept donated tickets and specifying the number of tickets they are willing to accept.

(2)   The written commitments are filed with the Department prior to any solicitation.

252

The contributions solicited for donated tickets shall not be more than the amount representing the number of ticket commitments received from persons and filed with the Department. At least seven days before the date of the event, the solicitor shall give all donated tickets to each person that made the written commitment to accept them. (1993 (Reg. Sess., 1994), c. 759, s. 2; 1995 (Reg. Sess., 1996), c. 748, s. 1.2.)

§ 131F-18. Requirements of coventurers.

(a)   Written Consent. - Prior to the commencement of any charitable sales promotion or sponsor sales promotion in this State conducted by a coventurer on behalf of a charitable organization or sponsor, the coventurer shall obtain the written consent of the charitable organization or sponsor whose name will be used during the charitable sales promotion or sponsor sales promotion.

(b)   Rules. - The Department may adopt rules requiring disclosure in advertising for a charitable sales promotion or sponsor sales promotion of information relating to the portion or amount that will benefit the charitable organization or sponsor or the charitable purpose or sponsor purpose.

(c)   Final Accounting. - A final accounting for each charitable sales promotion or sponsor sales promotion shall be prepared by the coventurer following completion. The final accounting shall be provided to the charitable organization or sponsor on whose behalf the sales promotion was conducted within 10 days after a request by the charitable organization or sponsor. The final accounting shall be kept by the coventurer for a period of three years, unless the coventurer and the charitable organization or sponsor mutually agree that the accounting should be kept by the charitable organization or sponsor instead of the coventurer. A copy of the final accounting shall be provided to the Department no later than 10 days after the Department requests it. (1993 (Reg. Sess., 1994), c. 759, s. 2.)

§ 131F-19. Reserved for future codification purposes.

Article 4.

Prohibited Acts and Enforcement.

§ 131F-20. Prohibited acts.

It is unlawful for any person to:

(1)   Violate or fail to comply with the requirements of this Chapter.

(2)   Act as a fund-raising consultant or solicitor after the expiration, suspension, or revocation of that person's license.

(3)   Enter into any contract or agreement with or employ a fund-raising consultant or solicitor unless that fund-raising consultant or solicitor is licensed by the Department.

(4)   Knowingly file false or misleading information in any document required to be filed with the Department or in response to any request or investigation by the Department or the Attorney General.

(5)   Make misrepresentations or misleading statements to the effect that any other person sponsors or endorses the solicitation, approves of its purpose, or is connected therewith, when that person has not given written consent to the use of that person's name.

(6)   Represent that a contribution is for or on behalf of a charitable organization or sponsor, or to use any emblem, device, or printed matter belonging to or associated with a charitable organization or sponsor, without first being authorized in writing to do so by the charitable organization or sponsor.

(7)   Use a name, symbol, emblem, device, service mark, or statement so closely related or similar to that used by another charitable organization or sponsor that the use would mislead the public.

(8)   Falsely state that the person is a member of or a representative of a charitable organization or sponsor or falsely state or represent that the person is a member of or represents law enforcement officers or emergency service employees.

(9)   Misrepresent or mislead anyone by any manner, means, practice, or device to believe that the person on whose behalf the solicitation or sale is being conducted is a charitable organization or sponsor, or that any of the proceeds of the solicitation or sale will be used for charitable or sponsor purposes.

(10)   Represent that a charitable organization or sponsor will receive a fixed or estimated percentage of the gross revenue from a solicitation campaign greater than that identified in filings with the Department under this Chapter, or that a charitable organization or sponsor will receive an actual or estimated dollar amount or percentage per unit of goods or services purchased or used in the charitable or sponsor sales promotion that is greater than that agreed to by the coventurer and the charitable organization or sponsor.

(11)   Use or exploit the fact of registration or the filing of any report with any governmental agency to lead any person to believe that the registration in any manner constitutes an endorsement or approval by the State. However, use of the statement required in G.S. 131F-9(c) or G.S. 131F-17(a)(3) is not a prohibited use or exploitation.

(12)   Make misrepresentations or misleading statements to the effect that the donation of a contribution or the display of any sticker, emblem, or insignia offered to contributors shall entitle a person to any special treatment by emergency service employees or law enforcement officers in the performance of their official duties.

(13)   Solicit contributions from another person while wearing the uniform of an emergency service employee or law enforcement officer, or while on duty as an emergency service employee or law enforcement officer, except where the solicitation is for a charitable organization or sponsor or except when soliciting contributions to benefit an emergency service employee or law enforcement officer who has been injured in the line of duty or to benefit the family or dependents of an emergency service employee or law enforcement officer who has been killed in the line of duty.

(14)   Solicit contributions on behalf of another person using any statement that the failure to make a contribution shall result in a reduced level of law enforcement services being provided to the public or the person solicited.

(15)   Employ in any solicitation any device or scheme to defraud or to obtain a contribution by means of any deception, false pretense, misrepresentation, or false promise.

(16)   Notify any other person by any means, as part of an advertising scheme or plan, that the other person has won a prize, received an award, or has been selected or is eligible to receive anything of value if the other person is required

to purchase goods or services, pay any money to participate in, or submit to a promotion effort.

(17)   Fail to provide complete and timely payment to a charitable organization or sponsor of the proceeds from a solicitation campaign or a charitable or sponsor sales promotion.

(18)   Fail to apply contributions in a manner substantially consistent with the solicitation.

(19)   Fail to identify the professional relationship to the person for whom the solicitation is being made.

(20)   To send to any person a writing which simulates or resembles an invoice unless the intended recipient has contracted for goods, property, or services from the charitable organization or solicitor who sends the writing. (1981, c. 886, s. 1; 1993 (Reg. Sess., 1994), c. 759, s. 2.)

§ 131F-21. Violation as deceptive or unfair trade practice.

Any person who commits an act or practice that violates any provision of this Chapter engages in an unfair trade practice in violation of G.S. 75-1.1. (1993 (Reg. Sess., 1994), c. 759, s. 2.)

§ 131F-22. Criminal penalties.

Except as otherwise provided in this Chapter and in addition to any administrative or civil penalties, any person who willfully and knowingly violates a provision of this Chapter commits a Class 1 misdemeanor. (1981, c. 886, s. 1; 1993, c. 539, s. 952; 1993 (Reg. Sess., 1994), c. 759, s. 2.)

§ 131F-23. Enforcement.

(a)   Investigation. - The Department may conduct an investigation of any person whenever there is an allegation or appearance, either upon complaint or otherwise, that a violation of this Chapter or of any rule adopted or of any order issued pursuant to this Chapter has occurred or is about to occur.

(b)   Subpoena Power. - The Department may issue and serve subpoenas and subpoenas duces tecum to compel the attendance of witnesses and the production of all books, accounts, records, and other documents and materials relevant to an examination or investigation. The Department, or its duly authorized representative, may administer oaths and affirmations to any person.

(c)   Court Action. - In the event of substantial noncompliance with a subpoena or subpoena duces tecum issued or caused to be issued by the Department, the Department may petition the superior court of the county in which the person subpoenaed resides or has the principal place of business for an order requiring the subpoenaed person to appear and testify and to produce any books, accounts, records, and other documents as are specified in the subpoena duces tecum. The court may grant injunctive relief restraining the person from collecting contributions and any other relief, including the restraint by injunction or appointment of a receiver, or any transfer, pledge, assignment, or other disposition of the person's assets, or any concealment, alteration, destruction, or other disposition of subpoenaed books, accounts, records, or other documents and materials as the court deems appropriate, until the person or organization has fully complied with the subpoena or subpoena duces tecum and the Department has completed its investigation or examination. The court may also order the person to produce a financial statement that has been audited by an independent certified public accountant. Costs incurred by the Department to obtain an order granting, in whole or in part, a petition for enforcement of a subpoena or subpoena duces tecum shall be taxed against the subpoenaed person and failure to comply with the order shall be contempt of court.

(d)   Violations. - The Department may enter an order imposing one or more of the penalties set forth in subsection (e) of this section if the Department finds that a charitable organization, sponsor, fund-raising consultant, or solicitor, or their officers, agents, directors, or employees have engaged in any of the following acts:

(1)   Violated or is operating in violation of any of the provisions of this Chapter or of the rules adopted or orders issued under this Chapter.

(2)   Made a false statement in an application, statement, or report required to be filed under this Chapter.

(3)   Refused or failed, after notice, to produce any records or to disclose any information required to be disclosed under this Chapter or the rules adopted by the Department.

(4)   Made a false statement in response to any request or investigation by the Department or the Attorney General.

(e)   Penalties. - Upon a finding as set forth in subsection (d) of this section, the Department may enter an order as follows:

(1)   Imposing an administrative penalty not to exceed one thousand dollars ($1,000) for each act or omission which constitutes a violation of this Chapter or a rule or an order.

(2)   Issuing a cease and desist order that directs that the person cease and desist specified fund-raising activities.

(3)   Refusing to register or cancelling or suspending a registration.

(4)   Placing the registrant on probation for a period of time, subject to such conditions as the Department may specify.

(5)   Issuing of a letter of concern.

(6)   Cancelling an exemption granted under G.S. 131F-3.

(f)   Procedures. - Except as otherwise provided in this section, the administrative proceedings which could result in the entry of an order imposing any of the penalties specified in subsection (e) of this section are governed by Chapter 150B of the General Statutes.

(g)   Disposition of Penalties. - The clear proceeds of penalties provided for in subsection (e) of this section shall be remitted to the Civil Penalty and Forfeiture Fund in accordance with G.S. 115C-457.2. (1993 (Reg. Sess., 1994), c. 759, s. 2; 1998-215, s. 81.)

§ 131F-24. Civil remedies and enforcement.

(a)   Civil Remedies. - In addition to other remedies authorized by law, the Attorney General may bring a civil action in superior court to enforce this Chapter. Upon a finding that any person has violated this Chapter, a court may make any necessary order or enter a judgment, including a temporary or permanent injunction, a declaratory judgment, the appointment of a master or receiver, the sequestration of assets, the reimbursement of persons from whom contributions have been unlawfully solicited, the distribution of contributions in accordance with the charitable or sponsor purpose expressed in the registration statement or in accordance with the representations made to the person solicited, the reimbursement of the Department for attorneys' fees and costs, including investigative costs, and any other equitable relief the court finds appropriate. Upon a finding that any person has violated any provision of this Chapter, a court may enter an order imposing a civil penalty in an amount not to exceed ten thousand dollars ($10,000) per violation.

The clear proceeds of penalties imposed pursuant to this subsection shall be remitted to the Civil Penalty and Forfeiture Fund in accordance with G.S. 115C-457.2.

(b)   Attorney General. - The Attorney General may conduct any investigation necessary to bring a civil action under this section, including administering oaths and affirmations, subpoenaing witnesses or material, and collecting evidence.

(c)   Voluntary Compliance. - The Attorney General may terminate an investigation or an action upon acceptance of a person's written assurance of voluntary compliance with this Chapter. Acceptance of an assurance may be conditioned on commitment to reimburse donors or to take other appropriate corrective action. An assurance is not evidence of a prior violation of any of this Chapter. Unless an assurance has been rescinded by agreement of the parties or voided by a court for good cause, subsequent failure to comply with the terms of an assurance is prima facie evidence of a violation of this Chapter. (1993 (Reg. Sess., 1994), c. 759, s. 2; 1998-215, s. 82.)

§§ 131F-25 through 131F-29. Reserved for future codification purposes.

Article 5.

Miscellaneous.

§ 131F-30. Public information; annual report.

(a)   Public Information Program. - The Department shall develop a public information program to further the purposes of this Chapter. The purpose of the program is to help the public recognize unlawful, misleading, deceptive, or fraudulent solicitations and make knowledgeable, informed decisions concerning contributions.

(b)   Information to Be Included. - The program shall include information concerning:

(1)   The laws governing solicitations, including licensing and disclosure requirements, prohibited acts, and penalties.

(2)   The means by which the public can report suspected violations or file a complaint.

(3)   Any other information the Department believes will assist the public in making knowledgeable and informed decisions concerning contributions.

(c)   Annual Report. - The Department shall prepare an annual report to be submitted to the Governor, the President of the Senate, and the Speaker of the House of Representatives and to be made available to the public by publishing it on the Department's web site, summarizing the information filed under this Chapter which the Department determines will assist the public in making informed and knowledgeable decisions concerning contributions. The report shall include the following:

(1)   A list of complaints filed for which violations were found to have occurred in each of the following categories: charitable organizations, sponsors, solicitors, and fund-raising consultants.

(2)   A list of the number of investigations by the Department, enforcement actions commenced under this Chapter, and the disposition of those actions.

(3)   A list of those charitable organizations and sponsors that have voluntarily submitted an audited financial statement pursuant to G.S. 131F-6(a)(10) or an audit with an opinion prepared by an independent certified public accountant.

(4)   A list of all solicitors licensed under this Chapter and the fixed percentage of the gross revenue that the charitable organization or sponsor will receive as a benefit from the solicitation campaign, the reasonable estimate of the percentage of the gross revenue that the charitable organization or sponsor will receive as a benefit from the solicitation campaign, or the guaranteed minimum percentage of the gross revenue that the charitable solicitation or sponsor will receive as a benefit from the solicitation campaign as provided in the contract between the solicitor and the charitable organization or sponsor, whichever of these three amounts is least. This list shall appear in order of percentages, from lowest to highest.

(d)   Each year immediately following the submission of the report under subsection (c) of this section, the Secretary of State shall issue that report as a press release to all print and electronic news media that provide general coverage. (1993 (Reg. Sess., 1994), c. 759, s. 2; 2003-373, s. 1.)

§ 131F-31. Contributions solicited for, or accepted by or on behalf of, a named individual.

(a)   Trust Account Required. - Contributions solicited for, or accepted by or on behalf of, a named individual shall be deposited in a trust account opened by a trustee named in a properly established trust document.

(b)   Use of Trust Funds. - Contributions deposited in the trust fund may be used only for the purpose for which the contributions were solicited; if the contributions are no longer needed for the purpose for which they were solicited, they may be used for another similar charitable purpose. The trustee may disburse funds from the trust account only after making a written record verifying the purpose for which the funds will be used accompanied by documentation of the identity of the payee and the justification for the payment. The Trustee shall retain these records for each disbursement from the trust account for a period of three years after the disbursement. (1993 (Reg. Sess., 1994), c. 759, s. 2.)

§ 131F-32. Records.

Each charitable organization, sponsor, fund-raising consultant, and solicitor shall keep, for a period of at least three years, true and accurate records as to

261

their activities in the State. The records shall be made available to the Department for inspection and shall be furnished no later than 10 days after the request was made. (1981, c. 886, s. 1; 1993 (Reg. Sess., 1994), c. 759, s. 2.)

§ 131F-33. Rule-making authority.

The Department shall have the authority to adopt rules necessary for the implementation of this Chapter or to prevent false or deceptive statements or conduct in the solicitation of charitable contributions. (1981, c. 886, s. 1; 1993 (Reg. Sess., 1994), c. 759, s. 2.)

Chapter 132.

Public Records.

§ 132-1. "Public records" defined.

(a)   "Public record" or "public records" shall mean all documents, papers, letters, maps, books, photographs, films, sound recordings, magnetic or other tapes, electronic data-processing records, artifacts, or other documentary material, regardless of physical form or characteristics, made or received pursuant to law or ordinance in connection with the transaction of public business by any agency of North Carolina government or its subdivisions. Agency of North Carolina government or its subdivisions shall mean and include every public office, public officer or official (State or local, elected or appointed), institution, board, commission, bureau, council, department, authority or other unit of government of the State or of any county, unit, special district or other political subdivision of government.

(b)   The public records and public information compiled by the agencies of North Carolina government or its subdivisions are the property of the people. Therefore, it is the policy of this State that the people may obtain copies of their public records and public information free or at minimal cost unless otherwise specifically provided by law. As used herein, "minimal cost" shall mean the actual cost of reproducing the public record or public information. (1935, c. 265, s. 1; 1975, c. 787, s. 1; 1995, c. 388, s. 1.)

262

§ 132-1.1. Confidential communications by legal counsel to public board or agency; State tax information; public enterprise billing information; Address Confidentiality Program information.

(a)   Confidential Communications. - Public records, as defined in G.S. 132-1, shall not include written communications (and copies thereof) to any public board, council, commission or other governmental body of the State or of any county, municipality or other political subdivision or unit of government, made within the scope of the attorney-client relationship by any attorney-at-law serving any such governmental body, concerning any claim against or on behalf of the governmental body or the governmental entity for which such body acts, or concerning the prosecution, defense, settlement or litigation of any judicial action, or any administrative or other type of proceeding to which the governmental body is a party or by which it is or may be directly affected. Such written communication and copies thereof shall not be open to public inspection, examination or copying unless specifically made public by the governmental body receiving such written communications; provided, however, that such written communications and copies thereof shall become public records as defined in G.S. 132-1 three years from the date such communication was received by such public board, council, commission or other governmental body.

(b)   State and Local Tax Information. - Tax information may not be disclosed except as provided in G.S. 105-259. As used in this subsection, "tax information" has the same meaning as in G.S. 105-259. Local tax records that contain information about a taxpayer's income or receipts may not be disclosed except as provided in G.S. 153A-148.1 and G.S. 160A-208.1.

(c)   Public Enterprise Billing Information. - Billing information compiled and maintained by a city or county or other public entity providing utility services in connection with the ownership or operation of a public enterprise, excluding airports, is not a public record as defined in G.S. 132-1. Nothing contained herein is intended to limit public disclosure by a city or county of billing information:

(1)   That the city or county determines will be useful or necessary to assist bond counsel, bond underwriters, underwriters' counsel, rating agencies or investors or potential investors in making informed decisions regarding bonds or other obligations incurred or to be incurred with respect to the public enterprise;

(2)   That is necessary to assist the city, county, State, or public enterprise to maintain the integrity and quality of services it provides; or

263

(3)   That is necessary to assist law enforcement, public safety, fire protection, rescue, emergency management, or judicial officers in the performance of their duties.

As used herein, "billing information" means any record or information, in whatever form, compiled or maintained with respect to individual customers by any owner or operator of a public enterprise, as defined in G.S. 160A-311, excluding subdivision (9), and G.S. 153A-274, excluding subdivision (4), or other public entity providing utility services, excluding airports, relating to services it provides or will provide to the customer.

(d)   Address Confidentiality Program Information. - The actual address and telephone number of a program participant in the Address Confidentiality Program established under Chapter 15C of the General Statutes is not a public record within the meaning of Chapter 132. The actual address and telephone number of a program participant may not be disclosed except as provided in Chapter 15C of the General Statutes.

(e)   Controlled Substances Reporting System Information. - Information compiled or maintained in the Controlled Substances Reporting System established under Article 5E of Chapter 90 of the General Statutes is not a public record as defined in G.S. 132-1 and may be released only as provided under Article 5E of Chapter 90 of the General Statutes.

(f)   Personally Identifiable Admissions Information. - Records maintained by The University of North Carolina or any constituent institution, or by the Community Colleges System Office or any community college, which contain personally identifiable information from or about an applicant for admission to one or more constituent institutions or to one or more community colleges shall be confidential and shall not be subject to public disclosure pursuant to G.S. 132-6(a). Notwithstanding the preceding sentence, any letter of recommendation or record containing a communication from an elected official to The University of North Carolina, any of its constituent institutions, or to a community college, concerning an applicant for admission who has not enrolled as a student shall be considered a public record subject to disclosure pursuant to G.S. 132-6(a). Nothing in this subsection is intended to limit the disclosure of public records that do not contain personally identifiable information, including aggregated data, guidelines, instructions, summaries, or reports that do not contain personally identifiable information or from which it is feasible to redact any personally identifiable information that the record contains. As used in this subsection, the term "community college" is as defined in G.S. 115D-2(2), the

264

term "constituent institution" is as defined in G.S. 116-2(4), and the term "Community Colleges System Office" is as defined in G.S. 115D-3.

(g)   Public Agency Proprietary Computer Code. - Proprietary computer code written by and for use by an agency of North Carolina government or its subdivisions is not a public record as defined in G.S. 132-1. (1975, c. 662; 1993, c. 485, s. 38; 1995 (Reg. Sess., 1996), c. 646, s. 21; 2001-473, s. 1; 2002-171, s. 7; 2003-287, s. 1; 2005-276, s. 10.36(b); 2007-372, s. 2; 2013-96, s. 1.)

§ 132-1.2. Confidential information.

Nothing in this Chapter shall be construed to require or authorize a public agency or its subdivision to disclose any information that:

(1)   Meets all of the following conditions:

a.   Constitutes a "trade secret" as defined in G.S. 66-152(3).

b.   Is the property of a private "person" as defined in G.S. 66-152(2).

c.   Is disclosed or furnished to the public agency in connection with the owner's performance of a public contract or in connection with a bid, application, proposal, industrial development project, or in compliance with laws, regulations, rules, or ordinances of the United States, the State, or political subdivisions of the State.

d.   Is designated or indicated as "confidential" or as a "trade secret" at the time of its initial disclosure to the public agency.

(2)   Reveals an account number for electronic payment as defined in G.S. 147-86.20 and obtained pursuant to Articles 6A or 6B of Chapter 147 of the General Statutes or G.S. 159-32.1.

(3)   Reveals a document, file number, password, or any other information maintained by the Secretary of State pursuant to Article 21 of Chapter 130A of the General Statutes.

(4)   Reveals the electronically captured image of an individual's signature, date of birth, drivers license number, or a portion of an individual's social security number if the agency has those items because they are on a voter registration document.

(5)   Reveals the seal of a licensed design professional who is licensed under Chapter 83A or Chapter 89C of the General Statutes that has been submitted for project approval to (i) a municipality under Part 5 of Article 19 of Chapter 160A of the General Statutes or (ii) to a county under Part 4 of Article 18 of Chapter 153A of the General Statutes. Notwithstanding this exemption, a municipality or county that receives a request for a document submitted for project approval that contains the seal of a licensed design professional who is licensed under Chapter 83A or Chapter 89C of the General Statutes and that is otherwise a public record by G.S. 132-1 shall allow a copy of the document without the seal of the licensed design professional to be examined and copied, consistent with any rules adopted by the licensing board under Chapter 83A or Chapter 89C of the General Statutes regarding an unsealed document. (1989, c. 269; 1991, c. 745, s. 3; 1999-434, s. 7; 2001-455, s. 2; 2001-513, s. 30(b); 2003-226, s. 5; 2004-127, s. 17(b); 2009-346, s. 1.)

§ 132-1.3. Settlements made by or on behalf of public agencies, public officials, or public employees; public records.

(a)   Public records, as defined in G.S. 132-1, shall include all settlement documents in any suit, administrative proceeding or arbitration instituted against any agency of North Carolina government or its subdivisions, as defined in G.S. 132-1, in connection with or arising out of such agency's official actions, duties or responsibilities, except in an action for medical malpractice against a hospital facility. No agency of North Carolina government or its subdivisions, nor any counsel, insurance company or other representative acting on behalf of such agency, shall approve, accept or enter into any settlement of any such suit, arbitration or proceeding if the settlement provides that its terms and conditions shall be confidential, except in an action for medical malpractice against a hospital facility. No settlement document sealed under subsection (b) of this section shall be open for public inspection.

(b)   No judge, administrative judge or administrative hearing officer of this State, nor any board or commission, nor any arbitrator appointed pursuant to the laws of North Carolina, shall order or permit the sealing of any settlement document in any proceeding described herein except on the basis of a written order concluding that (1) the presumption of openness is overcome by an overriding interest and (2) that such overriding interest cannot be protected by any measure short of sealing the settlement. Such order shall articulate the overriding interest and shall include findings of fact that are sufficiently specific to permit a reviewing court to determine whether the order was proper.

(c)   Except for confidential communications as provided in G.S. 132-1.1, the term "settlement documents," as used herein, shall include all documents which reflect, or which are made or utilized in connection with, the terms and conditions upon which any proceedings described in this section are compromised, settled, terminated or dismissed, including but not limited to correspondence, settlement agreements, consent orders, checks, and bank drafts. (1989, c. 326.)

§ 132-1.4. Criminal investigations; intelligence information records; Innocence Inquiry Commission records.

(a)   Records of criminal investigations conducted by public law enforcement agencies, records of criminal intelligence information compiled by public law enforcement agencies, and records of investigations conducted by the North Carolina Innocence Inquiry Commission, are not public records as defined by G.S. 132-1. Records of criminal investigations conducted by public law enforcement agencies or records of criminal intelligence information may be released by order of a court of competent jurisdiction.

(b)   As used in this section:

(1)   "Records of criminal investigations" means all records or any information that pertains to a person or group of persons that is compiled by public law enforcement agencies for the purpose of attempting to prevent or solve violations of the law, including information derived from witnesses, laboratory tests, surveillance, investigators, confidential informants, photographs, and measurements. The term also includes any records, worksheets, reports, or analyses prepared or conducted by the North Carolina State Crime Laboratory at the request of any public law enforcement agency in connection with a criminal investigation.

(2)   "Records of criminal intelligence information" means records or information that pertain to a person or group of persons that is compiled by a public law enforcement agency in an effort to anticipate, prevent, or monitor possible violations of the law.

(3)   "Public law enforcement agency" means a municipal police department, a county police department, a sheriff's department, a company police agency commissioned by the Attorney General pursuant to G.S. 74E-1, et seq., and any State or local agency, force, department, or unit responsible for investigating, preventing, or solving violations of the law.

(4)   "Violations of the law" means crimes and offenses that are prosecutable in the criminal courts in this State or the United States and infractions as defined in G.S. 14-3.1.

(5)   "Complaining witness" means an alleged victim or other person who reports a violation or apparent violation of the law to a public law enforcement agency.

(c)   Notwithstanding the provisions of this section, and unless otherwise prohibited by law, the following information shall be public records within the meaning of G.S. 132-1.

(1)   The time, date, location, and nature of a violation or apparent violation of the law reported to a public law enforcement agency.

(2)   The name, sex, age, address, employment, and alleged violation of law of a person arrested, charged, or indicted.

(3)   The circumstances surrounding an arrest, including the time and place of the arrest, whether the arrest involved resistance, possession or use of weapons, or pursuit, and a description of any items seized in connection with the arrest.

(4)   The contents of "911" and other emergency telephone calls received by or on behalf of public law enforcement agencies, except for such contents that reveal the natural voice, name, address, telephone number, or other information that may identify the caller, victim, or witness. In order to protect the identity of the complaining witness, the contents of "911" and other emergency telephone calls may be released pursuant to this section in the form of a written transcript

or altered voice reproduction; provided that the original shall be provided under process to be used as evidence in any relevant civil or criminal proceeding.

(5)   The contents of communications between or among employees of public law enforcement agencies that are broadcast over the public airways.

(6)   The name, sex, age, and address of a complaining witness.

(d)   A public law enforcement agency shall temporarily withhold the name or address of a complaining witness if release of the information is reasonably likely to pose a threat to the mental health, physical health, or personal safety of the complaining witness or materially compromise a continuing or future criminal investigation or criminal intelligence operation. Information temporarily withheld under this subsection shall be made available for release to the public in accordance with G.S. 132-6 as soon as the circumstances that justify withholding it cease to exist. Any person denied access to information withheld under this subsection may apply to a court of competent jurisdiction for an order compelling disclosure of the information. In such action, the court shall balance the interests of the public in disclosure against the interests of the law enforcement agency and the alleged victim in withholding the information. Actions brought pursuant to this subsection shall be set down for immediate hearing, and subsequent proceedings in such actions shall be accorded priority by the trial and appellate courts.

(e)   If a public law enforcement agency believes that release of information that is a public record under subdivisions (c)(1) through (c)(5) of this section will jeopardize the right of the State to prosecute a defendant or the right of a defendant to receive a fair trial or will undermine an ongoing or future investigation, it may seek an order from a court of competent jurisdiction to prevent disclosure of the information. In such action the law enforcement agency shall have the burden of showing by a preponderance of the evidence that disclosure of the information in question will jeopardize the right of the State to prosecute a defendant or the right of a defendant to receive a fair trial or will undermine an ongoing or future investigation. Actions brought pursuant to this subsection shall be set down for immediate hearing, and subsequent proceedings in such actions shall be accorded priority by the trial and appellate courts.

(f)   Nothing in this section shall be construed as authorizing any public law enforcement agency to prohibit or prevent another public agency having custody of a public record from permitting the inspection, examination, or copying of

269

such public record in compliance with G.S. 132-6. The use of a public record in connection with a criminal investigation or the gathering of criminal intelligence shall not affect its status as a public record.

(g)   Disclosure of records of criminal investigations and criminal intelligence information that have been transmitted to a district attorney or other attorney authorized to prosecute a violation of law shall be governed by this section and Chapter 15A of the General Statutes.

(h)   Nothing in this section shall be construed as requiring law enforcement agencies to disclose the following:

(1)   Information that would not be required to be disclosed under Chapter 15A of the General Statutes; or

(2)   Information that is reasonably likely to identify a confidential informant.

(i)   Law enforcement agencies shall not be required to maintain any tape recordings of "911" or other communications for more than 30 days from the time of the call, unless a court of competent jurisdiction orders a portion sealed.

(j)   When information that is not a public record under the provisions of this section is deleted from a document, tape recording, or other record, the law enforcement agency shall make clear that a deletion has been made. Nothing in this subsection shall authorize the destruction of the original record.

(k)   The following court records are public records and may be withheld only when sealed by court order: arrest and search warrants that have been returned by law enforcement agencies, indictments, criminal summons, and nontestimonial identification orders.

(l)   Records of investigations of alleged child abuse shall be governed by Article 29 of Chapter 7B of the General Statutes. (1993, c. 461, s. 1; 1998-202, s. 13(jj); 2006-184, s. 7; 2010-171, s. 5; 2011-321, s. 1; 2013-360, s. 17.6(o).)

§ 132-1.5. 911 database.

Automatic number identification and automatic location identification information that consists of the name, address, and telephone numbers of telephone subscribers, or the e-mail addresses of subscribers to an electronic emergency notification or reverse 911 system, that is contained in a county or municipal 911 database, or in a county or municipal telephonic or electronic emergency notification or reverse 911 system, is confidential and is not a public record as defined by Chapter 132 of the General Statutes if that information is required to be confidential by the agreement with the telephone company by which the information was obtained. Dissemination of the information contained in the 911, electronic emergency notification or reverse 911 system, or automatic number and automatic location database is prohibited except on a call-by-call basis only for the purpose of handling emergency calls or for training, and any permanent record of the information shall be secured by the public safety answering points and disposed of in a manner which will retain that security except as otherwise required by applicable law. (1997-287, s. 1; 2007-107, s. 3.2(a).)

§ 132-1.6. Emergency response plans.

Emergency response plans adopted by a constituent institution of The University of North Carolina, a community college, or a public hospital as defined in G.S. 159-39 and the records related to the planning and development of these emergency response plans are not public records as defined by G.S. 132-1 and shall not be subject to inspection and examination under G.S. 132-6. (2001-500, s. 3.1.)

§ 132-1.7. Sensitive public security information.

(a)   Public records, as defined in G.S. 132-1, shall not include information containing specific details of public security plans and arrangements or the detailed plans and drawings of public buildings and infrastructure facilities.

(b)   Public records as defined in G.S. 132-1 do not include plans to prevent or respond to terrorist activity, to the extent such records set forth vulnerability and risk assessments, potential targets, specific tactics, or specific security or emergency procedures, the disclosure of which would jeopardize the safety of governmental personnel or the general public or the security of any governmental facility, building, structure, or information storage system.

271

(c)   Information relating to the general adoption of public security plans and arrangements, and budgetary information concerning the authorization or expenditure of public funds to implement public security plans and arrangements, or for the construction, renovation, or repair of public buildings and infrastructure facilities shall be public records. (2001-516, s. 3; 2003-180, s. 1.)

§ 132-1.8. Confidentiality of photographs and video or audio recordings made pursuant to autopsy.

Except as otherwise provided in G.S. 130A-389.1, a photograph or video or audio recording of an official autopsy is not a public record as defined by G.S. 132-1. However, the text of an official autopsy report, including any findings and interpretations prepared in accordance with G.S. 130A-389(a), is a public record and fully accessible by the public. For purposes of this section, an official autopsy is an autopsy performed pursuant to G.S. 130A-389(a). (2005-393, s. 1.)

§ 132-1.9. Trial preparation materials.

(a)   Scope. - A request to inspect, examine, or copy a public record that is also trial preparation material is governed by this section, and, to the extent this section conflicts with any other provision of law, this section applies.

(b)   Right to Deny Access. - Except as otherwise provided in this section, a custodian may deny access to a public record that is also trial preparation material. If the denial is based on an assertion that the public record is trial preparation material that was prepared in anticipation of a legal proceeding that has not commenced, the custodian shall, upon request, provide a written justification for the assertion that the public record was prepared in anticipation of a legal proceeding.

(c)   Trial Preparation Material Prepared in Anticipation of a Legal Proceeding. - Any person who is denied access to a public record that is also claimed to be trial preparation material that was prepared in anticipation of a legal proceeding that has not yet been commenced may petition the court pursuant to G.S. 132-9 for determination as to whether the public record is trial preparation material that was prepared in anticipation of a legal proceeding.

(d)   During a Legal Proceeding. -

(1)   When a legal proceeding is subject to G.S. 1A-1, Rule 26(b)(3), or subject to Rule 26(b)(3) of the Federal Rules of Civil Procedure, a party to the pending legal proceeding, including any appeals and postjudgment proceedings, who is denied access to a public record that is also claimed to be trial preparation material that pertains to the pending proceeding may seek access to such record only by motion made in the pending legal proceeding and pursuant to the procedural and substantive standards that apply to that proceeding. A party to the pending legal proceeding may not directly or indirectly commence a separate proceeding for release of such record pursuant to G.S. 132-9 in any other court or tribunal.

(2)   When a legal proceeding is not subject to G.S. 1A-1, Rule 26(b)(3), and not subject to Rule 26(b)(3) of the Federal Rules of Civil Procedure, a party to the pending legal proceeding, including any appeals and postjudgment proceedings, who is denied access to a public record that is also claimed to be trial preparation material that pertains to the pending legal proceeding may petition the court pursuant to G.S. 132-9 for access to such record. In determining whether to require the custodian to provide access to all or any portion of the record, the court or other tribunal shall apply the provisions of G.S. 1A-1, Rule 26(b)(3).

(3)   Any person who is denied access to a public record that is also claimed to be trial preparation material and who is not a party to the pending legal proceeding to which such record pertains, and who is not acting in concert with or as an agent for any party to the pending legal proceeding, may petition the court pursuant to G.S. 132-9 for a determination as to whether the public record is trial preparation material.

(e)   Following a Legal Proceeding. - Upon the conclusion of a legal proceeding, including the completion of all appeals and postjudgment proceedings, or, in the case where no legal proceeding has been commenced, upon the expiration of all applicable statutes of limitations and periods of repose, the custodian of a public record that is also claimed to be trial preparation material shall permit the inspection, examination, or copying of such record if any law that is applicable so provides.

273

(f)   Effect of Disclosure. - Disclosure pursuant to this section of all or any portion of a public record that is also trial preparation material, whether voluntary or pursuant to an order issued by a court, or issued by an officer in an administrative or quasi-judicial legal proceeding, shall not constitute a waiver of the right to claim that any other document or record constitutes trial preparation material.

(g)   Trial Preparation Materials That Are Not Public Records. - This section does not require disclosure, or authorize a court to require disclosure, of trial preparation material that is not also a public record or that is under other provisions of this Chapter exempted or protected from disclosure by law or by an order issued by a court, or by an officer in an administrative or quasi-judicial legal proceeding.

(h)   Definitions. - As used in this section, the following definitions apply:

(1)   Legal proceeding. - Civil proceedings in any federal or State court. Legal proceeding also includes any federal, State, or local government administrative or quasi-judicial proceeding that is not expressly subject to the provisions of Chapter 1A of the General Statutes or the Federal Rules of Civil Procedure.

(2)   Trial preparation material. - Any record, wherever located and in whatever form, that is trial preparation material within the meaning of G.S. 1A-1, Rule 26(b)(3), any comparable material prepared for any other legal proceeding, and any comparable material exchanged pursuant to a joint defense, joint prosecution, or joint interest agreement in connection with any pending or anticipated legal proceeding. (2005-332, s. 1; 2005-414, s. 4.)

§ 132-1.10. Social security numbers and other personal identifying information.

(a)   The General Assembly finds the following:

(1)   The social security number can be used as a tool to perpetuate fraud against a person and to acquire sensitive personal, financial, medical, and familial information, the release of which could cause great financial or personal harm to an individual. While the social security number was intended to be used solely for the administration of the federal Social Security System, over time this unique numeric identifier has been used extensively for identity verification purposes and other legitimate consensual purposes.

(2)   Although there are legitimate reasons for State and local government agencies to collect social security numbers and other personal identifying information from individuals, government should collect the information only for legitimate purposes or when required by law.

(3)   When State and local government agencies possess social security numbers or other personal identifying information, the governments should minimize the instances this information is disseminated either internally within government or externally with the general public.

(b)   Except as provided in subsections (c) and (d) of this section, no agency of the State or its political subdivisions, or any agent or employee of a government agency, shall do any of the following:

(1)   Collect a social security number from an individual unless authorized by law to do so or unless the collection of the social security number is otherwise imperative for the performance of that agency's duties and responsibilities as prescribed by law. Social security numbers collected by an agency must be relevant to the purpose for which collected and shall not be collected until and unless the need for social security numbers has been clearly documented.

(2)   Fail, when collecting a social security number from an individual, to segregate that number on a separate page from the rest of the record, or as otherwise appropriate, in order that the social security number can be more easily redacted pursuant to a valid public records request.

(3)   Fail, when collecting a social security number from an individual, to provide, at the time of or prior to the actual collection of the social security number by that agency, that individual, upon request, with a statement of the purpose or purposes for which the social security number is being collected and used.

(4)   Use the social security number for any purpose other than the purpose stated.

(5)   (For applicability date - See Editor's note) Intentionally communicate or otherwise make available to the general public a person's social security number or other identifying information. "Identifying information", as used in this subdivision, shall have the same meaning as in G.S. 14-113.20(b), except it shall not include electronic identification numbers, electronic mail names or addresses, Internet account numbers, Internet identification names, parent's

legal surname prior to marriage, or drivers license numbers appearing on law enforcement records. Identifying information shall be confidential and not be a public record under this Chapter. A record, with identifying information removed or redacted, is a public record if it would otherwise be a public record under this Chapter but for the identifying information. The presence of identifying information in a public record does not change the nature of the public record. If all other public records requirements are met under this Chapter, the agency of the State or its political subdivisions shall respond to a public records request, even if the records contain identifying information, as promptly as possible, by providing the public record with the identifying information removed or redacted.

(6)   Intentionally print or imbed an individual's social security number on any card required for the individual to access government services.

(7)   Require an individual to transmit the individual's social security number over the Internet, unless the connection is secure or the social security number is encrypted.

(8)   Require an individual to use the individual's social security number to access an Internet Web site, unless a password or unique personal identification number or other authentication device is also required to access the Internet Web site.

(9)   Print an individual's social security number on any materials that are mailed to the individual, unless state or federal law required that the social security number be on the document to be mailed. A social security number that is permitted to be mailed under this subdivision may not be printed, in whole or in part, on a postcard or other mailer not requiring an envelope, or visible on the envelope or without the envelope having been opened.

(c)   Subsection (b) of this section does not apply in the following circumstances:

(1)   To social security numbers or other identifying information disclosed to another governmental entity or its agents, employees, or contractors if disclosure is necessary for the receiving entity to perform its duties and responsibilities. The receiving governmental entity and its agents, employees, and contractors shall maintain the confidential and exempt status of such numbers.

276

(2)   To social security numbers or other identifying information disclosed pursuant to a court order, warrant, or subpoena.

(3)   To social security numbers or other identifying information disclosed for public health purposes pursuant to and in compliance with Chapter 130A of the General Statutes.

(4)   To social security numbers or other identifying information that have been redacted.

(5)   To certified copies of vital records issued by the State Registrar and other authorized officials pursuant to G.S. 130A-93(c). The State Registrar may disclose any identifying information other than social security numbers on any uncertified vital record.

(6)   To any recorded document in the official records of the register of deeds of the county.

(7)   To any document filed in the official records of the courts.

(c1)   If an agency of the State or its political subdivisions, or any agent or employee of a government agency, experiences a security breach, as defined in Article 2A of Chapter 75 of the General Statutes, the agency shall comply with the requirements of G.S. 75-65.

(d)   No person preparing or filing a document to be recorded or filed in the official records of the register of deeds, the Department of the Secretary of State, or of the courts may include any person's social security, employer taxpayer identification, drivers license, state identification, passport, checking account, savings account, credit card, or debit card number, or personal identification (PIN) code or passwords in that document, unless otherwise expressly required by law or court order, adopted by the State Registrar on records of vital events, or redacted. Any loan closing instruction that requires the inclusion of a person's social security number on a document to be recorded shall be void. Any person who violates this subsection shall be guilty of an infraction, punishable by a fine not to exceed five hundred dollars ($500.00) for each violation.

(e)   The validity of an instrument as between the parties to the instrument is not affected by the inclusion of personal information on a document recorded or filed with the official records of the register of deeds or the Department of the

277

Secretary of State. The register of deeds or the Department of the Secretary of State may not reject an instrument presented for recording because the instrument contains an individual's personal information.

(f)   Any person has the right to request that a register of deeds or clerk of court remove, from an image or copy of an official record placed on a register of deeds' or court's Internet Website available to the general public or an Internet Web site available to the general public used by a register of deeds or court to display public records by the register of deeds or clerk of court, the person's social security, employer taxpayer identification, drivers license, state identification, passport, checking account, savings account, credit card, or debit card number, or personal identification (PIN) code or passwords contained in that official record. The request must be made in writing, legibly signed by the requester, and delivered by mail, facsimile, or electronic transmission, or delivered in person to the register of deeds or clerk of court. The request must specify the personal information to be redacted, information that identifies the document that contains the personal information and unique information that identifies the location within the document that contains the social security, employer taxpayer identification, drivers license, state identification, passport, checking account, savings account, credit card, or debit card number, or personal identification (PIN) code or passwords to be redacted. The request for redaction shall be considered a public record with access restricted to the register of deeds, the clerk of court, their staff, or upon order of the court. The register of deeds or clerk of court shall have no duty to inquire beyond the written request to verify the identity of a person requesting redaction and shall have no duty to remove redaction for any reason upon subsequent request by an individual or by order of the court, if impossible to do so. No fee will be charged for the redaction pursuant to such request. Any person who requests a redaction without proper authority to do so shall be guilty of an infraction, punishable by a fine not to exceed five hundred dollars ($500.00) for each violation.

(f1)   Without a request made pursuant to subsection (f) of this section, a register of deeds or clerk of court may remove from an image or copy of an official record placed on a register of deeds' or clerk of court's Internet Web site available to the general public, or placed on an Internet Web site available to the general public used by a register of deeds or clerk of court to display public records, a person's social security or drivers license number contained in that official record. Registers of deeds and clerks of court may apply optical character recognition technology or other reasonably available technology to official records placed on Internet Web sites available to the general public in

278

order to, in good faith, identify and redact social security and drivers license numbers.

(g)   A register of deeds or clerk of court shall immediately and conspicuously post signs throughout his or her offices for public viewing and shall immediately and conspicuously post a notice on any Internet Web site available to the general public used by a register of deeds or clerk of court a notice stating, in substantially similar form, the following:

(1)   Any person preparing or filing a document for recordation or filing in the official records may not include a social security, employer taxpayer identification, drivers license, state identification, passport, checking account, savings account, credit card, or debit card number, or personal identification (PIN) code or passwords in the document, unless expressly required by law or court order, adopted by the State Registrar on records of vital events, or redacted so that no more than the last four digits of the identification number is included.

(2)   Any person has a right to request a register of deeds or clerk of court to remove, from an image or copy of an official record placed on a register of deeds' or clerk of court's Internet Web site available to the general public or on an Internet Web site available to the general public used by a register of deeds or clerk of court to display public records, any social security, employer taxpayer identification, drivers license, state identification, passport, checking account, savings account, credit card, or debit card number, or personal identification (PIN) code or passwords contained in an official record. The request must be made in writing and delivered by mail, facsimile, or electronic transmission, or delivered in person, to the register of deeds or clerk of court. The request must specify the personal information to be redacted, information that identifies the document that contains the personal information and unique information that identifies the location within the document that contains the social security, employer taxpayer identification, drivers license, state identification, passport, checking account, savings account, credit card, or debit card number, or personal identification (PIN) code or passwords to be redacted. No fee will be charged for the redaction pursuant to such a request. Any person who requests a redaction without proper authority to do so shall be guilty of an infraction, punishable by a fine not to exceed five hundred dollars ($500.00) for each violation.

(h)   Any affected person may petition the court for an order directing compliance with this section. No liability shall accrue to a register of deeds or

279

clerk of court or to his or her agent for any action related to provisions of this section or for any claims or damages that might result from a social security number or other identifying information on the public record or on a register of deeds' or clerk of court's Internet website available to the general public or an Internet Web site available to the general public used by a register of deeds or clerk of court. (2005-414, s. 4; 2006-173, ss. 1-7; 2009-355, s. 3.)

§ 132-1.11. Economic development incentives.

(a)   Assumptions and Methodologies. - Subject to the provisions of this Chapter regarding confidential information and the withholding of public records relating to the proposed expansion or location of specific business or industrial projects when the release of those records would frustrate the purpose for which they were created, whenever a public agency or its subdivision performs a cost-benefit analysis or similar assessment with respect to economic development incentives offered to a specific business or industrial project, the agency or its subdivision must describe in detail the assumptions and methodologies used in completing the analysis or assessment. This description is a public record and is subject to all provisions of this Chapter and other law regarding public records.

(b)   Disclosure of Public Records Requirements. - Whenever an agency or its subdivision first proposes, negotiates, or accepts an application for economic development incentives with respect to a specific industrial or business project, the agency or subdivision must disclose that any information obtained by the agency or subdivision is subject to laws regarding disclosure of public records. In addition, the agency or subdivision must fully and accurately describe the instances in which confidential information may be withheld from disclosure, the types of information that qualify as confidential information, and the methods for ensuring that confidential information is not disclosed. (2005-429, s. 1.2.)

§ 132-1.11A. Limited access to identifying information of minors participating in local government programs and programs funded by the North Carolina Partnership for Children, Inc., or a local partnership in certain localities.

(a)   A public record, as defined by G.S. 132-1, does not include, as to any minor participating in a program sponsored by a local government or combination of local governments, a program funded by the North Carolina

Partnership for Children, Inc., under G.S. 143B-168.12, or a program funded by a local partnership under G.S. 143B-168.14, any of the following information as to that minor participant: (i) name, (ii) address, (iii) age, (iv) date of birth, (v) telephone number, (vi) the name or address of that minor participant's parent or legal guardian, (vii) e-mail address, or (viii) any other identifying information on an application to participate in such program or other records related to that program. Notwithstanding this subsection, the name of a minor who has received a scholarship or other local government-funded award of a financial nature from a local government is a public record.

(b)   The county, municipality, and zip code of residence of each participating minor covered by subsection (a) of this section is a public record, with the information listed in subsection (a) of this section redacted.

(c)   Nothing in this section makes the information listed in subsection (a) of this section confidential information.

(d)   This section applies to the County of Chatham, the Towns of Apex, Cary, Fuquay-Varina, Garner, Holly Springs, Knightdale, Morrisville, Rolesville, Wake Forest, Wendell, and Zebulon, and the City of Raleigh only. (2008-126, s. 1; 2012-67, s. 1; 2012-139, s. 1(a), (b); 2012-194, s. 70.5(a), (c).)

§ 132-1.12. Limited access to identifying information of minors participating in local government parks and recreation programs and programs funded by the North Carolina Partnership for Children, Inc., or a local partnership in other localities.

(a)   A public record, as defined by G.S. 132-1, does not include, as to any minor participating in a park or recreation program sponsored by a local government or combination of local governments, a program funded by the North Carolina Partnership for Children, Inc., under G.S. 143B-168.12, or a program funded by a local partnership under G.S. 143B-168.14, any of the following information as to that minor participant: (i) name, (ii) address, (iii) age, (iv) date of birth, (v) telephone number, (vi) the name or address of that minor participant's parent or legal guardian, or (vii) any other identifying information on an application to participate in such program or other records related to that program.

(b)   The county, municipality, and zip code of residence of each participating minor covered by subsection (a) of this section is a public record, with the information listed in subsection (a) of this section redacted.

(c)   Nothing in this section makes the information listed in subsection (a) of this section confidential information. (2008-126, s. 1; 2012-67, s. 1.)

§ 132-1.13. Electronic lists of subscribers open for inspection but not available for copying.

(a)   Notwithstanding this chapter, when a unit of local government maintains an electronic mail list of individual subscribers, this chapter does not require that unit of local government to provide a copy of the list. The list shall be available for public inspection in either printed or electronic format or both as the unit of local government elects.

(b)   If a unit of local government maintains an electronic mail list of individual subscribers, the unit of local government and its employees and officers may use that list only: (i) for the purpose for which it was subscribed to; (ii) to notify subscribers of an emergency to the public health or public safety; or (iii) in case of deletion of that list, to notify subscribers of the existence of any similar lists to subscribe to.

(c)   Repealed by Session Laws 2011-54, s. 1, effective April 28, 2011. (2010-83, ss. 1-3; 2011-54, s. 1.)

§ 132-1.14: Reserved for future codification purposes.

§ 132-1.15: Reserved for future codification purposes.

§ 132-1.16: Reserved for future codification purposes.

§ 132-1.17: Reserved for future codification purposes.

§ 132-1.18: Reserved for future codification purposes.

§ 132-1.19: Reserved for future codification purposes.

§ 132-1.20: Reserved for future codification purposes.

§ 132-1.21: Reserved for future codification purposes.

§ 132-1.22: Reserved for future codification purposes.

§ 132-1.23. Eugenics program records.

(a)   Records in the custody of the State, including those in the custody of the Office of Justice for Sterilization Victims, concerning the Eugenics Board of North Carolina's program are confidential and are not public records, including the records identifying (i) individuals impacted by the program, (ii) individuals, or their guardians or authorized agents, inquiring about the impact of the program on the individuals, or (iii) individuals, or their guardians or authorized agents, inquiring about the potential impact of the program on others.

(b)   Notwithstanding subsection (a) of this section, an individual impacted by the program, or a guardian or authorized agent of that individual, may obtain that individual's records under the program upon execution of a proper release authorization.

(c)   Notwithstanding subsections (a) and (b) of this section, minutes or reports of the Eugenics Board of North Carolina, for which identifying information of the individuals impacted by the program have been redacted, may be released to any person. As used in this subsection, "identifying information" shall include the name, street address, birth day and month, and any other information the State believes may lead to the identity of any individual impacted by the program, or of any relative of an individual impacted by the program. (2011-188, s. 1; 2013-360, s. 6.18(c).)

§ 132-2. Custodian designated.

The public official in charge of an office having public records shall be the custodian thereof. (1935, c. 265, s. 2.)

§ 132-3. Destruction of records regulated.

(a)   Prohibition. - No public official may destroy, sell, loan, or otherwise dispose of any public record, except in accordance with G.S. 121-5 and G.S. 130A-99, without the consent of the Department of Cultural Resources. Whoever unlawfully removes a public record from the office where it is usually kept, or alters, defaces, mutilates or destroys it shall be guilty of a Class 3 misdemeanor and upon conviction only fined not less than ten dollars ($10.00) nor more than five hundred dollars ($500.00).

(b)   Revenue Records. - Notwithstanding subsection (a) of this section and G.S. 121-5, when a record of the Department of Revenue has been copied in any manner, the original record may be destroyed upon the order of the Secretary of Revenue. If a record of the Department of Revenue has not been copied, the original record shall be preserved for at least three years. After three years the original record may be destroyed upon the order of the Secretary of Revenue.

(c)   Employment Security Records. - Notwithstanding subsection (a) of this section and G.S. 121-5, when a record of the Division of Employment Security has been copied in any manner, the original record may be destroyed upon the order of the Division. If a record of that Division has not been copied, the original record shall be preserved for at least three years. After three years the original record may be destroyed upon the order of the Assistant Secretary of Commerce. (1935, c. 265, s. 3; 1943, c. 237; 1953, c. 675, s. 17; 1957, c. 330, s. 2; 1973, c. 476, s. 48; 1993, c. 485, s. 39; c. 539, s. 966; 1994, Ex. Sess., c. 24, s. 14(c); 1997-309, s. 12; 2001-115, s. 2; 2011-401, s. 3.16.)

§ 132-4. Disposition of records at end of official's term.

Whoever has the custody of any public records shall, at the expiration of his term of office, deliver to his successor, or, if there be none, to the Department of Cultural Resources, all records, books, writings, letters and documents kept or received by him in the transaction of his official business; and any such person who shall refuse or neglect for the space of 10 days after request made in writing by any citizen of the State to deliver as herein required such public records to the person authorized to receive them shall be guilty of a Class 1 misdemeanor. (1935, c. 265, s. 4; 1943, c. 237; 1973, c. 476, s. 48; 1975, c. 696, s. 1; 1993, c. 539, s. 967; 1994, Ex. Sess., c. 24, s. 14(c).)

§ 132-5. Demanding custody.

Whoever is entitled to the custody of public records shall demand them from any person having illegal possession of them, who shall forthwith deliver the same to him. If the person who unlawfully possesses public records shall without just cause refuse or neglect for 10 days after a request made in writing by any citizen of the State to deliver such records to their lawful custodian, he shall be guilty of a Class 1 misdemeanor. (1935, c. 265, s. 5; 1975, c. 696, s. 2; 1993, c. 539, s. 968; 1994, Ex. Sess., c. 24, s. 14(c).)

§ 132-5.1. Regaining custody; civil remedies.

(a)   The Secretary of the Department of Cultural Resources or his designated representative or any public official who is the custodian of public records which are in the possession of a person or agency not authorized by the custodian or by law to possess such public records may petition the superior court in the county in which the person holding such records resides or in which the materials in issue, or any part thereof, are located for the return of such public records. The court may order such public records to be delivered to the petitioner upon finding that the materials in issue are public records and that such public records are in the possession of a person not authorized by the custodian of the public records or by law to possess such public records. If the order of delivery does not receive compliance, the petitioner may request that the court enforce such order through its contempt power and procedures.

(b)   At any time after the filing of the petition set out in subsection (a) or contemporaneous with such filing, the public official seeking the return of the public records may by ex parte petition request the judge or the court in which the action was filed to grant one of the following provisional remedies:

(1)   An order directed at the sheriff commanding him to seize the materials which are the subject of the action and deliver the same to the court under the circumstances hereinafter set forth; or

(2)   A preliminary injunction preventing the sale, removal, disposal or destruction of or damage to such public records pending a final judgment by the court.

(c)   The judge or court aforesaid shall issue an order of seizure or grant a preliminary injunction upon receipt of an affidavit from the petitioner which alleges that the materials at issue are public records and that unless one of said provisional remedies is granted, there is a danger that such materials shall be sold, secreted, removed out of the State or otherwise disposed of so as not to be forthcoming to answer the final judgment of the court respecting the same; or that such property may be destroyed or materially damaged or injured if not seized or if injunctive relief is not granted.

(d)   The aforementioned order of seizure or preliminary injunction shall issue without notice to the respondent and without the posting of any bond or other security by the petitioner. (1975, c. 787, s. 2.)

§ 132-6. Inspection and examination of records.

(a)   Every custodian of public records shall permit any record in the custodian's custody to be inspected and examined at reasonable times and under reasonable supervision by any person, and shall, as promptly as possible, furnish copies thereof upon payment of any fees as may be prescribed by law. As used herein, "custodian" does not mean an agency that holds the public records of other agencies solely for purposes of storage or safekeeping or solely to provide data processing.

(b)   No person requesting to inspect and examine public records, or to obtain copies thereof, shall be required to disclose the purpose or motive for the request.

(c)   No request to inspect, examine, or obtain copies of public records shall be denied on the grounds that confidential information is commingled with the requested nonconfidential information. If it is necessary to separate confidential from nonconfidential information in order to permit the inspection, examination, or copying of the public records, the public agency shall bear the cost of such separation on the following schedule:

State agencies after June 30, 1996;

Municipalities with populations of 10,000 or more, counties with populations of 25,000 or more, as determined by the 1990 U.S. Census, and public hospitals in those counties, after June 30, 1997;

Municipalities with populations of less than 10,000, counties with populations of less than 25,000, as determined by the 1990 U.S. Census, and public hospitals in those counties, after June 30, 1998;

Political subdivisions and their agencies that are not otherwise covered by this schedule, after June 30, 1998.

(d)   Notwithstanding the provisions of subsections (a) and (b) of this section, public records relating to the proposed expansion or location of specific business or industrial projects may be withheld so long as their inspection, examination or copying would frustrate the purpose for which such public records were created; provided, however, that nothing herein shall be construed to permit the withholding of public records relating to general economic development policies or activities. Once the State, a local government, or the specific business has announced a commitment by the business to expand or locate a specific project in this State or a final decision not to do so and the business has communicated that commitment or decision to the State or local government agency involved with the project, the provisions of this subsection allowing public records to be withheld by the agency no longer apply. Once the provisions of this subsection no longer apply, the agency shall disclose as soon as practicable, and within 25 business days, public records requested for the announced project that are not otherwise made confidential by law. An announcement that a business or industrial project has committed to expand or locate in the State shall not require disclosure of local government records relating to the project if the business has not selected a specific location within the State for the project. Once a specific location for the project has been determined, local government records must be disclosed, upon request, in accordance with the provisions of this section. For purposes of this section, "local government records" include records maintained by the State that relate to a local government's efforts to attract the project.

(e)   The application of this Chapter is subject to the provisions of Article 1 of Chapter 121 of the General Statutes, the North Carolina Archives and History Act.

(f)   Notwithstanding the provisions of subsection (a) of this section, the inspection or copying of any public record which, because of its age or condition could be damaged during inspection or copying, may be made subject to reasonable restrictions intended to preserve the particular record. (1935, c. 265, s. 6; 1987, c. 835, s. 1; 1995, c. 388, s. 2; 2005-429, s. 1.1.)

287

§ 132-6.1. Electronic data-processing records.

(a)   After June 30, 1996, no public agency shall purchase, lease, create, or otherwise acquire any electronic data-processing system for the storage, manipulation, or retrieval of public records unless it first determines that the system will not impair or impede the agency's ability to permit the public inspection and examination, and to provide electronic copies of such records. Nothing in this subsection shall be construed to require the retention by the public agency of obsolete hardware or software.

(b)   Every public agency shall create an index of computer databases compiled or created by a public agency on the following schedule:

State agencies by July 1, 1996;

Municipalities with populations of 10,000 or more, counties with populations of 25,000 or more, as determined by the 1990 U.S. Census, and public hospitals in those counties, by July 1, 1997;

Municipalities with populations of less than 10,000, counties with populations of less than 25,000, as determined by the 1990 U.S. Census, and public hospitals in those counties, by July 1, 1998;

Political subdivisions and their agencies that are not otherwise covered by this schedule, after June 30, 1998.

The index shall be a public record and shall include, at a minimum, the following information with respect to each database listed therein: a list of the data fields; a description of the format or record layout; information as to the frequency with which the database is updated; a list of any data fields to which public access is restricted; a description of each form in which the database can be copied or reproduced using the agency's computer facilities; and a schedule of fees for the production of copies in each available form. Electronic databases compiled or created prior to the date by which the index must be created in accordance with this subsection may be indexed at the public agency's option. The form, content, language, and guidelines for the index and the databases to be indexed shall be developed by the Office of Archives and History in consultation with officials at other public agencies.

(c)   Nothing in this section shall require a public agency to create a computer database that the public agency has not otherwise created or is not

288

otherwise required to be created. Nothing in this section requires a public agency to disclose security features of its electronic data processing systems, information technology systems, telecommunications networks, or electronic security systems, including hardware or software security, passwords, or security standards, procedures, processes, configurations, software, and codes.

(d)   The following definitions apply in this section:

(1)   Computer database. - A structured collection of data or documents residing in a database management program or spreadsheet software.

(2)   Computer hardware. - Any tangible machine or device utilized for the electronic storage, manipulation, or retrieval of data.

(3)   Computer program. - A series of instructions or statements that permit the storage, manipulation, and retrieval of data within an electronic data-processing system, together with any associated documentation. The term does not include the original data, or any analysis, compilation, or manipulated form of the original data produced by the use of the program or software.

(4)   Computer software. - Any set or combination of computer programs. The term does not include the original data, or any analysis, compilation, or manipulated form of the original data produced by the use of the program or software.

(5)   Electronic data-processing system. - Computer hardware, computer software, or computer programs or any combination thereof, regardless of kind or origin. (1995, c. 388, s. 3; 2000-71, s. 1; 2002-159, s. 35(i).)

§ 132-6.2. Provisions for copies of public records; fees.

(a)   Persons requesting copies of public records may elect to obtain them in any and all media in which the public agency is capable of providing them. No request for copies of public records in a particular medium shall be denied on the grounds that the custodian has made or prefers to make the public records available in another medium. The public agency may assess different fees for different media as prescribed by law.

(b)   Persons requesting copies of public records may request that the copies be certified or uncertified. The fees for certifying copies of public records shall be as provided by law. Except as otherwise provided by law, no public agency shall charge a fee for an uncertified copy of a public record that exceeds the actual cost to the public agency of making the copy. For purposes of this subsection, "actual cost" is limited to direct, chargeable costs related to the reproduction of a public record as determined by generally accepted accounting principles and does not include costs that would have been incurred by the public agency if a request to reproduce a public record had not been made. Notwithstanding the provisions of this subsection, if the request is such as to require extensive use of information technology resources or extensive clerical or supervisory assistance by personnel of the agency involved, or if producing the record in the medium requested results in a greater use of information technology resources than that established by the agency for reproduction of the volume of information requested, then the agency may charge, in addition to the actual cost of duplication, a special service charge, which shall be reasonable and shall be based on the actual cost incurred for such extensive use of information technology resources or the labor costs of the personnel providing the services, or for a greater use of information technology resources that is actually incurred by the agency or attributable to the agency. If anyone requesting public information from any public agency is charged a fee that the requester believes to be unfair or unreasonable, the requester may ask the State Chief Information Officer or his designee to mediate the dispute.

(c)   Persons requesting copies of computer databases may be required to make or submit such requests in writing. Custodians of public records shall respond to all such requests as promptly as possible. If the request is granted, the copies shall be provided as soon as reasonably possible. If the request is denied, the denial shall be accompanied by an explanation of the basis for the denial. If asked to do so, the person denying the request shall, as promptly as possible, reduce the explanation for the denial to writing.

(d)   Nothing in this section shall be construed to require a public agency to respond to requests for copies of public records outside of its usual business hours.

(e)   Nothing in this section shall be construed to require a public agency to respond to a request for a copy of a public record by creating or compiling a record that does not exist. If a public agency, as a service to the requester, voluntarily elects to create or compile a record, it may negotiate a reasonable charge for the service with the requester. Nothing in this section shall be construed to require a public agency to put into electronic medium a record that is not kept in electronic medium. (1995, c. 388, s. 3; 2004-129, s. 38.)

§ 132-7. Keeping records in safe places; copying or repairing; certified copies.

Insofar as possible, custodians of public records shall keep them in fireproof safes, vaults, or rooms fitted with noncombustible materials and in such arrangement as to be easily accessible for convenient use. All public records should be kept in the buildings in which they are ordinarily used. Record books should be copied or repaired, renovated or rebound if worn, mutilated, damaged or difficult to read. Whenever any State, county, or municipal records are in need of repair, restoration, or rebinding, the head of such State agency, department, board, or commission, the board of county commissioners of such county, or the governing body of such municipality may authorize that the records in need of repair, restoration, or rebinding be removed from the building or office in which such records are ordinarily kept, for the length of time required to repair, restore, or rebind them. Any public official who causes a record book to be copied shall attest it and shall certify on oath that it is an accurate copy of the original book. The copy shall then have the force of the original. (1935, c. 265, s. 7; 1951, c. 294.)

§ 132-8. Assistance by and to Department of Cultural Resources.

The Department of Cultural Resources shall have the right to examine into the condition of public records and shall give advice and assistance to public officials in the solution of their problems of preserving, filing and making available the public records in their custody. When requested by the Department of Cultural Resources, public officials shall assist the Department in the preparation of an inclusive inventory of records in their custody, to which shall be attached a schedule, approved by the head of the governmental unit or agency having custody of the records and the Secretary of Cultural Resources, establishing a time period for the retention or disposal of each series of records. Upon the completion of the inventory and schedule, the Department of Cultural Resources shall (subject to the availability of necessary space, staff, and other facilities for such purposes) make available space in its Records Center for the filing of semicurrent records so scheduled and in its archives for noncurrent records of permanent value, and shall render such other assistance as needed,

291

including the microfilming of records so scheduled. (1935, c. 265, s. 8; 1943, c. 237; 1959, c. 68, s. 2; 1973, c. 476, s. 48.)

§ 132-8.1. Records management program administered by Department of Cultural Resources; establishment of standards, procedures, etc.; surveys.

A records management program for the application of efficient and economical management methods to the creation, utilization, maintenance, retention, preservation, and disposal of official records shall be administered by the Department of Cultural Resources. It shall be the duty of that Department, in cooperation with and with the approval of the Department of Administration, to establish standards, procedures, and techniques for effective management of public records, to make continuing surveys of paper work operations, and to recommend improvements in current records management practices including the use of space, equipment, and supplies employed in creating, maintaining, and servicing records. It shall be the duty of the head of each State agency and the governing body of each county, municipality and other subdivision of government to cooperate with the Department of Cultural Resources in conducting surveys and to establish and maintain an active, continuing program for the economical and efficient management of the records of said agency, county, municipality, or other subdivision of government. (1961, c. 1041; 1973, c. 476, s. 48.)

§ 132-8.2. Selection and preservation of records considered essential; making or designation of preservation duplicates; force and effect of duplicates or copies thereof.

In cooperation with the head of each State agency and the governing body of each county, municipality, and other subdivision of government, the Department of Cultural Resources shall establish and maintain a program for the selection and preservation of public records considered essential to the operation of government and to the protection of the rights and interests of persons, and, within the limitations of funds available for the purpose, shall make or cause to be made preservation duplicates or designate as preservation duplicates existing copies of such essential public records. Preservation duplicates shall be durable, accurate, complete and clear, and such duplicates made by a photographic, photostatic, microfilm, micro card, miniature photographic, or

292

other process which accurately reproduces and forms a durable medium for so reproducing the original shall have the same force and effect for all purposes as the original record whether the original record is in existence or not. A transcript, exemplification, or certified copy of such preservation duplicate shall be deemed for all purposes to be a transcript, exemplification, or certified copy of the original record. Such preservation duplicates shall be preserved in the place and manner of safekeeping prescribed by the Department of Cultural Resources. (1961, c. 1041; 1973, c. 476, s. 48.)

§ 132-9. Access to records.

(a)   Any person who is denied access to public records for purposes of inspection and examination, or who is denied copies of public records, may apply to the appropriate division of the General Court of Justice for an order compelling disclosure or copying, and the court shall have jurisdiction to issue such orders if the person has complied with G.S. 7A-38.3E. Actions brought pursuant to this section shall be set down for immediate hearing, and subsequent proceedings in such actions shall be accorded priority by the trial and appellate courts.

(b)   In an action to compel disclosure of public records which have been withheld pursuant to the provisions of G.S. 132-6 concerning public records relating to the proposed expansion or location of particular businesses and industrial projects, the burden shall be on the custodian withholding the records to show that disclosure would frustrate the purpose of attracting that particular business or industrial project.

(c)   In any action brought pursuant to this section in which a party successfully compels the disclosure of public records, the court shall allow a party seeking disclosure of public records who substantially prevails to recover its reasonable attorneys' fees if attributed to those public records. The court may not assess attorneys' fees against the governmental body or governmental unit if the court finds that the governmental body or governmental unit acted in reasonable reliance on any of the following:

(1)   A judgment or an order of a court applicable to the governmental unit or governmental body.

293

(2)   The published opinion of an appellate court, an order of the North Carolina Business Court, or a final order of the Trial Division of the General Court of Justice.

(3)   A written opinion, decision, or letter of the Attorney General.

Any attorneys' fees assessed against a public agency under this section shall be charged against the operating expenses of the agency; provided, however, that the court may order that all or any portion of any attorneys' fees so assessed be paid personally by any public employee or public official found by the court to have knowingly or intentionally committed, caused, permitted, suborned, or participated in a violation of this Article. No order against any public employee or public official shall issue in any case where the public employee or public official seeks the advice of an attorney and such advice is followed.

(d)   If the court determines that an action brought pursuant to this section was filed in bad faith or was frivolous, the court shall assess a reasonable attorney's fee against the person or persons instituting the action and award it to the public agency as part of the costs.

(e)   Notwithstanding subsection (c) of this section, the court may not assess attorneys' fees against a public hospital created under Article 2 of Chapter 131E of the General Statutes if the court finds that the action was brought by or on behalf of a competing health care provider for obtaining information to be used to gain a competitive advantage. (1935, c. 265, s. 9; 1975, c. 787, s. 3; 1987, c. 835, s. 2; 1995, c. 388, s. 4; 2005-332, s. 2; 2010-169, s. 21(c).)

§ 132-10. Qualified exception for geographical information systems.

Geographical information systems databases and data files developed and operated by counties and cities are public records within the meaning of this Chapter. The county or city shall provide public access to such systems by public access terminals or other output devices. Upon request, the county or city shall furnish copies, in documentary or electronic form, to anyone requesting them at reasonable cost. As a condition of furnishing an electronic copy, whether on magnetic tape, magnetic disk, compact disk, or photo-optical device, a county or city may require that the person obtaining the copy agree in writing that the copy will not be resold or otherwise used for trade or commercial purposes. For purposes of this section, publication or broadcast by the news media, real estate trade associations, or Multiple Listing Services operated by real estate trade associations shall not constitute a resale or use of the data for trade or commercial purposes and use of information without resale by a licensed professional in the course of practicing the professional's profession shall not constitute use for a commercial purpose. For purposes of this section, resale at cost by a real estate trade association or Multiple Listing Services operated by a real estate trade association shall not constitute a resale or use of the data for trade or commercial purposes. (1995, c. 388, s. 5; 1997-193, s. 1.)

Vision Books Order Form

Fax Orders:	1-980-299-5965
Phone Orders:	1-704-898-0770
E-mail Orders:	www.visionbooks.org
Mail Orders:	Vision Books, LLC P.O. Box 42406 Charlotte, NC 28215

Shipp To:
Name_____
Address_____
City_____State_____Zip_____
Phone_____Fax_____
Email_____@_____

Bill To: We can bill a third party on your behalf.
Name_____
Address_____
City_____State_____Zip_____
Phone___(_____)_____Fax_____
Email_____@_____

Pamphlet Number ($15.00 Each)	Qty	Total Cost
_____	_____	_____
_____	_____	_____
_____	_____	_____
_____	_____	_____
_____	_____	_____
_____	_____	_____
_____	_____	_____
_____	_____	_____
Full Volume Set 1-92	92 Pamphlets	1,380.00

Free Shipping & Handling on Full Volume Orders
Add $1.00 Shipping & Handling per pamphlet $_____

Total Cost $_____

Thank you for your support. Management!

DID YOU ENJOY THIS BOOK?

Vision Books, LLC would like to hear from you! If you or someone you know has been fasely imprisoned, we would like to hear your story. If the 'North Carolina Criminal Law and Procedure' has had an effect in your life or if you have suggestions, we would like to hear from you. Send your letters to:

Vision Books, LLC
Attn: Staff Writers
P.O. Box 42406
Charlotte, NC 28215
Email: staff@visionbooks.org

Order Additional Copies:

Fax Orders: 1-980-299-5965

Phone Orders: 1-704-898-0770

E-mail Orders: www.visionbooks.org

Mail Orders: Vision Books, LLC
                       P.O. Box 42406
                       Charlotte, NC 28215

www.ingramcontent.com/pod-product-compliance
Lightning Source LLC
Chambersburg PA
CBHW051631170526
45167CB00001B/139